M.J. Trow studied history at university, after which he has spent years teaching. He is also an established crime writer; a biographer, with a reputation as a scholar who peels away legend to reveal the truth. Originally from Rhondda, South Wales, he lives on the Isle of Wight.

Highlights from the series

A BRIEF HISTORY OF

VAMPIRES

M.J. TROW

ROBINSON   RUNNING PRESS
PHILADELPHIA · LONDON

Constable & Robinson Ltd
3 The Lanchesters
162 Fulham Palace Road
London W6 9ER
www.constablerobinson.com

First published in the UK by Robinson,
an imprint of Constable & Robinson, 2010

A copy of the British Library Cataloguing in Publication
Data is available from the British Library

UK ISBN 978-1-84901-336-9

1 3 5 7 9 10 8 6 4 2

First published in the United States in 2010 by Running Press Book Publishers

US Library of Congress Control Number: 2009943292
US ISBN 978-0-7624-3988-1

Running Press Book Publishers
2300 Chestnut Street
Philadelphia, PA 19103-4371

Visit us on the web!
www.runningpress.com

Typeset by TW Typesetting, Plymouth, Devon
Printed and bound in the EU

Pace voua, morti nostri

Rest in peace, our dead.

CONTENTS

ACKNOWLEDGEMENTS

I would like to offer my sincere thanks to everyone involved in the creation of *A Brief History of Vampires*: to Leo Hollis and his team at Constable & Robinson; to Andrew Lownie; to my ex-colleague Brian Bond; to the library staff at the School of Slavonic Studies, London University; to Taliesin Trow, whose knowledge of films on the undead is truly scary; but most of all, as always, to my wife Carol, a busy writer herself, who did more than anyone else to shape this book.

PROLOGUE

DRACULA
THE MYTH AND THE MAN

Over time we have become hardened to horror, especially when we watch it on the screen. A long time ago I watched Alfred Hitchcock's *The Birds* with a student friend who had not seen it before. When the credits rolled, he breathed a sigh of relief and pulled a steel comb from his pocket. So gripped had he been that he had bent the comb almost in half. Scroll back half a century to the time a great aunt of mine went to 'the pictures' to see Lon Chaney in *Phantom of the Opera*. So terrified was she at the first appearance of the Phantom's unmasked face that her false teeth flew across the aisle and could not be found until the next day.

We *love* to be frightened. As long as the actual terror belongs to someone else, as long as we can get our kicks secondhand by reading a ghost story or watching a 'slasher' movie, we are in our element. And we have a long list of fictional and cinematic bogeymen to leap metaphorically out from under the stairs: Freddie Kruger in the *Nightmare on*

Elm Street series of films; Michael Myers in the *Halloween* sagas; Frankenstein's monster; Dracula ...

And thereby hangs a tale. Because Freddie, Michael and the bolt-necked freak that was the new Prometheus created in a laboratory are all invention.

Dracula was real.

Long before man created celluloid or began to write fiction, long before he used horror stories as entertainment, bogeymen were real too. The anonymous Cornish prayer 'From ghoulies and ghosties and long-leggity beasties, And things that go bump in the night, Good Lord, deliver us!' is a reminder of the terror that once existed in all of us. When Reginald Scot produced his 'exposé' *A Discoverie of Witches* in 1584, he reeled off a long list of 'bull-beggars' of which country people, in particular, were afraid. There were nearly 200 of them, although some were probably regional dialect variants of the same thing. To us now they are quaint and incomprehensible – to our ancestors they were real. They came knocking on doors, curdling milk, destroying corn. They hid in haylofts and lurked in forests or the darkness of caves. Night was their time – the time of blackness and the unknown; and generations of children were terrified into obedience by the mere mention of their names: Man-in-the-oak; Tom-tumbler; Dick-a-Tuesday; Jack-in-the-Wad; Peg Powler; Doppleganger; Gabriel-hound; Kit-in-the-Canstick.

Modern science has dispersed those demons; they have vanished, like will o' the wisps in the face of cold logic and reason. But they have come back in other forms, not to haunt us, but to delight. We can laugh at them now because we know they were not there in the first place.

Dracula was there.

Eccentric cleric Montague Summers wrote in 1927:

In all the darkest pages of the malign supernatural there is no more terrible tradition than that of the Vampire, a pariah even among demons. Foul are his ravages; gruesome and seemingly barbaric are the ancient and approved methods by which folk must rid themselves of this hideous pest.

Reginald Scot, writing of English folkloric experience in the sixteenth century, would have been generally unfamiliar with the vampire, although he would have understood the stock from which he came. The *Shorter English Dictionary* today defines 'vampire' as: 'A ghost, monster or reanimated corpse supposed to leave its grave at night to suck the blood of sleeping people, often represented as a human figure with long, pointed canine teeth.' Most of the folkloric examples of vampires, which we will meet in this book, come from Central Europe, although many cultures worldwide have such creatures as part of their mythology.

In 1897, the Irish civil servant Bram Stoker wrote his best known work *Dracula*, introducing to the world the mysterious undead Count from Transylvania, a land of wolves and forests and dark horror. It was by no means the first fictional appearance of the vampire – some would say it was not even the best – but it struck a chord with a large readership wanting to be shocked by the story's sense of terror and sexuality, and it spawned a film industry which catered for its audiences in the same way.

Bram Stoker found his anti-hero, the Count, from the pages of history. The name 'Dracula', in its native Wallachian (now Romanian), means son of the dragon, or son of the devil (*Dracul* can mean either, just as the dragon/serpent *is* the devil in biblical and other sources). And Stoker was writing about the most notorious scion of the Draculesti clan, Vlad III, known in his time as Țepeș, which translates as 'the Impaler'. He was not a count, but a voivod, a warrior-prince who ruled Wallachia three times in the fifteenth century. Legend and actual evidence have conspired to make this man one of the most feared and bloodthirsty psychopaths in history. Most Stoker/vampire experts today dismiss the link between the Impaler and Stoker's Count. They say that Stoker merely pinched the name because he liked the sound of it and that there is no vampiric tradition associated with the real Dracula at all. This book challenges that view. We cannot understand vampires or their history without a detailed understanding of the life and times of Vlad Ţepeş.

Part 1

Like most areas open to re-evaluation, our concept of vampirism, the belief in the existence of vampires, is constantly changing. Part 1 looks at the cultural development of vampires going backwards in time. Chapter 1, California Screaming, investigates the state of play today. We look at the current vogue of the *Twilight* series, both in book and film format, and discover it is actually a Romeo and Juliet style romance with a hint of menace. To paraphrase the tag line of a schmaltzy movie of forty years ago, 'Love means never having to say you're scary.' But today's vampirism has its darker side too, a whole generation given to wearing black and believing themselves to be a subspecies who are able to communicate after dark on the Internet. At its nastiest end lurk dangerous cults and even the occasional sadistic murderer.

Chapter 2, Reel Vampires, looks at the celluloid vampire. In a society which reads less than ever before, films have a profound influence. From *New Moon* (2009) we delve back in the film archive to the genuinely terrifying *Nosferatu* (1922) and beyond.

Chapter 3, Bram Stoker's *Dracula*, is a turning point in the history of the vampire myth. The chapter looks at more recent vampire works (which in themselves are often 'the book of the film') before examining the enormous impact of the undead Count created by the living civil servant. The fangs, the lack of reflection, the cloak and the fear of sunlight are all etched indelibly on our minds and they are all the creation of Stoker. So is van Helsing, the vampire hunter and precursor of Buffy.

When reading Stoker we can lose ourselves in Transylvania and listen to the howling of the 'children of the night'.

But Stoker did not create the vampire myth and Chapter 4, Fantasmagoria, takes us back to the earlier authors who influenced him. Sheridan le Fanu wrote *Carmilla* in the 1870s, introducing the whole side issue of then taboo lesbian relationships. *Varney the Vampire* ran as a part-work thriller to titillate and terrify the middle class readership of the 1840s. And Dr John Polidori, confidante of the Romantic poet Lord Byron, went into print with his own version twenty years before that.

What all these literati were doing was basing their work, consciously or otherwise, on the ancient folklore of the vampire in Europe. Chapter 5, Kiss and Kin, and Chapter 6, Vampyr, focus on this fascinating area before I turn the spotlight on the flesh and blood man I believe lies at the heart of all this.

Part 2
Chapters 7–13 focus on the biographical details of Vlad Ţepeş, establishing the kind of society into which he was born and the various interpretations of him that exist. He was one of the first topics for the newly invented printing press and stories of his barbarism and cruelty were only outsold in his own time by the Bible. The Saxon stories call him a madman and a monster given to unspeakable perversions in which, among other things, human beings were impaled alive like insects on pins. The Russian stories of Vlad are more balanced – he was cruel but it was a cruel age and Dracula's ends justified his means. The Romanian stories see him as a crusader knight, the nationalist champion of his people, the hero on the white horse.

The last three chapters of the book evaluate the real Vlad and place him in the context of vampirism. Far from being a mere footnote and a coincidence happened upon by Bram Stoker, Vlad Ţepeş *is* Dracula and the greatest vampire of them all.

PART 1:
VAMPIRES IN MYTH AND THE IMAGINATION

I

CALIFORNIA SCREAMING
VAMPIRES IN THE TWENTY-FIRST CENTURY

> I was born Miles Prockofiev. In the year 1542 I was a tailor and
> clothier in Pozsony, a town at the foot of the Carpathian
> Mountains . . . Zlatan opened his mouth and in an instant a pair
> of dagger-like fangs extended past his lips and plunged into my
> neck. No longer was I the tailor Miles Prockofiev; I was the
> vampire Miles Prockofiev . . . I arrived on Ellis Island on April
> 17 1907 [and] I discovered many new enthusiasms: capitalism,
> automobiles, the Charleston.[1]

This extract from *The New Vampires' Handbook* encapsulates
a brief history of vampires with its tongue (and presumably,
fangs) firmly in its cheek. From a haunted time in a far
country, the notion of the vampire had been transformed and
translated into modernity. What was once actually believed –
that there are creatures of the night who are neither dead nor
alive and who feast on blood; what was once an unspoken
taboo – is now virtually commonplace. The vampires of the
most recent screen craze based on the bestselling novels by

Stephenie Meyer – the Cullen family in the *Twilight* series – are certainly odd, but they hold down jobs, attend schools and even play their own ultra high-speed version of baseball.

Today there are an estimated 10,000 'Real Vampires' in the United States, although that figure, and the exact nature of a 'real vampire' are open to interpretation. *Bizarre* magazine wrote in May 1997 that today's vampires:

> cannot trace their 'immortal souls' back to Vlad Dracula or any other real figure, because they believe in a creature invented by novelists and film-makers.[2]

In the twenty-first century, when we have (at least in the West) freedom of expression and a steadily declining lack of awareness of our real past, it is possible for thousands of people to claim in censuses to be Jedi knights.

So who are these people who claim to be vampires but have never heard of Vlad the Impaler? Some of them are teenagers, 'wannabees' who are not quite sure what they actually wannabee. Cinematic and literary influences will be discussed elsewhere, but most devotees of the current craze of vampirism are girls between the ages of twelve and eighteen. While researching for this book I met an ex-colleague who told me her sixteen-year-old daughter had seen *New Moon*, the second film in the *Twilight* saga, four times. 'At least,' she told me, 'it's getting her to read as well.' So some good, it seems, comes out of something that has always been supposed to be evil!

Among this group it is difficult to be sure of the precise focus of their interest. Is it the vampire Edward Cullen, with his moody distance, superhuman strength, aching loneliness, glistening skin and ever-changing iris colour? Or is it Robert Pattinson, with his gelled hair, smouldering good looks and tight T-shirt? There is no doubt that sex plays a huge part in modern vampirism in all its manifestations. Stephenie Meyer's series of books may be sexless (it is said because of her strict

Mormon beliefs) but the sexual tension on screen is palpable.[3] So it was half a generation ago when teenage girls swooned over David Boreanaz in the TV series *Buffy the Vampire Slayer* and its spin-off, *Angel*. And there was no doubt a frisson back in the 1960s when 'tall, dark and gruesome' Christopher Lee strutted his stuff with cloak, red eyes and widow's peak as the creepy Count in a series of films for Hammer. Perhaps Bela Lugosi's heavily accented performance in the classic 1931 *Dracula* did not cause the same shudder, but no doubt he too had his female following.

Teenage girls also identify with the leading female in the *Twilight* saga. Bella Swan, played by Kristen Stewart, is the sensitive girl who falls in love with a vampire, as did Sarah Michelle Geller (Buffy) despite the fact that she is supposed to be killing the 'sub species'. The plotline on *Twilight*'s DVD case explains some of the motivation behind the teen-age fan base: '*Twilight* adds a dangerous twist to the classic story of star-crossed lovers.' So, in essence, the new vampire craze is simply an old-fashioned love story, of the kind that has hooked young female audiences and readers long before CGI, Hollywood, Hammer House of Horror or even Bram Stoker.

But there is another sense in which the modern vampire craze grips this teenaged group. 'When you can live forever,' says *Twilight*'s tag-line, 'what do you live for?' Today, when so many young people are the displaced products of broken homes, there is a sort of comfort in the 'forever-ness' of the vampire. Bella comes from just such a home. She usually lives with her mother in a sunlit Arizona before moving to a wet, dark, Carpathian-looking Washington State to live with her father. The vampire Cullen family, however, is nuclear and, because they are different, closer than most.

'How old are you?' Bella asks Edward.

'Seventeen,' he replies.

'How long have you been seventeen?'

'A while.'

The vampire cannot die[4] so that unlike the fragmented relationships that litter many tangled lives, the love of a vampire is eternal.

The next group that follows the current vampire obsession is the horror buff, slightly older, perhaps, and of both sexes, who batten on the strange, the weird, the gore-drenched. One example from dozens of 'fanzines' available on mainstream bookshelves is *SciFi Now* styling itself 'the premier sci-fi, fantasy horror and cult TV magazine'. Leaving aside the purely science fiction element from the edition of November 2009, we are told that there will soon be a return to the *Lost Boys*[5] franchise by Corey Feldman and Jameson Newlander. There is a remake on the way of *Nightmare on Elm Street* in which homicidal Freddie Kruger with his nasty fingernails reappears as the 'iconic bogeyman'. *Jennifer's Body* is yet another piece of schlock fantasy featuring an impossibly attractive high school cheerleader. *Zombieland* revisits *Shaun of the Dead* country where the blood is spilt for laughs all over the supermarket. *Drag Me to Hell* tells the story of a (young, impossibly attractive) bank clerk who is cursed by a gypsy woman in the street. The editor's verdict is that this film has 'just the right balance of gross-out schlock and jumpy scares'. It is 'horror at its silliest'. *The Uninvited* is a psychological horror movie and in *Inside* the 'blood flows fast, thick and endlessly'. This is the fascination of the vampire cult for some – one strand in the web of terror created by the cinema and computer game franchises.

Beyond this broad fan base is the club scene, which in itself is very wide. Here, as with the horror buffs, the line of interest blurs with social interaction, sex, drugs and heavy metal music. These come and go with astonishing rapidity. Indeed one of the problems is to pin them down (rather like the undead for which they exist). Probably no one has succeeded in doing this as effectively as Tony Thorne, Language and Innovation Consultant to King's College, London and author of *Children of the Night*. Most of the American clubs at the

Millennium were New York-based – the Batcave, the Realm, the Bank, Click-and-Drag etc., but there was a secondary outcrop on the West Coast, especially the Fang Club in Beverley Hills. To make the point that vampirism is universal, there are also clubs in Poland, Britain, Germany, Holland, Australia and Canada.

Some of the clubbers are there to dress up. Few of them wear the traditional capes and fangs of Bela Lugosi's Dracula, but many of them are goths, with their pale skin, dark makeup and black clothes. Some are there for the music – 'death metal' thumping with so many decibels that it hurts the chest. Others have come for sex, to chat up girls/men in the stabbing lights and cacophony of noise as best they can. A few are there to drink blood.

Usually a distinction is made between the easy-going 'vampyres' – with a 'y' – who may be, in Tony Thorne's phrase, 'surfers in summer, goths in winter' and the vampires with an 'i' who often see themselves as a subspecies, alienated from the mainstream of humanity.

The sense of being different felt by some individuals is important. Of the interviewees contacted by Thorne for his book[6] most claimed an aversion to sunlight (a concept created by Bram Stoker), hyper-sensitive skin, reversed body-clock and a craving for human blood. Some claimed to be born vampires; others experienced tendencies in their early teens; most expressed an intense loneliness. Thorne is kind to his interviewees and rarely attempts to analyse an individual's response to his questions, but sociologists and psychologists would recognize in them standard teenage behaviour.

The onset of puberty can cause hormonal imbalances that children find difficult to control. It is textbook behaviour for a fourteen-year-old to kick over the traces and to rebel. When that rather aged teenager Marlon Brando was asked in the film *The Wild One* what he was rebelling against, his famous answer was, 'What have you got?' Parents, teachers and authority figures generally are the targets of the young. Each generation is supremely egotistical; it is better, more clever, wiser than the one that went before and it has a terrifying fear that it might turn into it. The would-be vampires have gone a stage further. They see themselves as beyond the pale, outside the norms of society, unloved and completely misunderstood. Most of them are of above-average intelligence and by definition sensitive, but the alienation aspect means that they have a built-in excuse if they fail, either academically or in the world of work.

Those who believe they are vampires also identify themselves as having heightened powers. While some droop around shunning sunlight and feeling listless, others claim telepathic abilities, vastly improved eyesight, smell and hearing; an ability to control people, situations and even the weather.

The 'psi-vamps' are those who in the past were known as 'psychic sponges'. The usual definition is: 'a person who preys on the life energy of others.' Sub-groups here are the emotional, sexual and 'pranic' or energy types who gain attention and thus power in a complex variety of ways.

The loneliness of today's vampire has been lessened by a sort of acceptance of the concept by mainstream society and because of the Internet. Rather like homosexuals in countries where such activity is or was against the law, the Net is a social meeting place where like minds can find some comfort and support. And of course the Net is a hugely powerful – some would say dangerous – manipulator of minds. It is particularly 'good' at spreading the contagion of fear. So all the scare stories of the past thirty years, mostly created and certainly exaggerated by the media – can be perpetuated at the click of a button or the drag of a mouse in everybody's living room. The pernicious example that Tony Thorne quotes is the sudden emergence in the America of 1973 of MPD, Multiple Personality Disorder (now usually referred to as DID – Dissociative Identity Disorder). This involved regression hypnosis under which numerous people 'remembered' experiences of child abuse and satanic worship, the revelation of which did untold damage to families. Now recognized as false memory syndrome and actually a mish-mash of late night horror film reminiscences and half-understood conversations, the oxygen of publicity afforded to this nonsense meant that the number of cases discovered rose from fifty to 20,000 in the space of a few years. Since then, some researchers have estimated that cases of DID could represent a staggering 10 per cent of the total of the psychiatric population of the US, a figure which, if correct, could imply nearly seven million sufferers.

A number of websites today have 'rules' by which vampires live. These are a conglomeration of philosophies drawn from a number of different sources. The best known is the Black Veil code, created by Sebastian Todd in 1998 and updated by Michelle Belanger in 2003, and featured on many vampire websites. Under the heading 'Discretion', vampires are encouraged to respect themselves and to recognize that they are part of a community with responsibilities. They should reveal themselves only to those who can understand. 'Diversity' covers the many shades of vampirism: 'no single one of us can have all the answers.' 'Control' warns vampires not to allow their darkness to consume them: 'Never feed because you think it makes you powerful; feed because this is what you must do.' Under the heading 'Elders' we learn that they should be respected, but 'Leaders' should be guiders, not dictators. 'Behaviour' states that recklessness is not encouraged; wisdom and commonsense must prevail. The vampire world is a 'Community'; ideas should be exchanged and support given.

It is in the 'Donors' section that we deal with the most dangerous aspect of modern vampirism. The code states:

> Feeding should occur between consenting adults. Allow donors to make an informed decision before they give of themselves to you. Do not take rapaciously from others, but seek to have an exchange that is pleasant and beneficial for all ... Do not engage in illegal activity, for this can endanger us all.

Blood-fetishism is at the hard-core end of vampirism. Whereas most of the multi-faceted genre is about lonely people looking for friends, mixed-up asocial teenagers looking for themselves, even a generation trying to find a new faith after the collapse of the old conventions, blood-fetishism is a high risk activity and opens the door to that very illegality that the Black Veil code warns against. A number of Tony Thorne's correspondents spoke openly about their cravings: the taste of blood, how they acquire it, the effect it has on them. Older ones spoke of the hysteria engendered – again, out of all proportion by the media – by the AIDS outbreak in the 1980s. Today, all donors are regularly screened. No one spoke in terms of committing assaults or even murder to obtain blood, because that is contrary to the code.

But the code can be broken. The Christian West has long held the ten commandments to be a moral blueprint to make society work, but the commandments are broken daily by millions and the sixth, 'thou shalt not kill', is ignored by a tiny minority. No one contends that modern vampires are blood-sucking night prowlers, but the self-description of one vampire quoted by Tony Thorne reads:

> I am coming out of the coffin . . . I am a vampire. I am lonely, depressed, heartbroken and mad as hell.

It is the madness of the tiny minority that grabs the headlines. Journalist Susan Walsh, carrying out research into vampire cults in New York State, disappeared without a trace in July 1996, leaving behind an eleven-year-old son. We do not know if she is alive or dead. Her body has never been found. In the same area in 1980, a young mother was detained for life in a psychiatric unit for killing her four-year-old daughter and drinking her blood. The late 1990s (the centenary of the publication of Bram Stoker's *Dracula*) saw a spate of vampire-associated assaults on both sides of the Atlantic. Wayne Phelps' vampire group, based in Weymouth, England, a quiet seaside town, took drugs and formed a coven inspired by the vampire film *The Lost Boys* and the real-life story of Charles Manson's 'family' who were responsible for the 'Helter Skelter' murders on the West Coast of the US in 1969. In 1996 Jon C. Bush of Virginia Beach, USA, was arrested for picking up high school girls in the local shopping mall and forcing them to join his vampire group and indulge in oral sex. He was sentenced to twenty-six years' imprisonment. Three years earlier, in Sunderland, England, a fifteen-year-old girl was attacked and raped by an assailant who licked the blood from her wounds; drifter Malcolm Foster, glue-sniffer and paint-drinker, was sentenced to nine years. He was found to have a morbid fascination with 'Countess Dracula', Elizabeth Báthory, the sixteenth-century child-murderer from the Carpathians (see Chapter 15).

In 1992 Paul Watts, from London, became convinced that his father and brother were vampires and killed them both with a carving knife. In the same city in the same year French chef Georges Castillio stabbed Myra Myers thirty-seven times for the same reason. Three years earlier, scaffolder Michael Ireland from Northampton, England, hit eleven-year-old Susan Giles with a brick and then tried to drain her blood. Amazingly, the girl survived and Ireland was detained indefinitely.

More recently, and more disturbingly, a German couple, twenty-three-year-old Manuela Ruda and her husband David, were found guilty in 2003 of ritual vampiric murder. The trial, held at Bochum in Germany's industrial heartland, produced weeks of lurid and graphic testimony which would not be out of place in any vampire film and which no Victorian 'penny dreadful' writer would have been allowed to publish. Claiming to have learnt the art of devil-worship and blood-sucking in Scotland and England, the pair, appearing in the dock with shaven heads and wearing chains, admitted freely that they killed Frank Haegen and carved a Satanic star on his chest with a razor. Haegen died as a result of sixty-six slash wounds from a machete and demolition of his skull with a sledge-hammer. Prosecutor Dieter Justinsky tried his best to sum up the enormous callousness of the crime:

> I have never, ever, seen such a picture of cruelty and depravity before. They simply had a lust for murder . . . and . . . believed they would achieve immortality as vampires.

Manuela Ruda confessed in court, 'For the last two and a half years I have had Satan in my soul.'

The Ruda couple may be the tip of a pernicious iceberg. Tony Thorne estimates there are 6,000 hard-core devil worshippers in Germany today.

But it is not merely with regard to murder that modern examples of vampirism emerge. In 1993 the *Eventmental Ziliei*, one of Romania's most widely read newspapers, told its readers to prepare for St Andrew's Day, 30 November, by smearing their windows and doors with garlic to ward off werewolves and other 'children of the night'. This may have been reported in Britain's the *Independent* tongue in cheek, but there is no evidence that this was the case in the paper's home in Bucharest.

Even more telling was an incident in Stoke-on-Trent in January 1973. PC John Pye was called to investigate the death of Demetrios Myicuiria, a Polish immigrant in his seventies, living in a Victorian terrace in the heart of the Potteries. Old people die alone commonly enough, abandoned by friends and family years before, but there was something odd about this particular death. Pye noticed, by the light of his torch, that salt had been scattered around the room and especially around the old man's bed. A half-empty bag of salt lay between his legs and on his pillow, and a number of containers in the room were full of a mixture of salt and the dead man's urine.

The inquest reported at first that Myicuiria had choked to death on a pickled onion found wedged in his windpipe.

Closer examination revealed that the 'onion' was in fact a clove of garlic. Garlic, salt and the crucifix are the traditional symbols of good against evil. The coroner said:

> This man genuinely believed . . . I've been a lawyer for a long time, dealing with courtroom cases of all kinds. I've seen all sorts of depravity, all sorts of nonsense, but I can visualize what was behind this man. A lot of evil had happened to him [he had lost everything during the Second World War] . . . I am convinced, even after this inquest, that this man was genuinely afraid of vampires and [was] not trying to kill himself.[7]

Interestingly, in folklore, one of the reasons why some people become vampires in the first place is that they are predisposed to it. 'People who are different,' writes Paul Barber, 'unpopular or great sinners are apt to return from the dead, and they often die alone.'[8] We have no way of knowing whether Mr Myicuiria was unpopular or a sinner, but as a Polish refugee in Stoke-on-Trent in the 1970s, he was certainly different. It is rather ironic that in some societies a man terrified of vampires might be considered one himself.

The following year tales of the Highgate vampire reached the Press. Highgate cemetery is the burial place of the great and the good of high Victorian society, including the unlikely tomb of Karl Marx, whom many Victorians regarded as neither great nor good. Architect Stephen Geary had a field day in the 1830s and 1840s designing Egyptian Avenues and catacombs which could have come straight out of a Hammer vampire flick. This older part of the cemetery became the focus of disturbing events after reports of a seven-foot vampire seen prowling the Gothic tombs.[9]

Nearly a hundred vampire-hunters under the loose leadership of the High Priest of the Occult Society, David Farrant, descended on Highgate and the result was an orgy of tomb-smashing, with iron stakes being driven through corpses. Farrant's home was searched by the police who found salt, crucifixes and voodoo dolls in his apartment. He was officially charged with offering indignity to the dead 'to the great scandal and disgrace of religion, decency and morality'.[10] Defending himself, Farrant lost the case and the judge gave him five years.

Nowhere in modern vampirism with its sub species and dreamy, hallucinogenic sexuality is there room, it seems, for the Cult of the Count. In many ways, it is Bram Stoker's novel *Dracula* of 1896 that is nevertheless the source of much that is vampiric today. As we shall see, as we peel away the layers of commercialism and legend, there is an ancient, folkloric aspect to all this which modern acolytes have twisted and bastardized to their own ends.

And the heart of vampirism too, still beating after interment, and only to be stilled by the single blow of a hawthorn stake, is the lonely malevolence of 'that bloody madman', the Voivod of Wallachia, Vlad Dracula, son of the Devil.

2

REEL VAMPIRES
THE UNDEAD CINEMA

At the time of writing 'Twilight Moms' has become a major phenomenon in America, with similar groups appearing in Britain and elsewhere. Whereas most fans of the latest cinematic vampire offering are teenagers, there is a significant support group of frightening intensity to be found among the over-thirties who are themselves mothers.

In an article for *Stylist* magazine in November 2009, a few of these Moms, now with their own website, explained their obsession. They hold conventions, bake *Twilight* cakes and stalk the film's stars. Actor Kellan Lutz, who plays Emmett Cullen in *Twilight* says, 'It's the Moms who are the most full-on; I think some of them actually make their daughters stay at home. They come in big groups and battle to give us the best presents, like candy, picture frames, flowers, baskets of stuff.' And the suggestions he has received by email and post make him blush.

If teenage girls flock to the film's stars, like Robert Pattinson and Kristen Stewart, trying to obtain the impossible by watching their screen love story in cinemas, their mothers are trying to recapture a lost youth. 'Edward [Pattinson's character] is proof you can have the most intimate, romantic relationship in the world without any sex,' property manager Joanna, aged thirty-five, told the magazine. Forty-year-old Penny said, 'It brought back the joy of being utterly under someone's spell, when you talk on the phone for hours and while away whole days exchanging meaningful glances.'

It appears, then, that the huge success of *Twilight* and its most recent sequel *New Moon* is because this is just a bittersweet romance straight out of the Romeo and Juliet stable, with far greater appeal to females than to males. And it is certainly lucrative; to date, *Twilight* has grossed $382 million worldwide and made its creator, Stephenie Meyer, one of *Time* magazine's top one hundred most influential people.

In *Twilight* Bella Swan falls for vampire Edward Cullen, who is torn between loving her back and biting her neck. In *New Moon* Edward leaves Bella for her own safety, opening the door to the infinitely more dangerous Jacob Black, who is a werewolf (the vampire's alter ego) linked – and this is folklorically correct – with a local tribe of native Americans. The third in the trilogy, *Eclipse*, features the return of Edward and the inevitable clash between vampire and werewolf. The success of the *Twilight* series is such that more vampire films are planned – *Fangland* starring Hilary Swank is in production and *The Vampire Diaries* will air in Britain on ITV in 2010.

Not everybody is impressed with the *Twilight* series, however. In a one-star rating, the *Daily Mail*'s film critic Chris Tookey says that *New Moon* squanders the goodwill factor from the first film and is 'disastrous'. There are six extra minutes, he says, 'but it feels like six hours'. Dialogue is tedious, scenes develop at a snail's pace and the images of various Native Americans wandering stripped to their shorts in Washington State's woodland 'seem to be aimed more at confirmed bachelors than at teenage girls'.[1]

Various academics have been brought in by magazines to explain *Twilight*'s extraordinary success. Delia Konzett, Professor of English and Cinema Studies at the University of New Hampshire told the *Mail*'s *You* Magazine, 'Vampires are selfish, narcissistic, and usually pleasing in appearance and potentially immortal – all things teenagers want to be.' The films are also surprisingly innocent, without actual sex, drugs or even bad language.

The genre is also all things to all men. For Dr Thomas Garza of the Centre for Russian, East European and Eurasian Studies at the University of Texas, vampire stories reflect socio-economic turbulence, saying, 'Every time we have periods of economic stress, social disorder, war, these stories peak in interest.' By contrast, television's highly acclaimed drama *True Blood* starring Stephen Moyer has led to *True Blood* parties, an increase in Bloody Mary drinking and is generally assumed to be a metaphor for homophobia and racism. What stands out about the new wave of vampire films is that the vampires are now the goodies and the story elements focusing on persecuted minorities reflect real-life issues.

A recent 'classic' of the vampire cinema is arguably *Interview with the Vampire: the Vampire Chronicles*[2] based on the novels of Anne Rice and it shows how far we have wandered from the Dracula concept developed by Bram Stoker. Perhaps the most lavish 'dead undead' film made to date, it focuses on the vampire Lestat, played by an elegantly pale Tom Cruise, 'exquisitely miscast' according to Thorne,[3] who takes us through two centuries of his 'life', centring on the murky night people of Paris and New Orleans.

'Drink from me and live forever' said the film's posters, but most critics were unimpressed by its intended longevity. The critic for the *London Evening Standard* wrote:

> For fear, it substitutes disgust. It's such a dishonest, hypocritical film. Largely an exercise in sado-masochism, it uses the traditional trappings of vampire legend as licence for its own

fixation on an array of modern perversions it would be hard to
get permission to show if they were performed in modern dress
and contemporary times.[4]

Presumably the perversions that Alexander Walker is referring
to are the inevitable obsession with blood, the homoerotic
subtext of the relationship between Cruise and Brad Pitt and
the potential paedophilia involving the little girl vampire
played by Kirsten Dunst. Interestingly, even though *Interview* does not feature Dracula at all, an even vaster array of
perversions has been laid at the Impaler's door, as we shall see.
Critic Joe Queenan's comment was that the film was 'best
thought of as a lycanthropic *The Odd Couple*' and it was
noticeable that in the Academy Award and BAFTA nomina-
tions, credit was given to the music and photography, not the
writing, direction or performances.

The criticisms of *Interview* and the storyline of the film
itself expose the problem for vampire film-makers in the
twenty-first century; we have seen it all before and it is
difficult to find anything new to say. With our jaded cinematic
appetites, cloyed by years of television repeats and DVDs 'to
rent and buy', are we seriously going to be frightened and
shocked by a traditional vampire film? Directors and screenplay writers are, inevitably perhaps, bound to look for
something else, something more pulse-quickening, to draw
their audiences. If the straightforward bite to the neck does
not work anymore, what if the bite belongs to Tom Cruise and
the neck to Brad Pitt? It adds a dimension of the exotic and the
forbidden which is actually an attempt to recreate the impact
of Bram Stoker's original *Dracula* novel and strangely takes us
back to the repellent and shocking tales that were already
circulating about the Impaler during his lifetime. Ironically of
course, the *Twilight* series has nothing new to say, merely
wallowing in sickly nostalgia for old-fashioned romance.

With this problem in mind and moving back in time as we
remove the layers of legend, film producers, mostly from

Hollywood, in the 1970s and 1980s created vampire stories that were modern in their setting, 'alongside the yuppie, the geek, the trailerpark and the shopping mall'.[5] *Interview*'s brooding nineteenth-century New Orleans backstreets have a sinister surrealism of their own, but that very surrealism means that it cannot frighten us like the folksy 1980s town of *Salem's Lot* or the tawdry seaside fairground in *The Lost Boys*.

Originally a two-part drama made for American television, *Salem's Lot*[6] was based on a novel by horror writer Stephen King and a screenplay by Paul Monash. The hero is a famous writer played by David Soul who returns to his home only to find that it is infested with vampires, themselves the undead victims of the mysterious Mr Barlow, a hideous gigantic ghoul who is brought to life by the sinister James Mason – 'You'll enjoy Mr Barlow – and he'll enjoy you.' Although it cannot compare with *Interview* in terms of its budget or scope, *Salem's Lot* is a genuine attempt to implement the terror process by making the setting so mundane. Bram Stoker did the same thing by bringing his undead Count to the prosaic Yorkshire fishing village of Whitby.

The Lost Boys,[7] with a screenplay by Janice Fischer, James Jeremias and Jeffrey Boam, has as much to do with gang warfare, teenage status and the attention-seeking of America's disaffected youth as with vampirism. As director Joel Schumacher said in an interview at the time of the film's opening:

> Vampires bring up a lot of stuff. In the Victorian period, when people lived such repressed lives, a lot of sexual fantasies were lived out through these stories. But I don't think our movie deals with any of those things at all. I think it just says 'Hey! There are still Vampires, they just dress better!'[8]

However we rate *The Lost Boys* and *Salem's Lot*, they were both serious attempts to return spine-chilling effects to a genre that was waning almost as though, without Dracula, the films served no purpose and without the shadowy figure of the Impaler, the genre had lost its way.

The *Blade* series was an exception, one of the first to look at vampires as a dangerous sub species who were *everywhere*. So ubiquitous were they, and so dangerous, that Wesley Snipes and Kris Kristofferson are employed to control the menace. The original film opens in a vampire club, like the ones described in Chapter 1, with blood squirting from the sprinkler system. The remainder of the film is a combination of the gritty reality of New York street life with the clever camera techniques of the best martial arts movies. The Snipes character, Daywalker, is a sort of van Helsing-cum-Buffy and was more charismatic than Hugh Jackman's attempt at the real Abraham van Helsing in the 2004 film. The fact that he is the offspring of a human mother and vampire father is an example of the evolving nature of the vampire in film and fiction.

Before these, as we peel back the layers of time, vampire film-makers had gone in two directions – the comic and the pornographic. In 1972, the first black horror film was made, with the Shakespearean actor William Marshal as *Blacula*.[9] The product of a pre-politically correct era, in which black American stars were big box office *because* they were black, the film attempted to link Transylvania in the early nineteenth century to 1970s Los Angeles, via an unlikely visit by an African prince.

Going for the comic jugular with a more slapstick approach was Roman Polanski in *The Fearless Vampire Killers or Pardon Me Your Teeth Are In My Neck*[10] released in 1967. *Halliwell's Film Guide* is dismissive:

> Heavy, slow spoof ... most of which shows that sense of humour is very personal; a few effective moments hardly compensate for the prevailing stodge.[11]

The critic Tom Milne found the film 'an engaging oddity' and its blue screen Carpathian Mountains and polystyrene snow were not to everyone's taste. Tony Thorne reminds us, however, that there is more to Polanski than this. The director had endured the horrors of a Nazi concentration camp as a child and two years after the release of *Vampire Killers*, its female lead (and Polanski's wife) Sharon Tate would be decapitated by the deranged 'family' of serial killer Charles Manson. Her unborn baby died with her in a barrage of sixteen stab wounds eerily redolent of the impalements of Vlad Țepeș. One of the killers, Tex Watson said, appropriately, 'I am the devil come to do the devil's work.' Another, Susan Atkins, claimed to have drunk Sharon Tate's blood:

> It felt so good the first time I stabbed her. When she screamed at me, it did something to me, sent a rush through me and I stabbed her again . . . it was like a sexual release, especially when you see the blood. It's better than a climax.[12]

The vicarious thrill of such blood-letting and the notion of doing the devil's work have obvious echoes of the vampire tradition and Vlad Țepeș.

Even more of a flop than *Vampire Killers* was *Dracula: Dead and Loving It*[13] written by Mel Brooks on the strength of his hugely successful *Young Frankenstein*. 'You'll die laughing,' promised the film's hype, 'Then you'll rise from the dead and laugh once more.' With a plot that followed Bram Stoker's novel surprisingly closely, it starred former 'heavy'-turned-comedian Leslie Nielsen as the Count, complete with ludicrous silver wig. The *Sunday Times* was unimpressed, finding it as 'thin as a bat wing'.[14]

If comedy was not the natural home of the vampire film, what about pornography? There was certainly a pornographic element in Stoker's novel and in many of the literary works that preceded it. To many, the tortures enjoyed by Vlad Țepeș have heavily erotic overtones, depending on the motives they ascribe to them. Two vampire films in recent years had sections left on the cutting room floor after the censors took over. Both from 1970 and considered pure sexploitation, *The Vampire Lovers*[15] and *Lust for a Vampire*[16] attempted to breathe titillation into a tired theme. *The Vampire Lovers* was directed by Roy Baker and apart from the opening dream-like scene was based entirely on Sheridan Le Fanu's *Carmilla* (see Chapter 4) which predated Stoker's novel. It is worth remembering that before the vampire of fiction became 'distorted by the overwhelming influence of that middle-aged gentleman, Count Dracula',[17] it was 'again as a *femme fatale*, a lady, that she was cast'.[18] Jimmy Sangster's *Lust for a Vampire* was not actually a sequel to Baker's work, but it took the idea of vampire and sex-goddess a stage further.

Most of the sex-vampire films of the 1960s and 1970s were in fact French, like Jean Rollin's *La Vampire Nue* with its elements of nudity, blood and sadomasochism. We are increasingly drifting away here from that 'middle-aged gentleman' and still further from his fifteenth-century original, but the films of the previous generation were altogether more faithful.

For many, the archetypal vampire films were made by the British company, Hammer, by Hollywood standards a tiny film studio, housed at Bray on the Thames. The success of these turned Hammer into the biggest money-spinner in the British film industry. Founded in 1947, the studio specialized in low budget B-features with a price tag of under £20,000. The stock sets were immediately recognizable as was the stable of actors who filled the minor roles. The undoubted star of the Hammer series, however, was the 'tall, dark and gruesome' Christopher Lee, who first played Bram Stoker's malignant Count in *Dracula*[19] in 1958. Lee was a natural. As author and critic David Pirie writes,[20] Lee is:

> himself an aristocrat of Italian origin and claims to be able to trace his family tree back to the Emperor Charlemagne. His slightly demonic good looks and tall statuesque physique made him ideal for the role and after nearly ten years of supporting parts in movies, he put everything into it.

It seems bizarre today that one of the *Carry On* comedy team, Bernard Bresslaw, was also in the running for the part. Lee himself sums up the cinematic Dracula brilliantly:

> He offers the illusion of immortality, the subconscious wish we all have for limitless power, a man of tremendous brain and physical strength with a strange dark heroism. He is either a reincarnation or he has never died ... He is a superman image with an erotic appeal for women who find him totally alluring. In many ways he is everything people would like to be, the anti-hero, the heroic villain ... part-saint and part-sinner. Men find him irresistible because they cannot stop him and, to women, he represents the complete abandonment to the power of a man.[21]

As horror expert Christopher Frayling put it in a Radio Scotland feature *The Usual Suspects* in December 1997:

> ... gorgeous Christopher Lee coming slowly towards you across the carpet, with this incredible voice saying, 'I am here. You have called me, my dear, and I am here.' They [Dracula's victims] just throw back the covers and seem to say 'Have me! Have me!' And he does.[22]

Journalist and horror-expert Basil Copper was particularly impressed by Lee's blood-filled eyeballs (a red contact lens technique which Lee himself thought over-done) and 'particularly his agonies in disintegration'.[23]

No less distinguished was Peter Cushing as Professor van Helsing, the vampire-hunter and a force for good, an altogether more suave character than Bram Stoker created, doomed to spend his life with immense courage and folkloric knowledge in equal quantities, before at last driving the inevitable stake through Lee's heart. There were no official complaints about this violence in late 1950s Britain, although audiences were equally thrilled and appalled by the erotic overtones of Lee sinking his fangs into all-too-welcoming throats and Cushing driving home his whitethorn spike with a mallet. 'Who will be his bride tonight?' the film's posters asked.

Of all the later Hammer productions on the vampire theme, *Dracula, Prince of Darkness*[24] released in 1966 stands out. Film critic Judith Crist dismissed it at that time as 'run-of-the-coffin stuff ... only for ardent fangs-and-cross fans', but this ignored the rather more tempestuous background to its creation. Lee was not keen to 'resurrect' the role after eight years since his first appearance, but censorship problems also accrued. Richard Matheson's vampire novel *I am Legend* was due to be made by the company, but the British Board of Film Censors (BBFC) warned that it would ban it if production went ahead. Produced in this climate, *Prince of Darkness* was therefore a much more timid effort than it might otherwise have been.

Vampire films have always walked a fine line, exemplified by the friction between the mid-twentieth-century caution and even pomposity of the BBFC and the natural boundary-pushing creativity of Hammer's boss James Carreras, the 'king of nausea'. The original no-go areas for the BBFC in 1912, the year of its creation, were nudity and portrayals of Christ. In America, things had been much more lax, but the Hays Office, a self-regulating studio watchdog, clamped down severely in the 1920s, so that, unusually, attitudes towards vampire films were more or less in accord on both sides of the Atlantic.

From where had Carreras, Fisher and Hammer obtained their original inspiration? Stoker clearly, but a series of limp sequels throughout the 1930s and 1940s were the descendants of the best known Dracula of them all, Bela Lugosi. As Basil Copper wrote:

[Lugosi's] Dracula ... showed the powerful effect a serious approach to the vampiric could have on mass audiences. This, coupled with acting of integrity, impressive art work and the intelligent use of sound and atmosphere proved that the theme, though inherently distasteful to the person of average intelligence and sensibility, could thrill without becoming repulsive. This was an artistic approach which might well have been noted by those who followed.[25]

Hollywood's Universal Studio was, in the 1920s, outside the giants of the industry, with only the critically acclaimed *All Quiet on the Western Front* to its recent credit. The cut-throat economic competition between West Coast studios in the mid-1920s and the potentially catastrophic advent of sound nearly broke the company, but its boss, the German immigrant Carl Laemmle, survived by making low-budget westerns and comedies which played in the less prestigious theatres. Perhaps because of his mid-European background, Laemmle took the idea of the 1927 Broadway play *Dracula* and intended to give the lead to Lon Chaney, the most celebrated horror film star of his day. Chaney died of cancer in 1930, however, and actors Ian Keith, Conrad Veidt and William Powell were all considered for the role before it was finally won by Lugosi, whose Broadway theatricality was transferred to celluloid.

Bela Lugosi Blaske himself has become a character of legend. He was probably born in 1884 in Lugoj, in the Banat region of Romania (then a Hungarian province) and he was brought up in Hungary, arriving in America sometime in 1919. The fact that the character of Dracula was played by a Hungarian, one of the ancient enemy, outraged patriotic Romanians in 1931. He claimed to have been a Hussar officer in the Austro-Hungarian army, but this is unsubstantiated. His English was poor and in minor parts such as MGM's *The Thirteenth Chair* he had to learn his lines phonetically and often clearly had no real understanding of what he was saying. It worked admirably, however, in introducing pure Transylvanian evil to American audiences. As Tony Thorne nicely observes:

The Magyar actor actually brought a little bit of Hungary to Hollywood, itself a place that was deliberately and wilfully ignorant of the rest of the planet, even though many of its founders were refugees from the Vampire's homelands.

Lugosi's delivery, 'I am Dracula. I bid you welcome,'[26] has been much parodied over the years, contrasting sharply with Christopher Lee's public school sang-froid. It also contrasts sharply with Stoker's original[27] in which a much more subtle Dracula shakes Jonathan Harker's hand with, 'Welcome to my house. Come freely. Go safely. And leave something of the happiness you bring.'

Because of the power of the stage-play and the problems of censorship in what was, after all, a delicate area of sexual seduction,[28] much of the real action happens off set, with creepy shadows, cobwebbed vaults and bat motifs in abundance. Basil Copper writes:

> The opening of the production could hardly be bettered; the Count's lair, the dark, malodorous vaults, with the camera passing slowly past the melancholy scene . . . bones protruding from a shattered coffin; a rat gnawing listlessly at them . . . the coffin-lid lifts, a hand gropes . . .

Lugosi too, because of Garrett Ford's clumsy screenplay and his own limitations as an actor, exudes no ambiguity and very little charm. As David Pirie rightly says:

> He is a thug and as such his capacity to threaten is drastically limited . . . His exaggerated gestures and diction stand out with dazzling clarity from the pale and more modern shadows with which he is surrounded, making that looming malevolent shape into the ultimate stereotype of all heavies. As a personality, as a phenomenon, as a star, he was remarkable. As an influence on the emergent horror film, struggling for freedom from stage melodrama, he was disastrous.[29]

There are fascinating echoes here of the real Vlad Ţepeş, who many historians have dismissed merely as a 'thug'. This assessment, as we shall see, is naïve – the Impaler's 'capacity to threaten' was enormous.

Like many associated with the name of Dracula, Lugosi's career went downhill after making the film. Trapped in the ultimate of stereotypes, he resorted to recreating the Count (with no venom at all) in silly comedies like *Abbott and Costello Meet Frankenstein* in 1948 and *Old Mother Riley Meets the Vampire* in 1952. He claimed to be a heart-throb in his native Budapest, although there is no evidence for this and he died a largely forgotten morphine addict in 1956, the year in which his native country attempted to throw off the yoke of Russian Communism. He had pleaded to be taken into care and still continued to play minor roles in minor films, virtually sleepwalking through scenes. He was buried in the black, scarlet-lined cloak he had worn in *Dracula* and horror actor Peter Lorre murmured to his co-star Vincent Price at the graveside, 'Do you think we should drive a stake through his heart, just in case?' Lugosi is reputed to have made over $600,000 from his various films, but he died with only $3,000 to his name.[30]

The directorial creator of the Lugosi films was Todd Browning, who had worked with Lon Chaney and others in the silent film industry. Browning was a cinematic genius in his own right, but he was working in the decade that produced the first,[31] best and still the most truly frightening vampire film ever made, *Nosferatu*, released in 1922.

What terrifies in the film is the central performance delivered by Max Schreck. Because the name means 'fright' and the actor is so heavily made up, it was assumed for years that this was a one-off creation, and, like Lugosi, the actor was as much part of the legend as the Count himself. In fact, Schreck appeared in a number of other classics of the German silent cinema, though never with such effect. David Pirie explains our fascination with the man:

The well-groomed, demonic vampire of Stoker [and one might
add of Lugosi and Lee] is transformed into a skeletal, contorted
monster, who shuffles with senile purpose in and out of frame
... He resembles an animated corpse ... the long fingers
tapering away into little sticks of bone and nail; the broad,
domed, hairless scalp with grotesquely pale skin; the mongoloid
pointed ears, staring eyes and gap-toothed mouth.

Klaus Kinski's recreation of this role in 1979, *Nosferatu the
Vampyre*,[31] although stylish and slick, could not hold a candle
to the original.

There is little of Stoker and nothing of the Lugosi/Lee
tradition in *Nosferatu*. The vampire of folklore[32] has no
shadow and no reflection; Schreck has both. There is no
billowing cloak, no bloody fangs, almost no sexual atmosphere at all. Yet Schreck is compelling, unutterably creepy, to
the extent that *Shadow of the Vampire*[33] (2000), a fascinating
movie about the making of *Nosferatu*, has Willem Dafoe as
Schreck actually *being* a vampire. His fee? The right to bite his
heroine's neck.

In some ways, *Nosferatu* was a typical film of its time. It
was made cheaply and quickly by the Prana Company of
Berlin at a time when that city was in a state of anarchy as a
result of a lost war, the grip of economic chaos and the
street-fighting engendered by the Kapp Putsch, a threat to
overthrow the government. Chaotic, demoralized Germany
longed for escapism from the reality of Weimar and silent
greats such as *Waxworks*, *Metropolis* and *The Cabinet of Dr
Caligari* provided it. *Nosferatu*, the work of director F.W.
Murnau, and photographed by Fritz Wagner and Gunther
Krampf, was of the same stable, but its sets lacked the power
of those mentioned above.

It was the links with Stoker's *Dracula* that caused Murnau
and the Prana studios the greatest problems. Although 'the
Count' is called Orlock and his coffin-laden ship puts into the
German port of Bremen, rather than the Yorkshire port of

Whitby, its uncredited similarities to Bram Stoker's novel were sufficient to infuriate his widow, Florence, who promptly set out on the litigation warpath.

Realizing the extent of Prana's plagiarism two months after the film's release in March 1922, Florence successfully challenged the studio, although they kept appeals going for three years before declaring bankruptcy. In July 1925, all copies of the film were ordered to be destroyed, although prints made from an original negative were being shown in American cinemas four years later. The irony is that Florence Stoker had no real objection to her husband's work being filmed. She gave the green light to Hamilton Deane's Broadway play in 1927 and is believed to have approved Lugosi's film version four years after that. What annoyed her was that Henrik Galeen's script had taken liberties with the original and made no reference to Bram Stoker anywhere.

Before *Nosferatu*, there were perhaps a dozen vampire films, some of which have survived the ravages of time, damp, dust and studio collapse. There are twenty-four such films made between 1896 (*The Devil's Castle*) and 1922 (*The Blonde Vampire*). Most of these, however, were a mish-mash of horror and the 'vamp' in them was a heroine of the type made famous by the actress Theda Bara, a *femme fatale* intent on seducing men rather like the succubus of witchcraft and demonology. The film poster for Bara's *The Kiss of the Vampire* (1916) read, 'She just wanted to ruin her victims and then laugh at them. She was bad!'

Daniel Farson, British writer and broadcaster, wrote of the female vampire:

> She is described as voluptuous and wanton, irresistible, heartlessly cruel. Like the male vampire, she has full red lips – supposedly the result of sucking blood, but also traditionally regarded ... as a sign of excessive sensuality. Even the pure must succumb to her macabre charms.[34]

Vampires form the focus of films in countries as diverse as Italy and Malaysia, often drawing on their home-grown folkloric vampire (see Chapter 5) rather than the Transylvanian count. Sadly, it is beyond the scope of this book to follow this particular trail further, but some of the most interesting vampire films come from Turkey, in that several of them focus on the character of Vlad Dracula himself, the Ottoman Turks' enemy in the fifteenth century. *Drakula Istanbul-da* (Dracula in Istanbul) was made in 1953, the first serious Turkish horror flick and Vlad appeared as an actual vampire in *Kara Boga* in 1974.

Before the invention of moving pictures, Dracula was played many times on stage. Inevitably, the anti-hero is essentially Stoker's and bears as little relation to Vlad Ţepeş as his celluloid counterpart.

The most famous portrayal of Dracula on stage was the one first performed in the rather unlikely setting of the Grand Theatre in Derby in June 1924. An Irish actor-manager, Hamilton Deane, had been trying for years to turn his friend Bram Stoker's novel into a play and eventually did it himself. His Count was the twenty-two-year-old Raymond Huntley, a regular and reliable British film and television actor for many years afterwards. Deane himself played van Helsing, but Huntley was most impressed by the actor playing Renfield, an inmate from an asylum who falls under the Count's hypnotic spell – 'The outstanding performance . . . I would say, was that of an actor named Bernard Jukes – since dead – who played the fly-eating lunatic.'[35] As the curtain fell on the first night, Deane himself appeared front of house to send a suitable chill up the spines of the departing audience – 'Remember, there are such things.'[36] With a success on his hands, Deane took the play to the Little Theatre, London on St Valentine's Day, 1927 and it enjoyed one of the longest runs in theatrical history. For the Broadway version, American writer John L. Balderstone collaborated with Deane – although some accounts claim the two men detested each other – and the show opened at the

Shubert Theatre, New Haven, Connecticut in September of the same year. After Broadway, with Lugosi in the lead role, it toured the States for two years, breaking all previous records.[37]

Attempts to make films of the *real* Dracula, Vlad Ţepeş, the Impaler, have appeared only rarely in the West. An interesting piece, *In Search of Dracula*, was made in 1972 with Christopher Lee, looking very like the descriptions and portraits of Vlad with the well-known scarlet cap and sweeping black moustaches. But this was a documentary, intercut with scenes from various Hammer versions and must have been quite surreal. A version of Vlad's life was made, probably in Germany, in 1920 but it has not survived in the West and we had to wait until 1992 and *Bram Stoker's Dracula*[38] for the first Western attempt to explore Vlad on film.

Francis Ford Coppola directed Gary Oldman as the Count, but in this version the action starts in war-torn fifteenth-century Wallachia with Oldman as the Impaler cursing God and becoming a vampire as a result. Over a map of Wallachia and Transylvania, the shadow of the crescent representing the Ottoman Empire thrusts north-west and a narration tells us of 'A Romanian knight of the Sacred Order of the Dragon, known as Dracula.' In a surreal battle sequence, with silhouettes against a fire-red sky, Oldman's Dracula skewers Turks with his lance and impales them. His wife, given the fictional name Elizabeta, believing her husband has been killed, commits suicide by flinging herself from her castle tower into the river below.

Speaking Romanian and furious that Elizabeta is dead, Dracula renounces God, hacking his priests to death in front of an altar and vowing, 'I shall rise from my own death.' He drinks a chalice of the blood that is now flowing freely from the crucifix on the altar, and the credits roll *'Bram Stoker's Dracula'*, even though nothing we have seen so far has anything to do with Bram Stoker.

The film flashes forward 400 years by which time Oldman had transformed into the better-known Count complete with black cape and rather ludicrous Leslie Nielsen-style silver wig. His accent is pure Lugosi, however, and there is something quietly sinister in his delivery. We hear the wolves howling and he turns to the camera with the inevitable 'Ah, the children of the night.'

Dark Prince: The Legend of Dracula (2001) is of a different genre altogether. It is not at all a vampire film, but attempts to portray the life of the Impaler as authentically as the tastes of a modern audience will allow. Written intelligently by Tom Baum and directed by Joe Chappelle, the storyline remains true to the various legends of Vlad Ţepeş and was filmed on location in Romania with its idyllic painted churches and the brooding majesty of its mountains.

Much of the film is in flashback, with a smoulderingly handsome (but amazingly clean-shaven!) Rudolf Martin as Dracula explaining to a tribunal of the Orthodox Church that he is, in fact, more sinned against than sinning. We are introduced to Vlad Dracul, Dracula's father, and his slippery younger brother, Radu. The circumstances of the brothers' imprisonment by the Turks is historically incorrect, but intriguingly we see our first impaled victim in the Turkish camp.

Sultan Murad, slicing Radu's chest with a dagger and licking the blood, displays homosexual leanings towards the boy which have some basis in fact although historically these are attributed to his son, Mehmed, and Dracula is allowed to return to Wallachia, bent on revenge on the treacherous *boyars* (nobles) who killed his father by burying him alive.

Snagov Monastery, the presumed final resting place of Vlad, is correctly shown on a lake; the famous legends of the golden cup, the feast of the boyars and the nailing of the Turkish emissaries' turbans to their heads will be discussed later. Even János Hunyadi, the King of Hungary (an unlikely role for former The Who singer, Roger Daltry) is shown in his ambiguous relationship with Vlad, although his son Matthias Corvinus, who actually imprisoned Dracula in the 1460s, is not mentioned at all.

The love interest is provided by Lydia, the daughter of a double-dealing Wallachian *boyar* and she, marrying Dracula and giving birth to a son, commits suicide by leaping to her death because she cannot live with his barbaric cruelty. Dracula consistently denies committing the excesses with which he is usually credited, but one of the nastiest scenes in the film is the famous story of his eating a meal surrounded by the dying victims of his impalement. Filmed under a cloudless blue sky, with the flies of summer droning around the still-bleeding corpses, it has an air of grim reality.

Far more evil than Dracula, who is ambiguously portrayed as either messiah (the patriotic Romanian version) or anti-Christ (the view of the rest of the world) is Stefan, the Orthodox priest who, we learn, has spent years trying to kill Dracula because he believes him to be the anti-Christ. In the film, it is Stefan who engineers the death of the Impaler's father and conspires with Radu and the Turks to bring Dracula down. Vlad is finally killed in the monastery at Snagov, but reappears 'incorrupt and entire' as a result of his being excommunicated by Stefan and is thus unfit to rest in a Christian grave.

The 2004 film *Vlad* directed by Michael D. Sellers had poor reviews from horror fans who tend to be very one dimensional, looking only for blood, shocks and nudity. But the history of Vlad Ţepeş presented in the film is fairly accurate. The plotline, as in all horror yarns, is absurd; a group of post graduate students trek through Romania in search of the real Vlad and find more than they bargained for because one of them has a pendant that can bring the man back to life. Vlad is played by a grimly menacing Francisco Quinn, son of Hollywood legend Antony, and is probably more in keeping with the original Impaler than the smouldering Rudolf Martin.

Unlike vampire literature, most examples from the vampire cinema before 1980 have Dracula as their central character.

Whether he is villain or hero, messiah or anti-Christ, and the nature of van Helsing's role in relation to him are all subjects for debate. Dracula for both viewers and film-makers is the archetypal vampire of the silver screen. However, his immediate origins lie in the literature of an Irish civil-servant-turned-theatrical agent, Abraham Stoker, the subject of the next chapter.

3

BRAM STOKER'S *DRACULA*

THE DEFINITIVE VAMPIRE

By the time you read to the end of this sentence, two more copies of Stephenie Meyer's *Twilight* books will have been sold. Everything that applies to the film franchise also applies to the newest vampire literature. The novels, like the films, have their *Twilight* Mom fan base. One of the Moms, Andrea Hayes from Florida, has even written a book about her obsession, called predictably *Confessions of a Twilight Mom*. Lisa Hansen from Utah told *Stylist* magazine in November 2009, 'I was obsessed with the books – they were my shameful secret . . . I've read each of the four books nine times since January.' The four *Twilight* novels have been the UK's four bestselling children's titles in 2009 and that in itself is bizarre. In our sophisticated world children grow up fast, almost as if there is no gap between *The Hungry Caterpillar* and *Twilight*. Perhaps this is why the books were banned in many schools in Australia.

Vampire literature comprises adult books, most of which end up as series because of their popularity, juvenile fiction (into which the *Twilight* series fits), comic books and magazines. The magazines typically involve interviews with vampire actors and news relating to film or television series. Recent examples were *Journal of the Dark* and *Father Sebastian's Vampire Magazine* in America and *Crimson* and *The Velvet Vampyre* in Britain.

A whole library of vampire books has been written in the years since Bram Stoker penned *Dracula*; the most successful before Meyer was Anne Rice with *The Vampire Chronicles*. Rice's novels are blockbuster length, the *Boston Globe* referring to her as a 'wonderfully Gothic writer' with echoes of the eighteenth-century authors we shall meet in a later chapter. *The Washington Post* was even more glowing: 'Anne Rice offers more than just a story; she creates myth.'

Whereas Rice's books are meant to be taken as seriously as the genre allows, other writers have gone down the comedy route. Lynsay Sands, for example, has written such titles as *Bite Me If You Can* and *A Bite To Remember* although some of these books also have an occult detective theme.

The twenty-first- and twentieth-century vampire novels have extended the bounds of conventional vampire lore, so the running water which traditionally vampires could not cross is no longer problematical. In our irreligious society, crucifixes have also lost their power. In effect, these developments *had* to appear, otherwise the entire genre would not only have become stale, it would be static. Likewise, because of less censorship than in earlier generations, romance has become erotica in the less well-crafted tales.

Increasingly, there has been more fascination with the biology of the vampire. *The Hunger* written in 1981 and the sci-fi vampirism in *I Am Legend* (1954) explore the apocalyptic end of worlds in which the vampire sub species has become dominant and humans are in a minority of one. Crossovers into the realm of humour, science fiction, lycanthropy, zombism and a whole jumble of the occult are now conventional in almost all vampire literature.

* * *

In the wake of the most famous vampire novel ever written, a number of well known British writers went into print with short stories or novellas that covered the vampire theme. H.G. Wells' *The Flowering of the Strange Orchid* had a botanical vampire in which a strange plant from the Andaman Islands has a thirst for blood. Years later the idea would be transformed into the film and subsequent musical *Little Shop of Horrors*. In 1899, Fred M. White wrote a similar story *The Purple Terror* for *Strand Magazine* – this time poppies are the blood suckers.

E.F. Benson in 1912 wrote *The Room in the Tower* with grisly descriptions of a creature rotting in her shroud. Both Algernon Blackwood, the master of occult writing, and Arthur Conan Doyle, spiritualist and creator of Sherlock Holmes, wrote of 'psychic sponges' in their respective short stories *The Transfer* and *The Parasite* (although to be fair to Conan Doyle he wrote this two years before Stoker's *Dracula*). Psychic vampirism occurred again in Reginald Hodder's *The Vampire*.

Stanislas Eric, Count Stenbock, brought a touch of exotic aristocracy to the theme in *The True Story of a Vampire*. In his *The Other Side* we have a Draculaesque villain in Count Vardaleh:

My darling, I would fain spare thee; but thy life is my life and I must live, I who would rather die.

Far more ghoulish – and in line with the traditional fictional vampire – was F. Marion Crawford's *For the Blood is the Life*:

And the flickering light of the lantern played upon ... two deep, dead eyes that saw in spite of death ... upon gleaming teeth on which glistened a rosy drop.

Victor Roman's *Four Wooden Stakes* has the same imagery:

The lips were drawn back in a snarl disclosing two sets of pearly white teeth, the canines over developed and remarkably sharp.

However all these novels pale into insignificance in comparison with the huge influence of Stoker's *Dracula* itself.

Abraham Stoker was an unlikely creator of one of the world's most enduring monsters. An Irishman born in 1847 in Clontarf, County Dublin, his father was a third-class clerk in the Chief Secretary's office in Dublin Castle and as such the family was rooted in the Protestant Ascendancy that continued to dominate Irish history until the Troubles and partition in the years following the First World War. Ireland was a land of country estates owned by English landlords who were often absentees and which were run by less-than-scrupulous bailiffs. Three years before Stoker's birth, a blight had hit the staple potato crop and the 'praties' turned black and spongy in the ground. The result was the Famine – an estimated one million dead from starvation and disease.

As was not unusual in the Victorian period, Stoker's father was considerably older than his wife (a pattern the son would repeat in his own marriage). Abraham senior was forty-eight when his third child was born and his wife, Charlotte, thirty. All Stoker's brothers became doctors, William, the eldest, being knighted for his services to surgery in 1895. Charlotte was an inveterate charity worker, visiting workhouses and supporting women's rights at the dawn of feminine militancy.

For the first six years of his life, Stoker was largely bed-ridden and found walking difficult. In view of a very robust adulthood that was to follow, it is possible that the cause was psychosomatic. His illness may have led to his passion for reading, however, and he immersed himself in particular with Gaelic folklore and its female vampires, the *leannan-sidhe*.[1]

At Trinity College, Dublin, Stoker obtained an Honours degree in Mathematics, became president of the Philosophical

Society and won the college's athletic championship. He also met Oscar Wilde and was a frequent visitor at Wilde's parents' house in Merrion Square. Called to both Irish and English Bars, Stoker rather prosaically followed both his father and grandfather into service at Dublin Castle – 'the gingerbread castle of the viceroy' as Christopher Frayling calls it.[2] Here he worked as a junior civil servant, even publishing his first book on the subject, *The Duties of the Inspector in Petty Services*, in December 1879. It really is as dull as it sounds and serves to point up the curious paradox of the Count's creator. How could the man who wrote *Dracula* write this?

Two years earlier, Stoker had met the actor Henry Irving and this undoubtedly changed his life. Part of Stoker's curious personality is that he seemed intent on courting the attention of great men, drawing on their skills perhaps as a vampire drains his victims. For years he carried on a correspondence with the American poet and pacifist Walt Whitman, whose literary output at the time included subjects such as homosexuality that were taboo in nineteenth-century America and Britain.[3]

Irving had been a clerk in his early life, as had Whitman and Stoker, but had first trod the boards in Sunderland when Stoker was nine. His London debut was made at the St James's Theatre in 1866, but his Shakespearean triumphs at the Lyceum – *Hamlet* (1874), *Macbeth* (1875) and *Othello* (1876) – made him the greatest tragedian of his generation. Even so, when Stoker gave up the Dublin Castle post to become Irving's manager at the Lyceum, his mother was appalled. Stoker's pension had gone and he now worked for a 'strolling player'. The acting profession supposedly had been made respectable by David Garrick a century earlier, but Charlotte Stoker's attitude is proof enough that there were those who were less impressed; until the 1820s 'strolling players' risked a six month jail sentence.

Stoker's career took another direction in 1878. He married the 'exquisitely pretty' Florence Balcombe, who had been Oscar Wilde's sweetheart and who, many years later, would make life difficult for F.W. Murnau and the Prana Studio over the copyright issues in *Nosferatu* (see Chapter 2). Their only child, Noel, was born in 1879. Florence was a darling not only of literati like Wilde and Stoker, but also artists such as Edward Burne-Jones and Walter Osborne, anxious to capture her pre-Raphaelite, fin de siècle beauty.[4]

The novel *Dracula* was seven years in the making and was in many ways the culmination of short stories about the supernatural that Stoker had begun writing in the 1870s. The first of these, *The Chain of Destiny*, appeared in four parts in *The Shamrock* magazine in 1875 and was very much in the mode of his later short stories such as *The Burial of Rats* and *The Judge's House*, published posthumously by Florence in 1914. They are over-ripe and seem ludicrous today, although some writers place him as a 'minor master' in the field. The 1890s has a reputation of being a 'naughty' decade, one that saw the imprisonment of Oscar Wilde on homosexual charges, the illicit publication of the sexual 'biography' *Walter; My Secret Life* and a decadence which would resurface in Weimar Germany twenty years later to produce the extraordinary cinematic offerings of directors like Murnau.

What is odd, even parochial, about *Dracula* is Stoker's use of the minutiae of his own life. His holidays in Cruden Bay, Scotland and Whitby, Yorkshire with his family, all found their way eventually into the book. He made copious notes and buried himself in local libraries, soaking up the legends and folklore of the area. F.K. Robinson's *Glossary of Words Used in the Neighbourhood of Whitby* gave him 'barguests':

> Terrifying apparitions, taking shape human or animal . . . some say barguest signifies castle-spectre . . . whether dog or demon, glares with large eyes 'like burning coals' . . . it is a harbinger of death to those who happen to hear its shrieks in the night.[5]

It was very much an era of heightened interest in the supernatural. The Victorian fad for spiritualism was waning and would not be resurrected until the appalling slaughter on the Western Front made families desperate for contact with their dead loved ones. The controversy over burial versus cremation was all but resolved and the fascination with expensive, black-robed funerals in decline, but the sinister and the macabre were as popular as ever; witness the ghost stories of M.R. James and Algernon Blackwood. It may well be that, for Stoker, *Dracula* had its origins in the too generous helping of dressed crab for supper that he believed gave him nightmares in 1890, but it was his enduring fascination with the unknown that led to a full-blown novel.

Originally called *The Dead Undead*, the book was published as *Dracula* by Constable in June 1897. It had a print-run of 3,000 and a price of six shillings. Its re-issue in 1901 was in the form of a sixpenny paperback with a yellow cover featuring a crude drawing of a cloaked, white-haired Count descending vertically down a tower in Castle Dracula.

The book's narrative still has a surprisingly modern feel, told as it is through the journal-jottings of several of the main characters, all of them reacting to the fiendish Count himself. Jonathan Harker, a solicitor's clerk, goes to Castle Dracula in Transylvania to conclude a property purchase of Carfax Abbey on behalf of the Count. While there, he learns that Dracula is a vampire – one of the undead – and is imprisoned while the Count sails for England. When the ship arrives, drifting into Whitby harbour, all the crew are dead, except of course for the Count, asleep in his coffin below deck. Dracula attacks Lucy Westenra, the flirtatious friend of Harker's fiancée, Mina Murray, and despite the efforts of Lucy's three suitors, and the return of Jonathan from Transylvania, they cannot save the girl from becoming a vampire and she haunts Highgate Cemetery in search of lost souls. Even the learned Professor van Helsing cannot prevent this, but concentrates instead on saving Mina from Dracula's attentions. Pursuing the monster back to Transylvania, van Helsing, Harker and Lucy's suitors drive a stake through

Dracula's heart and lift the terrifying curse as the Count's body crumbles to dust.

Charlotte Stoker, Bram's mother, raved over the first edition:

> My dear, it is splendid, a thousand miles beyond anything you have written before and I feel certain will place you very high in the writers of the day ... No book since Mrs Shelley's *Frankenstein* [see below] or indeed any other at all has come near yours in originality or terror – Poe[6] is nowhere. I have read much but I have never met a book like it at all. In its terrible excitement it should make a widespread reputation and much money for you.[7]

As with the later landmark vampire films, the critics' reception to Stoker's book was less adulatory. The *Athanaeum* did not like it, finding the book 'wanting in the constructive art as well as in the higher literary sense'. *Punch* wrote that it was 'the very weirdest of weird tales'. The *Bookman* damned with faint praise: 'we read nearly the whole with rapt attention.'[8] Thirty years later, occultist Montague Summers (see Chapter 5) found the first sixty pages the best and believed that:

> many pages could have been compressed ... It is hardly possible to feel any great interest in the characters; they are labels rather than individuals.[9]

Summers was convinced (and he has a point) that horror stories should be short and any attempt to extend them to novel length is doomed to failure. For him, most of the creepy bits could be found in the first four chapters – Harker's journal – and after that, there are too many lapses into the average. Like any literary work that has caught the public imagination and survived, *Dracula* has been dissected over and over again and meaning given to its passages which it is most unlikely Bram Stoker ever intended. Maurice Richardson sums it up best perhaps – *Dracula* is 'a kind of incestuous, necrophiliac, oral-anal-sadistic all-in wrestling match'.[10] Christopher Frayling notes that it is possible to interpret the story in a variety of ways: as Freudian allegory, Marxist 'cosmic racial conflict', feminist gender politics and so on. The literary expert James Twitchell[11] wrote that *Dracula* was successful because it represented:

> sex without genitalia, sex without confusion, sex without responsibility, sex without guilt, sex without love – better yet, sex without mention.[12]

Stoker's own sexuality is a blank page. The gorgeous and adorable Florence seems to have withdrawn her favours after Noel's birth and this may have sent Bram into the beds of a number of young actresses keen to secure a plum role at the Lyceum. The late Dan Farson, himself a descendant of Stoker's, claimed in his biography of his forebear that Bram died of tertiary syphilis. A more recent biography by Barbara Bedford doubts this. The death certificate, issued on 20 April 1912 clearly says 'locomotor ataxi' which is commensurate with the strokes he had suffered in the weeks before his death. He died at home and there are no other medical records surrounding his last illness, but Farson contends that 'locomotor ataxi' is Edwardian medical-speak for syphilis, in that its euphemistic vagueness covers a multitude of sins and that polite society was just too nice to be more specific. If Farson is right, then Bram Stoker, like F.W. Murnau, killed in a car crash in Hollywood, and Bela Lugosi, a shadow of his former success, is another victim of the curse of Dracula. Tony Thorne wonders whether either the 'closet homosexual' or 'duplicitous, syphilitic frequenter of prostitutes' portrayals of Stoker is correct, seeing him more as a rather dull, hardworking family man. In a BBC broadcast for Radio Scotland,[13] Christopher Frayling had an altogether more interesting view:

> There isn't a single photo of Bram Stoker smiling . . . but there's
> something going on underneath. There's something about Bram
> Stoker that doesn't quite fit. None of the biographies have
> cracked him . . . They are the eyes of a frightened man.[14]

In one respect, Stoker's mother was wrong in her letter to him
shortly after *Dracula*'s publication. The book did not make
him a fortune. He left only £4,700 in his will – a comfortable
sum, certainly, but not what Charlotte Stoker expected. Never
again would her son produce anything as good as *Dracula* and
not even he could accept, hand on heart, her comparison with
Mary Shelley. The reality was that Stoker's upbringing and
contacts had paved the way for *Dracula* over a lifetime.

One of the most important of these contacts for our
purposes in removing the legend and finding the real Vlad
Ţepeş was Hermann Bamburger, who used a number of aliases
but is usually (and briefly) referred to in the Stoker bio-
graphies as the orientalist Arminius Vambery. He appears as
an aside of van Helsing: in *Dracula* itself – 'I have asked my
friend Arminius, of Buda-Pesth University . . . he must indeed
have been that Vovode Dracula who won his name against the
Turk.'[15] Vambery was born to orthodox Jewish parents in
March 1831, 400 years after Dracula, in the village of St
Georghem, then in Hungary. Short and, like the earlier
'vampire' Lord Byron (see Chapter 5), with a serious limp, he
was at once a hardworking, parsimonious social climber and
an incurable name-dropper. He was also a gifted linguist,
possibly fluent in at least sixteen languages and he travelled
widely throughout Afghanistan and Turkestan, invariably
with a donkey and disguised as a Dervish, using the name of
Hadji Rashid. By all accounts he had no sense of humour, bore
grudges and got progressively more bad-tempered as he got
older.

Vambery reached London in 1864 and promptly fell in love
with the city, Britain and with its Empire. He was awarded a
medal by the Royal Geographical Society six years later. His

travelogues were enormously popular, as were his two autobiographies; his lecture tours were sell-outs. He advised the nascent British Secret Service on matters relating to Russian aggression in Turkestan, but he was unlikely to have been a 'spy' in the usual sense of the term. Vambery first met Stoker at Sandringham in April 1889, where both men, together with Henry Irving, were the weekend guests of the Prince of Wales, whose favourite country house Sandringham was. A whole chapter on Vambery duly appeared in Stoker's biography of Irving in 1906.

Much of the correspondence between the two men has been lost to time, but it is likely that Vambery discussed his native Hungary with Stoker and probably suggested the books he would use in the reading room of the British Museum when researching the background to his novel *The Scottish Traveller*. Emily Gerard's *Land Beyond the Forest* (1888) gave Stoker the physical description of Transylvania that he needed, bearing in mind that, as Christopher Frayling has remarked, he 'never went further East than Whitby'.[16] Vambery was working in October 1889 on papers of Matthias Corvinus, the Hungarian king who imprisoned Vlad Dracula in the 1460s. *The Times* wrote:

> The Hungarian commission, which has been sent to Constantinople with Professor Arminius Vambery to explore the archives of the Imperial Library, has already made the important discovery of three volumes which belonged to the library of Matthias Corvinus.[17]

It is likely that Vambery suggested to Stoker William Wilkinson's *Account of the Principalities of Wallachia and Moldavia*, written in 1820 when Wilkinson was the British Consul in Bucharest. This in turn was based on the Oxford scholar Richard Knolles' work *The Generall History of the Turkes* (1603) where the 'notable but cruell prince' Vlad Dracula receives several pages of description. Vambery may well have pointed Stoker in the direction of the English translation of Sebastian Munster's *Cosmographia*, a sixteenth-century 'bestseller' which talked of '*der streng ja tyranisch man Dracula*'.[18] Vambery's colleague at Budapest and at Constantinople was a Dr Franknoi, an acknowledged expert on the reign of Mathias Corvinus and the Draculas of Wallachia.

Only the barest essentials of Vlad Ţepeş' history appear in Stoker's novel. He may have been intrigued by the name Dracula or Vambery's stories of barbarous cruelty that were associated with it, but the fact that Stoker's description of Vlad's lineage is reasonably accurate makes the point that he intended his undead Count to be associated with the Impaler himself.

We know from Stoker's notes, preserved in the Rosenbach Museum in Philadelphia, that he originally intended to set the story not in Vambery's Hungary or Emily Gerard's Transylvania, but in Styria, in his day a Duchy in the Austro-Hungarian Empire. And this is because he was intrigued by the area he had read about in J. Sheridan Le Fanu's famous story, *Carmilla*.

4

FANTASMAGORIA
VAMPIRES AND THE ROMANTICS

Joseph Sheridan Le Fanu was a grand-nephew of the playwright and Whig acolyte Richard Sheridan and was born into the same Irish Protestant Ascendancy as Stoker. This was 1814, when Robert Peel was Chief Secretary for Ireland. Sheridan's brother, William Richard Le Fanu was Commissioner of Public Works at Dublin Castle during Stoker's father's time. Le Fanu's father was an impoverished Protestant clergyman who twice became rector in the country's Catholic south. As such, his congregation and income was small and the family often at the centre of tension and resentment. Joseph read law at Trinity College, Dublin and although called to the Bar in 1839 was already dabbling in journalism and never practised. He wrote extensively in the 'Gothic Horror'-style so popular in his day, but always allowed a potentially natural explanation for the peculiar events in his plots. His first foray into vampire country came in 1839 with *A Strange Event in the Life of Schalken the Painter*, in which the revenant is also a demon lover with as much erotic overtone as the reading public and censorship would tolerate in that period. Four years later, he produced *Spalatro*, supposedly taken from the notebook of fictional vampire hunter Fra Giacomo, in which the hero is seduced by a deadly femme fatale who drinks blood.

Coincidentally, Le Fanu's son Thomas worked in the office next to Bram Stoker's and the aspiring novelist published his first short story *The Crystal Cup* in the *Dublin Evening Mail* of which Sheridan le Fanu had been editor. It was while Stoker was still at university that he read Le Fanu's *Carmilla*. Carmilla, aka Mircalla, aka Countess Karnstein, is clearly a reworking of the *Spalatro* heroine/villain (Le Fanu specialized in expansions like this in many of his works) and a number of stock characters who appear in later vampire books and films are there. The story is told in the first person (à la Stoker); there is not one, but two vampire hunters, Doctor Hesselius and Baron Vordenburg, and the whole tale is set in a background of ghostly castles, impenetrable forests (Styria, today's Austria) and has bitings galore. It is obvious from the text that Le Fanu had read Dom Calmet's *Treatise on Vampires and Revenants* (see Chapter 6), translated into English in 1850 as *The Phantom World* as well as two books by the Reverend Baring-Gould, *The Book of Werewolves* (1863) and a biography of Elizabeth Báthory (see Chapter 15).

Stoker must have been impressed by this, not only considering Le Fanu's Styria for his *Dracula* setting, but keeping the same sense of dreamy ennui that le Fanu uses:

Think me not cruel [says Carmilla], because I obey the irresistible law of my strength and weakness . . . In the rapture of my enormous humiliation, I live in your warm life and you shall die – die, sweetly die – into mine.[1]

Lesbian overtures were quite risqué for the time (*Carmilla* appeared as a short story in *The Dark Blue Magazine* in 1872):

Her hot lips travelled along my cheek in kisses and she would whisper almost in sobs, 'You are mine, you shall be mine and you and I are one forever.'

It is likely that Le Fanu, like Stoker, was brought up in the Irish Gaelic folklore of the *leannan-sidhe* (see Chapter 3), but other literary forces were also at work on him as an impressionable young man.

Varney the Vampire or the Feast of Blood hit a horror-hungry public in the winter of 1846. The potato famine was ravaging Ireland. England was shaken by the storm surrounding the repeal of the infamous Corn Laws and the collapse of Robert Peel's government. It was a hungry time in every sense with unemployment barely under control and gangs of navvies roaming the countryside building thousands of miles of track in what was erupting as 'railway mania'.

The authorship of *Varney* is still in dispute a century and a half later. One tradition has it that it is the work of Thomas Preskett Prest, a hack who churned out dozens of novels, some of them over a thousand pages long. They had delectable titles such as *The Goblet of Gore*, *The Skeleton Clutch* and *The Secret of the Grey Turrett*. Even so, Prest's name is known today for a number of tales featuring Sweeney Todd, the Demon Barber of Fleet Street. Another contender for the authorship of *Varney* is James Malcolm Rymer, a Scottish engineer who turned to writing the lurid 'penny dreadfuls' of his day as perhaps a more lucrative career. In 1928 author and 'clergyman' Montague Summers (see Chapter 5) had no doubts as to the authorship at all, writing: 'Who Rymer might be I cannot tell. *Varney the Vampire* was written by Thomas Preskett Prest.'[2] Also known as Errym and Merry (by which we may conclude that *all* the variants are pseudonyms), Rymer was paid one penny per line by his publishers, Edward Lloyd of Shoreditch. His description of the vampire has rather more in common with

Schreck's Orlock from the film *Nosferatu* than Stoker's
Dracula:

> The figure turns half round and the light falls upon the face. It
> is perfectly white – perfectly bloodless. The eyes look like
> polished tin; the lips are drawn back and the principal feature
> next to those dreadful eyes is the teeth – the fearful-looking
> teeth – projecting like those of some wild animal, hideously,
> glaringly white and fang-like. It approaches the bed with a
> strange, gliding movement. It clashes together the long nails
> that literally hang from the finger ends. No sound comes from
> its lips. Is she going mad – that young and beautiful girl exposed
> to so much terror?[3]

Bram Stoker was born in the year that *Varney*'s mammoth 868
pages and 220 chapters beguiled a fascinated readership.
Sheridan Le Fanu was already thirty-two. And whether Prest
or Rymer penned *Varney* they were working in the teeth of
fierce criticism from the more sophisticated middle classes
who worried that the 'penny dreadful' was dangerous to an
easily seduced youth. The 'Dime Novel' in America and the
British 'Newgate Novel' were believed to have the same effect
– they were the 'video nasties' of their day.

As Montague Summers points out, the problem with
assessing the vampire in literature is the exact meaning of the
term. M.R. James, one of the most successful short story
horror writers of the 1930s (and who was heavily influenced
by Le Fanu), has characters who may be ghosts or vampires –
Count Magnus for example – and this in itself reflects the
confusion in the 'true' accounts of vampirism we shall discuss
in later chapters.

But *Varney* was not the only vampire doing the rounds in
the mid-nineteenth century. In 1845, James Clerk Maxwell,
who would go on to become one of the most famous
theoretical physicists of the century, wrote 'The Vampyre', a
poem in Scottish dialect:

And the vampire suckis his gude lyfe blude,
She suckis him till hee dee.

It's hardly great poetry, but Maxwell was only fourteen at the time – a reminder that it is not only today's teens who are obsessed with the undead.

In the same year, the novel *The Last of the Vampires* by Smythe Upton appeared, showing that the writer had virtually no idea what a vampire was. One of the more interesting offshoots of the vampire craze appeared in 1858, supposedly written by 'The wife of a medical man'. *The Vampire* was a teetotal tract written at a time when the largely female Temperance Movement was attempting to curb the effects of the 'demon drink'. The villain here is not so much a person (undead or otherwise) but The Vampire Inn. The hero, driven frantic by a vampire pest, resorts to the pub to escape:

I dare not lie down! It bites – I die! Give me brandy – brandy – more brandy.

If we peel the layers back before *Varney* we have a number of writers using the term or the idea of the vampire. In America, Edgar Allen Poe introduced horrified readers to a succession of female vampires without using the word at all. Ligeia, Marella, Berenice and Madeleine Usher, they all fall into the succubi category (see Chapter 5) and in France, Théophile Gautier introduced a female vamp in *La Morte Amoreuse* in 1836. Alexandre Dumas *père* set his *Pale Faced Lady* in the Carpathian Mountains, within whose 'horseshoe' Stoker would build Castle Dracula sixty years later. In Britain, Charlotte Brontë's Bertha Rochester in *Jane Eyre* is described as 'that foul German spectre – the Vampyre'.[4]

And consciously or otherwise, these writers were drawing on older traditions still, particularly the Byronic vampire created by Dr John Polidori.

* * *

Europe opened its ports again after the days of *la gloire* that ended in Napoleon Bonaparte's defeat at Waterloo. Tourists, intrigued to see what had become of Paris in the days of the 'beast', flocked to the French capital and beyond. And a rather unlikely group ventured further east, through the Swiss Alps to Italy and more specifically to the Villa Diodati in the shadow of the 'haunted' Jura Mountains. The events of the night of 16 June 1816 have assumed a terror of their own, culminating in *Gothic*, directed by Ken Russell and dubbed by one critic 'the thinking man's *Nightmare on Elm Street*'.[5] Staying first at the Hotel d'Angleterre, the company rented a number of villas on the shores of Lake Geneva, but it was at the Diodati that the famous thunderstorm kept the group indoors. Trying to outscare each other like the overgrown schoolboys they were, Byron and Shelley decided to write ghost stories, building on the literary traditions of the 'Sensation' and Gothic novels still in vogue.

George Gordon, the sixth Baron Byron, would probably have been taken into care had he been born today. On his death, the artist John Constable wrote, 'The world is rid of him, but the deadly slime of his touch still remains.' Byron's father was the feckless eccentric Captain 'Mad Jack' Byron, a compulsive gambler who had blown his own and his wife's fortune by the time the future peer was born. His mother, Catherine, was a bitter and vulgar woman given to fits of violent temper which left their mark on young George. Educated at Harrow and Trinity College, Cambridge, the young man led the life of a Georgian rake, excelling at swimming and boxing and, perhaps unusually then for a Cambridge undergraduate, read, voraciously. In 1809, despite the war raging across the continent, Byron, with poems already published in the influential *Edinburgh Review*, went on the grand tour, that strange blend of culture, drinking and sex which served as a rite of passage for many young men of the aristocracy and gentry. While soaking up the sights and culture of Spain, Malta, the southern Balkans and the Aegean, he wrote the poem *Childe Harold* and returned as a gloomy man of mystery, impressing large numbers of fluttering ladies of society with his pronounced limp and striking good looks. The darling of London society in the days of the Prince Regent, he famously jilted the unbalanced Lady Caroline Lamb, married and left Anne Millbank and got out of England amid rumours of sexual flings with Augusta Leigh, his half sister, and of homosexual experimentation. It was in these enforced travels that he reached Diodati and met Shelley.

Percy Shelley was in his own way as subversive and rebellious a character as Byron. 'Mad Shelley', the 'Eton Atheist' wrote a Gothic novel in 1810 and at University College, Oxford, dressed and behaved outrageously before his expulsion from the university over *The Necessity of Atheism*, a pamphlet published the following year. He eloped with sixteen-year-old Harriet Westbrook, a friend of his sister; however in 1814 he fell in love with Mary Godwin. She, too, was sixteen and they too eloped, before returning to London to face financial disaster. They were on the road again by 1816 and reached Diodati.

At the villa on the night of the storm, having read excerpts from a book of ghost stories called *Fantasmagoria*:

Twelve o'clock's the Time of Night,
That the Graves, all gaping wide,
Quick send forth the airy Sprite
In the Church-way path to glide.

– it was Shelley who became hysterical and had to be sedated with cold water and ether, and it was Mary Shelley who created the monster of modern science in *Frankenstein*. It fell to the other male member of the party, Byron's physician John William Polidori, to create the vampire Lord Ruthven. In two senses, Ruthven was based on Byron. The poet had gone into print three years earlier with *The Giaour*:

But first on earth, as Vampyre sent,
Thy corpse shall from its toils be rent;
Then ghastly haunt thy native place,
And suck the blood of all thy race;
There from daughter, sister, wife,
At midnight drain the stream of life;
Yet loathe the banquet, which perforce
Must feed thy livid, living corpse.
Thy victims, ere they yet expire
Shall know the demon for their sire . . .
. . . Yet with thine own best blood shall drip
Thy gnashing tooth and haggard lip;
Then stalking to thy sullen grave
Go – and with Ghouls and Afrits rave,
Till these in horror shrink away
From spectre more accursed than they.

Ruthven was also Byron in that he was an arrogant libertine, seducer of gullible young women. Ironically, Polidori set Ruthven's 'death' in Greece, where Byron himself would die of marsh fever eight years later.

The darkly handsome Polidori was as highly strung as Byron or Shelley but he lacked the talent of either. The vampiric fragment that Byron produced at Diodati he later added to his poem *Mazeppa*, but it became the direct source for Polidori.

In a sense, the young doctor, ridiculed as 'Polly-Dolly' by the arrogant Byron, was very like Bram Stoker. Both men wrote of vampires; both men were overawed by the greatness of others. There is even a tangible link: Stoker knew Polidori's nephew, the poet Dante Gabriel Rossetti, who was a neighbour of the Irishman in Chelsea. Where Stoker and Polidori differ is that Polidori bore grudges. Educated by the Benedictines at Ampleforth and obtaining a medical diploma from Edinburgh University, Polidori had already specialized in the field that gave both Shelley and Stoker the jitters. He published a dissertation in the year before the events at

Diodati entitled *The Psychosomatic Effects of Sleepwalking and/or Nightmares*. He also kept a diary of his time with Byron, not published until nearly a century later, which made it clear that the doctor became paranoid because he was constantly the target of Byron's barbs. He couldn't bear Shelley, finding him 'bashful, shy, consumptive ... separated from his wife, keeps the two daughters of Godwin [Mary and Claire], who practice his theories [of free love]'.[6] Eventually, in the summer that *The Vampyre* was created, Polidori challenged Shelley to a duel. The rebel and atheist laughed it off, but Byron stepped in: 'Recollect, that although Shelley has some scruples about duelling, I have none, and shall be, at all times, ready to take his place.'[7]

By September, Polidori had had enough, but he was in fact dismissed by Byron before he could leave of his own accord. He drifted from Milan to Florence to Pisa and then back to England, where he briefly hung out his shingle in Norwich. In the meantime, his expanded short story *The Vampyre* was published in April 1819 in the *New Monthly Magazine* from the manuscript he had left behind in Geneva. Wrongly attributed to Byron himself – the German writer Goethe believed it to be the poet's finest work – the novella was hardly a success. Byron himself was furious that the hack piece should have been attributed to him. 'Damn the Vampyre,' he roared at his publisher, John Murray. 'What do I know of Vampyres?'[8]

In keeping with many of those associated with the vampire myth, John Polidori's end was tragic. Living as a recluse and becoming increasingly deranged, he rented rooms in Great Pulteney Street, London and was found dead there on 27 August 1821. He was twenty-five. The Coroner's Inquest was reported in *The Times* on 11 September, concluding:

> There being no further evidence adduced to prove how the deceased came to his death, the jury, under these circumstances, returned a verdict of – Died by the visitation of God.

Shelley the atheist would not have accepted that and clearly neither did Byron:

> When he was my physician he was always talking of prussic acid, oil of amber, blowing into veins, suffocating by charcoal and compounding poisons . . . It seems that disappointment was the cause of this rash act.[9]

If Polidori's patent suicide was the result of the failure of *The Vampyre*, it was a little ironic. It had already appeared on the French stage eighteen months before his death as *Lord Ruthven ou les Vampires* and it toured far more widely than the much later Hamilton Deane *Dracula* play (see Chapter 2), appearing in theatres as far apart as Venice and Baghdad. When Alexandre Dumas went to see it in Paris at the Thêatre de la Porte-Saint-Martin, three rival productions were running on other stages in the French capital. Montague Summers paraphrased Dumas in 1928:

> How the theatre applauded the lean livid mask of the Vampire, how I shuddered at his stealthy steps.[10]

And Polidori might have taken some pride in the fact that one of the lines in *Le Vampire* ran, 'Vampires . . . they come to us from England.' By August 1820 the vampire theatre was enjoying such success that there were operettas being performed, for example Martinet's *Le Vampire* in which the tag line in the libretto was '*Vivant les morts*' (the dead live) and many more followed suit. In Berlin in 1857, a Hungarian-set vampire ballet was produced, followed by another in Milan four years later. Dion Boucicault's *The Vampire* was a three-act play opening at the Princess's Theatre, London in June 1852. The critic Henry Morley didn't like it:

> To 'an honest ghost' one has no objection, but an animated corpse which goes about in Christian attire and . . . which

renews its odious life every hundred years by sucking a young lady's blood after fascinating her by motions which resemble mesmerism[11] burlesqued ... such a ghost as this passes all bounds of toleration.[12]

The literary genre in which Polidori, Byron and Mary Shelley were working in the 'haunted summer' of 1816 was that of the Gothic novel. Chris Baldock in *The Oxford Companion to Crime and Mystery Writing* defines such a work as one which 'arouses terror and dread, typically involving enclosed settings such as old castles or mansions and emphasising themes of imprisonment, persecution and decay'.[13] Poetry, as well as prose, became absorbed with these ideas. Edward Young, rector of Welwyn in Hertfordshire, produced *Night Thoughts* in the 1740s, occasioned by the death of his wife. All was gloom and doom, as it was in the 'churchyard school' of poetry initiated by the Scottish preacher Robert Blair in the same decade. From *The Castle of Otranto* written by Horace Walpole in 1764 to Charles Maturin's *Melmoth the Wanderer* in the year that *Le Vampire* appeared on the Paris stage, the genre was enormously popular. In the context of the central theme of this book, the word 'Gothic' fits like a glove – it is both medieval and barbaric, although the storylines of Walpole, Maturin and above all Anne Radcliffe are usually set in sixteenth- or seventeenth-century Europe and are obsessed with the Inquisition and the corruption of the Catholic Church. Mary Shelley's *Frankenstein; or the Modern Prometheus* published in 1818 is one of the few examples of the type that has stood the test of time, although most literary experts see Stoker's *Dracula* as a late flowering of the genre. The horror element present in the Gothic novel is again typified by Polidori's Lord Ruthven, Rymer's Sir Francis Varney and Stoker's Count Dracula. Female middle class innocence is pitted against an aristocratic and erotic past returned to haunt the living.

It was essentially the Romantic Movement that gave birth to the literary vampire in the late eighteenth century and examples can be found in Britain, France and Germany. In the German states, Heinrich Ossenfeller wrote *The Vampire* as early as 1748, Burger, *Lenore* (the name, at least, stolen by Poe) in 1773 and Goethe, *The Bride of Corinth* in 1797. Goethe, one of the German states' greatest writers, took his story from an ancient Greek version in which a young Athenian arrives at his fiancée's house to discover that the girl is a vampire.

Lenore became something of a household word once it was translated into English in 1796. Published in the influential Norwich *Monthly Review* it was discussed in literary circles throughout the country. The romantic novelist Walter Scott mentions it as having electrified the literati of Edinburgh sometime around 1794 so there must have been English versions available by that time. Scott was so taken with *Lenore* that he stayed up all night reading it – shades of the *Twilight* Moms here – and three different translations had appeared by 1797. There was even a pastiche, *Miss Kitty: A Parody on Lenora, a Ballad*, in the same year; history prefiguring itself again, as in the *New Moon* parody, *New Moan*, or The Harvard Lampoon's *Nightlight: A Parody*. For the historical figure who inspired Lenore see Chapter 14.

In this country, many of the great writers of their day, but especially poets, used the theme. Coleridge had his *Cristabel*; Shelley, *Cenci*; Keats, *The Eve of St Agnes* and *La Belle Dame Sans Merci*. The Germans accused Samuel Coleridge of stealing Burger's *Lenore* for *Christabel* but this seems unfounded. Shelley read *Lenore* to a company of friends with such skill that they were terrified and 'fully expected to see William stalk into the parlour'. Robert Southey in *Thabala the Destroyer* (1797) wrote:

When Moath, firm of heart,
Perform'd the bidding, through the vampire corpse

He thrust the lance; it fell,
And howling with the wound,
Its fiendish tenant fled.

Shelley, too, had done his homework. Notes accompanying *Thabala* refer to 'true' vampire tales of the eighteenth century:

> The Turks have an opinion that men that are buried have a sort of life in their graves. If any man makes affidavit before a judge that he heard a noise in a man's grave [the body] is dug up and chopped all to pieces.

John Stagg wrote *The Vampyre* six years before the events at Diodati:

With blood his visage was distain'd,
Ensanguin'd were his frightful eyes,
Each sign of former life remain'd,
Save that all motionless he lies.[14]

The oldest double reference to the twin themes of this book, the vampire myth and Vlad Ţepeş the man, can be found in Robert Browning's *The Pied Piper of Hamelin*.

In Tartary I freed the Cham,
Last June from his huge swarms of gnats;
I eased in Asia the Nizam
Of a monstrous brood of vampire bats.

This is the Piper's boast before he tackles Hamelin's acute rodent problem. More mysteriously, and possibly alluding to the 'dancing mania' which gripped parts of Europe in the Middle Ages and may partially explain the Children's Crusade of 1212:

And I must not omit to say

That in Transylvania there's a tribe
Of alien people that ascribe
Their outlandish ways and dress
On which their neighbours lay such stress,
To their fathers and mothers having risen
Out of some subterraneous prison
Into which they were trepanned
Long time ago in a mighty band
Out of Hamelin town in Brunswick land,
But how or why, they don't understand.

Stoker, Polidori and the others who wrote of vampires were drawing consciously or otherwise on earlier literary forms. They were also drawing on history. And they were drawing on legend; the folklore of the vampire forever linked via Stoker with Vlad Țepeș, the Impaler.

5

KISS AND KIN
FOLKLORE, SEXUALITY AND BLOODLUST

In all the darkest pages of the malign supernatural there is no
more terrible tradition than that of the Vampire, a pariah even
among demons. Foul are his ravages; gruesome and seemingly
barbaric are the ancient and approved methods by which folk
must rid themselves of this hideous pest.

So wrote Montague Summers in 1927. This odd, self-styled
Catholic priest (he converted to the Catholic Church in 1909
but never took holy orders) was in many ways a throwback
to the witch-hunting zealots of the Reformation. Everyone
who knew him found him fascinating and charming, but he
was a bigot with regard to the supernatural and brooked no
opposition to his belief. 'Tell me something strange,' he would
say when anyone visited him and that phrase is now incised
on his tombstone. He made a living by teaching classics in a
variety of boys' schools and editing Gothic novels from the
eighteenth century and the works of Jane Austen. He dressed
eccentrically, in flowing cloak and 'shovel' hat, and wore his

hair in such an odd style that many people assumed it was a wig.

On the face of it, the 1920s and 1930s seem an unusual time for a renewed interest in vampirism, but this was part of a much wider fascination with the macabre which is not only evident in films like *Nosferatu* and *Dracula* but the on-going cult of spiritualism and the notorious activities of Aleister Crowley, an acquaintance of Summers who styled himself 'the great beast'.

The importance of Summers to the vampire story is that he invested a vast amount of nonsense with the trappings of scholarship. He wrote extensively on witchcraft and the occult, larding his chapters with whole pages written in French, Latin and Greek, pretentiously assuming that his middle class readership could translate for themselves.

I will concentrate on *The Vampire: His Kith and Kin* written in 1928 not only because it deals with the central theme of this book, but also because it drags in all sorts of related topics, some of which explain the current state of vampirology today. Indubitably, much of Summers' research was based on folklore and I will discuss this elsewhere, but he also has a global element to his study, both in terms of sheer geography and in his interest in the related studies of witchcraft, lycanthropy and serial murder.

As a practising Catholic, Summers accepted the biblical and ecclesiastical tradition without demur. If the fathers of the Church wrote something in the fourth century then who are we to quibble? He states:

> We must bear in mind that these explanations come from the highest authority, one of the greatest Doctors of the Church . . .

He is talking, almost in hushed tones, about St Augustine, the first Archbishop of Canterbury, who died in 601. Few of us would quarrel with Augustine's piety, but his understanding of paranoid delusions must have been very limited. And we would certainly find difficulty in accepting Summers' view that Henry Kramer and James Sprenger were 'learned authors of the supremely authoritative' *Malleus Maleficarum* (Hammer of the Witches). This fifteenth-century witch-hunters' handbook will be discussed elsewhere, written as it was only eight years after the death of Vlad the Impaler, but it was certainly not learned. One modern commentator has described it as one of the most obscene books ever written, as it was largely the brainchild of two over-excitable and misogynist monks and was a virtual death warrant for thousands in the witch craze of the following century.

An entire chapter of Summers' book is devoted to the vampire in Assyria, the East 'and some ancient countries'. The Sumerians of the Fertile Crescent (today's Iran and Iraq) believed in an evil spirit known as *multaliku*, the wanderer. This was a creature unable to rest in his grave and doomed to walk the earth forever. He was shunned by the living and could not enter the House of Darkness (Hell). This concept of the undead fits exactly the European notion of the vampire.

Special prayers of exorcism were said for such revenants:

> He that lieth in a ditch; he that no grave covereth, he that lieth uncovered . . . The hero whom they have slain with the sword.

This last was to be the fate of Vlad the Impaler according to the nationalist Romanian view that saw him as a hero-warrior. The exorcism continued against the night-haunting demon:

> The Night-wraith that hath no husband,
> The Night-fiend that hath no wife.[1]

The Eastern vampire must not be touched or even looked at:

> Place not thy head upon his head; place not thy hand upon his hand . . . Look not behind thee.

A similar fear of 'spiritual contagion' could be found in southern Nigeria as late as the 1920s.

Summers quotes a variety of experts, but especially Dr R. Campbell-Thompson, an expert in Middle Eastern magic, and describes a drinking vessel and cylinder seals from ancient Assyria which appear to show a man copulating with a headless vampire. What made Campbell-Thompson think the headless body vampiric, Summers does not say. What he does say is that the Old Testament is full of references to the undead. Proverbs XXX 15 reads: 'the horse-leech has two daughters that say "Bring, bring."' The Latin version of horse-leech is *sanguisugae*, blood-sucking demon or vampire.

In Arabic, this creature became the *djinn*, a female ghoul, half-woman, half-fiend who infested graveyards looking for the newly dead to eat. This character appears often in *The Thousand and One Nights* of Arabian legend.

The Chinese vampire, Summers tells us, was *Ch'ing Shih*, who would preserve his own body by feeding on the blood of others. The Chinese believed that a man has two souls: *Hin* was the superior, positive and good force, *P'o* the inferior, malignant counterpart. Any part of the body remaining whole after burial could be utilized by the *P'o* to reconstitute the entire body, to create a revenant, as long as, in direct contrast to the modern variant of the European vampire myth, it is warmed by sunlight. *Ch'ing Shih* had 'red staring eyes, huge, sharp talons and crooked nails' and his entire body was covered with white hair. G. Willoughby-Meade, writing in the same year as Summers, presented a number of anecdotes about this vampire in *Chinese Ghouls and Goblins*, although few of these are actually vampires in the true sense. For instance, unlike the European tradition, in China the vampire did not infect the living and turn them into the undead like him.

The Indian *raksasha* is the nearest thing to a European vampire, but he is actually a demon, no matter how repulsive, not a subspecies that was once human. The word means destroyer and the creature was blue, green or yellow with slit eyes. It ate human and horse flesh and was impossibly rich, giving away vast wealth to a chosen few. The Victorian explorer and traveller Richard Burton wrote *Tales of Hindu Devilry* in 1870 and in it he discussed the *baital* or *vetala*, an evil spirit that animates dead bodies. It had a brown body and its ribs showed through its skin. It hung upside down, like a bat, by its toes. It had no blood, a goat's tail and its skin was the texture of a snake.

In Malaya (today's Malaysia) the *penanggalan* was a female human head with a stomach attached to it that fed on the blood of children. The *bajang* and *langsur* were male and female forms of demon-vampires, although their illness-carrying ability actually makes them more akin to European witches than vampires. To deal with this, the *pawang* (a shaman/witchdoctor/exorcist figure) was called in to find the culprit and kill him. The arrival of the British, Summers assures us, stopped this practice. The *langsir* was a gorgeous femme fatale common to the mythology of many cultures. She had long, beautiful nails and her black hair hung down to the ground, concealing until it was too late the hole in the back of her neck through which she sucked children's blood.

The Polynesians had their *tu*, a man or woman who struck a deal with a spirit in order to gain power (again, we see here the witchcraft link with the sixteenth-century pacts with Satan). To obtain this, the *tu* had to eat portions of a human body.

Among the Ashanti people of Africa the vampire was the *asasabonsam* who sat high in the tree tops and had iron teeth. It sucked the blood of children, could travel vast distances by night and was very common in the community.

Summers also found vampire traditions in ancient Mexico, where the *cinateteo* fitted the bill. They were exclusively women who had died in their first childbirth and wandered about infecting other children in a kind of warped revenge. They hated crossroads and temples and had white faces, arms and hands. They met regularly at an undead version of the sabbat[2] and wore priestly robes like those of *Tlazolteotl*, goddess of sorcery, lust and evil. Another Mexican variant was the lord of *Mictlayia*, the Region of the Dead. He was depicted in art as a skeleton, blue-grey with the talons of the vampire. He and his 'wife' fed on human flesh. When the Spanish conquistadors settled in Central and South America and brought with them the uncompromising terror of the Inquisition, one of the priests' first questions of the suspected idolator was, 'Are you a sorcerer? Do you suck the blood of others?'

Moving north-east into the West Indies, Summers reminds his readers that the vampire myth associated with voodoo is actually African in origin because of the transportation of slaves by white settlers in the seventeenth and eighteenth centuries. The *loogaroo* was a variant of the Guinea-French *loupgarou*, the werewolf (we shall discuss the vampire–wolf link in this and other chapters). They hung their pelts on the silk-cotton tree, known as the Devil's tree, and travelled the night as sulphurous fire balls in search of human prey. Summers cites the story of H.J. Bell, writing from Haiti in 1893:

> Dreadful accounts reach us of thousands of negroes having gone back to a perfectly savage life in the woods, going about stark naked, and having replaced the Christian religion by Voodooism and fetish worship. Cases of cannibalism have even been reported . . .[3]

'It is hard to believe,' wrote a gullible Summers:

> that a phenomenon which has had so complete a hold over nations both young and old, in all parts of the world, at all times of history, has not some underlying and terrible truth however rare this may be in its more remarkable manifestations.[4]

Totally undeterred by little things like relevance Summers also looks at 'orrible murder as part of the kith and kin of the vampire story. From our point of view, looking at Vlad the Impaler as the *fons et origo* of the vampire myth, this probably has little bearing. It might seem perverse to introduce this section with a look at the erotic overtones of the vampire myth, but the majority of the cases Summers cites are of sexual sadism, so it is a reasonable starting point.

> The vampire is . . . generally believed to embrace his victim who has been thrown into a trance-like sleep and after greedily kissing the throat suddenly to bite deep into the jugular vein and absorb the warm crimson blood. It has long been recognized by medico-psychologists that there exists a definite connexion between the fascination of blood and sexual excitation.[5]

He quotes his friend, the psychologist Havelock Ellis, who wrote:

> It is probable that the motive of sexual murders is nearly always to shed blood and not to cause death.[6]

It starts with a kiss. In a bizarre article, written in 1897, anthropologist Paul d'Enjoy defined a kiss as a bite and a suction. Havelock Ellis agreed:

> The impulse to bite is also a part of the tactile element which lies at the origin of kissing.[7]

This is the love-bite and the snobbish scholar Summers cannot resist giving us two whole pages of Latin and French verse extolling the naughtiness of the kiss. The eighteenth-century poet Dryden's translation of Ovid reads:

> Why do your locks and rumpled head-clothes show
> 'Tis more than usual sleep that made them so?
> Why are the kisses which he gave betrayed,
> By the impression which his teeth has made?

Summers positively slavers over the fact that the *Kama Sutra* spends one whole chapter on the love-bite and another Eastern sex manual, the *Perfumed Garden*, has umpteen references to it. 'Biting in amorous braces,' Summers noted, was particularly common among the southern Slavs, where vampirism was most rife. G. Alonzi, an Italian psychologist, was fascinated by the behaviour of peasant mothers in his native Sicily. They would kiss their children so hard that they drew blood, biting them on the face, neck and ears. And Summers quotes a case in London in 1894 in which a thirty-year-old man was on trial for abusing his wife's daughter over several months. The girl was three. Police had found her covered in bruises, especially to her lips, eyes and hands and her apron was bloodstained. The police report included the sentence, 'Defendant admitted he had bitten the child because he loved it.'

The polite, respectable middle class England in which Montague Summers grew up (and the same could be said of Bram Stoker's Ireland) did not acknowledge violent sex. Even orgasm was something which men only were supposed to enjoy and running through late Victorian middle class society is the general tenet that loving relationships within the family had little to do with sex. Intercourse was a duty for most women and childbirth the by-product of a lack of effective contraception. For actual enjoyment, a man would visit the high class courtesans of Duke Street in London, or bordellos like Kate Hamilton's in the Haymarket, depending on his financial circumstances. If he was poor, he would have to make do with the whores of Whitechapel.

All this is reflected in the literature of the time. When Thomas Hardy wrote *Tess of the Durbervilles* (1894) he was forced by his editor to rewrite a scene in which Tess is carried over a huge puddle by the hero, Angel Clare. Society would be horrified by the proximity of their bodies. So, in the original printed version, Tess obligingly hops into a handy wheelbarrow and Angel pushes her across. Only in pornography like *The Lustful Turk* (1827) and 'Walter's' *My Secret Life* (c.1884) could sex acts be described. All this, of course, makes it astonishing that Stoker and earlier writers on the vampire theme could even hint at the sexual aspects of the vampire.

From the kiss to violent sex to rape to sexual murder – this is the pattern that Summers essentially follows. He cites a writer called Plumröder in 1830 as the first to link sexual passions and blood and goes on to quote Dr T. Claye Shaw in the *Lancet* of 1909 in an article called *A Prominent Motive in Murder* where he coined the term 'haemothymia'. Normally, Havelock Ellis said, the powerful constraints of society and upbringing keep this blood lust in check, but in the case of high-profile serial killers, those constraints do not work.

Early examples that Summers quotes are actually necrophagia (cannibalism) and have more of a link, arguably, to the other manifestation of the vampire, the werewolf. He cites New World examples, for instance in the voodoo culture of the West Indies and among the Kwakiutl Inuit of British Columbia. Their *hamatsas* (secret societies) tore corpses apart and bit the living. Stephenie Meyer revisits them in the *Twilight* series. The Handa Indians of the Queen Charlotte Islands were also biters and the Bibiunga Aborigines in Australia ate the dead so that they could be reincarnated.

The European examples that Summers gives are well documented. Four Frenchmen admitted to transforming themselves into wolves in 1538 and killing children. In a related case, three others stripped children of their clothes in local woods and ate them. There are Russian and Spanish examples of organized, ritualistic cannibalism, but one of the oddest must be the Scotsman Sawney Beane. Unfortunately for historical truth, the man's story was taken up by Thomas Preskett Prest, whom we met in Chapter 4. Since he was a prolific writer of 'penny dreadfuls' or 'shockers', any hope of finding hard truth in his farrago of nonsense is limited. Beane was the son of peasants in East Lothian and made his living by robbing travellers on the road to Edinburgh. He lived with his wife and their growing brood of delinquents in a cave so skilfully hidden that it was twenty-five years before he was caught, the entire family being executed in Edinburgh in 1435, when Vlad the Impaler was a little boy. Summers concedes that it was probably starvation that led to the first cannibalistic act but that it became 'a mad passion. The children born into such conditions would be cannibalistic as a matter of course.'[8]

Summers' assertions of widespread cannibalism – he cites Roman and Irish examples – seem far-fetched, but there is probably an element of truth in them. Andre Chikatillo, a quiet Russian factory worker, killed fifty-five people between 1979 and 1991, eating certain body parts. As a child in the 1930s, his family had been exposed to chronic starvation and the link between murder and eating may have begun then. The problem is that the whole subject is so horrific that information – especially causation – is difficult to come by. Criminologist Brian Masters rightly uses the term 'the last taboo' as the tag line for his 1992[9] book and nowhere does he refer to the vampire's alter-ego, the werewolf.

Summers, of course, does. He cites W.A.F. Browne, Commissioner for Lunacy in Scotland in the 1870s who wrote of a West Indian case where two women hung around graveyards at night.

The abodes of the dead had been visited, violated, the exhumed corpses, or parts of them, have been kissed, caressed ... and carried to the homes of the ravisher, although belonging to total strangers.[10]

As a student, Browne had come across self-confessed female vampires, 'anaemic and dejected' in the Paris slums, a century and a half before such emotions were fashionable.

It is when he strays into sexual sadistic murder that Summers becomes most interesting. Psychiatry was still a relatively new science in the 1920s and the motivations of serial killers only partly understood because they were so rare.

He is suitably vague about Elizabeth Báthory, '*la comtesse hongroise sanguinare*' and I shall discuss her 'necro-sadistic abominations' in later chapters. Joseph Vacher is much better documented, but Summers got it wrong. One of Vacher's many victims (he killed young males and females indiscriminately between 1894 and 1897) was a thirteen-year-old shepherd boy, Pierre Laurent. Summers says, 'the body was indescribably hacked and bitten,' but this is not true. There is no doubt that Vacher was deeply disturbed – like the Whitechapel murderer known as Jack the Ripper he strangled, cut throats and mutilated genitals – but there is no evidence that he bit his victims, still less tried to eat them.

Summers explores a number of early nineteenth-century French cases, quoting extensively in French to impress us, but, clearly, two recent cases that fascinated him were those of Leopold and Loeb and Fritz Haarmann. Again, Summers is stretching a point. Nathan Leopold and Richard Loeb were two spoilt rich teenagers who killed fourteen-year-old Bobby Franks in Kenwood, Chicago in May 1924. They were thrill-seekers *par excellence*, an arrogant pair of sociopaths who had such lofty ideas of their own intelligence that they set out to murder almost as an academic exercise. They bashed Franks' skull with a chisel, held him underwater and poured hydrochloric acid over his face to disfigure it. Bloodstains in the car and Leopold's spectacles dropped at the crime scene ended all talk of their Nietzschean 'superman' persona and only the brilliant defence by Clarence Darrow saved them from the gas chamber. Summers' belief that the crime was an example of necrosadism was probably picked up from the hysterical press coverage at the time:

> They had exhausted every erotic emotion and sought something to thrill their jaded nerves.[11]

So appalled was Summers by the crimes of Fritz Haarmann that he devotes over five pages of his book to him. The *Daily*

Express of 17 April 1925 carried the news that Haarmann had been executed the previous day, but that:

> owing to the exceptional character of the crimes – most of Haarmann's victims were bitten to death ... it is probable that [the] brain will be removed and preserved by the [Gottingen] University authorities.[12]

The *News of the World* carried a similar article, in much more detail, with the banner headline 'Vampire's Victims'. Haarmann had a history of child molestation and petty theft and, with a pimp called Hans Grans, hung around Hanover's railway station picking up teenage boys and taking them back to his apartment. Here, he and Grans sodomized and murdered them. By 1919, with Germany in a state of near-anarchy after the country's collapse in the First World War, Haarmann had no difficulty finding suitable victims and cut the bodies up to sell as meat at his butcher's stall. He told police:

> I would throw myself on top of these boys and bite through the Adam's apple, throttling them at the same time.[13]

Summers wrote:

> The violent eroticism, the fatal bite in the throat, are typical of the vampire and it was perhaps something more than mere coincidence that the mode of execution should be the severing of the head from the body [with a sword] since this was one of the most efficacious methods of destroying a vampire.[14]

The examples of the sadistic sexual killer which Summers does not mention (because neither man had yet been caught when he wrote *Kith and Kin*) were Albert Fish and Peter Kurten. Fish was a masochistic degenerate who was executed by electric chair in Sing Sing prison in January 1936. The crime for which he died (although he was guilty of many others) was the murder of ten-year-old Grace Budd in June 1928. In a letter to her mother Fish wrote, 'Grace sat in my lap and kissed me. I made up my mind to eat her.' He raped her first and ate the body over a nine day period. 'How sweet and tender her little ass was roasted in the oven.'[15]

Peter Kurtin was the sadist to top all others. Dubbed the Monster of Dusseldorf, he carried out a horrific series of assaults and murders in the late 1920s, possibly killing his first victim by drowning when he was only nine years old. There is no doubt that he had an obsession with blood, decapitating swans and stabbing sheep just to see their blood flow. He was executed by guillotine on 2 July 1931 and famously told the psychiatrist who examined him, 'I hope I hear my own blood gurgle. That would be the greatest thrill of all.'

In discussing serial killers of the twentieth century, we seem to have wandered a long way from the vampire, but this is precisely the point. Everything about the vampire in film and literature is loose, vague, imprecise. It is a mish-mash of garbled folk legend and money-spinning titillation. 'Here,' says Montague Summers rather loftily, 'we have descended to mere quackery.' To put the vampire back into focus, we have to look at the ancient legends that predate Bram Stoker and the greatest vampire of them all – Vlad Ţepeş.

6

VAMPYR

VAMPIRES IN EUROPEAN FOLK TRADITION

The ghostly psychic terrain of the vampire is a nocturnal dreamscape of crossroads, foggy burial-grounds and graveyard paths, dark forests, windy heights, desolate heaths, lonely marshes where spectral will-o-the-wisps hover over black, moonlit pools and flicker around the weathered stones of ancient tombs.[1]

The atmosphere of the vampire folk-myth cannot be better summed up. Elements of all the above pepper the literary world of vampires, from Polidori and Stoker to Rice and Meyer. But the vampire of folklore is very different from that of fiction. The vampire comes to us from belief. Scientific secular culture dismisses such things with the contempt inherent in words like 'myth' and 'superstition'. However, less than a hundred years ago, significant numbers of people in Eastern Europe *knew* that vampires were real. Ironically, it was another myth, the advent of Communism, which finally weakened belief in vampires.

Chambers Etymological Dictionary of 1885, which predates Stoker's *Dracula* by twelve years, provides the following definition of a vampire: 'in the superstition of Eastern Europe, a ghost which sucks the blood of its sleeping victim.' In that sense, the vampire is synonymous with the succubi, the night-haunting demons believed to be real by the Catholic and Orthodox Churches and the subject of papal bulls dating from the time of Vlad Ţepeş.

The 1920s *Oxford English Dictionary*'s definition reads:

A preternatural being of a malignant nature (in the original and usual form of the belief in an animated corpse) supposed to seek nourishment and do harm by sucking the blood of sleeping persons; a man or woman abnormally endowed with similar habits.

Samuel Johnson's definition of 1755 was as follows:

Pretended demon, said to delight in sucking human blood and to animate the bodies of dead persons which, when dug up, are said to be found florid and full of blood.

Before that, as early as 1741, the word was used as a metaphor; Charles Forman's *Observations on the Revolution in 1688* has the line, 'These are the vampires of the Publick and riflers of the kingdom.'

Mankind has endless fun playing with words. In the nineteenth century a vampire trap was a double-leaved spring trapdoor, not unlike that of the gallows, which enabled characters in a theatre to leave the stage quickly (presumably in a cloud of smoke for maximum effect). False vampires refer to bats of the *Megadermatidae* family, insectivorous creatures from Africa, Asia and Australia that are not related closely to the *Desmondontidae*, the actual vampire bats of South America. Vampiredom is the state of being a vampire; vampiric, pertaining to vampires (the adverb is vampirically);

vampirism is the belief in the existence of vampires; and to vampirize means to behave like a vampire.

The vampire of folklore is found universally in pre-Christian times and non-Christian countries, but it survived long after Christ's Church imposed itself on superstitious societies throughout the world. So the cynic François Voltaire,[2] one of the most rational products of the Enlightenment, wrote:

> What! Is it in our eighteenth century that vampires exist? Is it after the reigns of Locke, Shaftesbury, Trenchard and Collins?[3]

Voltaire should not have been surprised. The eighteenth century has been dubbed the age of reason, and it followed the scientific revolution of the previous century. Towering over all the scholars of that period, Isaac Newton has come down to us as one of the greatest physicists of all time. His chemistry, however, was almost medieval mumbo jumbo. The eighteenth century also saw the rise, as we have seen, of the Gothic novel, a continuing belief in the reality of hell-fire and infamous poltergeist activity in Cock Lane, London and Samuel Wesley's rectory at Epworth, Lincolnshire. The Cock Lane ghost manifested itself in Clerkenwell, London in 1761 in the form of 'Scratching Fanny'. It was actually poltergeist activity focused on eleven-year-old Elizabeth Parsons. Dr Samuel Johnson was one of the 'committee of gentlemen' appointed to investigate. Fifty years earlier, similar activity centred on the younger sister of future Methodist leader John Wesley. Although both cases are today regarded as hoaxes, at the time they were thought to be proofs of pure evil. All his life (he did not die until 1791) John Wesley believed implicitly in the power of witches to do harm.

Scholars like Johann Zopfius and Karl von Dalen wrote of vampires as matters of factual reality when Voltaire was already a young man. In *Dissertatio de Vampyris Serviensibus*, published at Halle in 1733, they defined the species as follows:

Vampires issue forth from their graves in the night, attack people sleeping quietly in their beds, suck out all the blood from their bodies and destroy them. They beset men, women and children alike, sparing neither age nor sex. Those who are under the fatal malignity of their influence complain of suffocation and a total deficiency of spirits, after which they soon expire. Some who, when at the point of death, have been asked if they can tell what is causing their decease, reply that such and such persons, lately dead, have arisen from the tomb to torment and torture them.[4]

The most authoritative eighteenth-century work on vampires was published in 1746 by Dom Augustin Calmet. A prolific writer of the Benedictine order, Calmet's *Traité sur les Apparitions des Esprits et sur les Vampires* examined the 'horrid attacks' of vampires and described the traditional methods of killing them. It was not a work of gullible superstition, however. Calmet noted that most of the vampire stories came from Eastern Europe:

where people, being badly fed, are subject to certain disorders occasioned by the climate and the food, and augmented by prejudice, fancy and fright, which are capable of producing or of increasing the most dangerous maladies.

'These vampires,' wrote Calmet:

visibly appear to men, they knock loudly at their doors and cause the sound to re-echo throughout the whole house and once they have gained a foothold, death generally follows. To this sort of apparition is given the name Vampire or Oupire, which in the Slavonic tongues means a bloodsucker.

He goes on to take an oddly modern approach to the 'problem' for a Catholic priest writing 200 years ago:

If [vampirism] be an error and an illusion, it follows in the interests of religion that those who credit it must be undeceived and that we should expose a groundless superstition, a fallacy, which may easily have very serious and very dangerous consequences.[5]

The folkloric vampire has two definitions although they overlap continually. The first, and older, tradition is of the night-haunting ghost of a wizard or witch (the Turkish word *uber*, from which vampire is derived, literally means a witch which threatens whole communities). The second, and the variant that Stoker used (although physically it was more obvious in Murnau's *Nosferatu*), was the tradition of the walking corpse, the revenant who has led an evil life and cannot find rest in the grave.

The origins of the vampire myth take us into paganism and shamanic spirituality in which the dark, because it could not be explained or even readily understood, was filled with nameless terrors against which men must protect themselves. The shamans or witch doctors of the hunter-gatherer groups of Paleolithic society probably went into trances not unlike those of aboriginal tribesmen or Haitians under the grip of voodoo today. The trance symbolized death and the spirits of the dead could walk again through the shaman. There are links, too, with the sensation of flight and the concept of shape-shifting.

The idea of flight is associated with late medieval witchcraft in which thousands of terrified, tortured people 'confessed' to flying to the witches' sabbat on goats, horses and broomsticks. Much of this was nonsense and the result of the application of the excruciating torture implements of the Inquisition, but it may also have its root in religious ecstasy and trance-like states, with or without the narcotic, hallucinatory addition of hedge-row plants like hemlock. 'Root of hemlock, digg'd in the dark,' is one of the ingredients of Shakespeare's witches' cauldron in *Macbeth*. Ingested, it was highly toxic, but, mashed to a paste and smeared over the skin, it entered through the pores into the bloodstream and became a powerful hallucinogen.

Time and again in the vampire folkloric tradition the lines between vampirism and witchcraft are blurred as we saw in Chapter 5. In 1898, two years after Stoker's novel hit the bookshelves, Julian Jaworskij in *Südrussiche Vampyre* wrote:

> The power of the vampire is very great and many-sided, even in his lifetime. He can kill people and even eat them alive; can bring in to being or remove various sicknesses and epidemics, storms, rain and hail. He casts spells on the cows and their milk, the crops and the husbandry generally. He knows all secrets and the future. Besides this, he can make himself invisible or transform himself into various objects, especially into animal forms.

Jaworskij was describing Galician or southern Russian folklore and the list of animal forms from other traditions is extensive. Vampires could become donkeys, goats, dogs, cats, chickens, frogs, wolves, butterflies, owls, mice or even haystacks. What is noteworthy here is the reference to 'in his lifetime'. The vampire of fiction only has these phenomenal powers in his undead state – witches could access them at will. Witches were believed to be able to kill and cure people, cause storms and predict the future. The list of animals equates with the imps or familiars sent by the devil to serve the witch.

The shape-shifting metaphor links, especially in Eastern Europe, the vampire with the werewolf. Developed as a separate strand of horror by twentieth-century film-makers, according to Ukrainian and Russian folklore, wolfmen will simply become vampires unless exorcised. Writer and researcher Ian Woodward notes:

> In Siberia the vampire and the werewolf are known collectively as one creature, the *vulkodlak* and these are most active during the bleakest winter months. At their annual gatherings they strip off their wolf skins and hang them on the nearby trees. If any of them succeeds in getting hold of another's skin and

burning it, the *vulkodlak* whose skin it was will be freed for
ever from its fiendish enchantment.[6]

Belief in vampires was a cultural feature of the earliest
Indo-European nomads who emerged from the steppes north
of the Caspian Sea some 3,000 years before Christ. Migrating
bands of these peoples spread east into the Urals and Asia
Minor, along the Indus and the Ganges into India and west
along the Danube into the heartlands of the Balkans and what
would become Germany. They brought with them the
mythology of the 'Terrifying Sovereign', god of death and
magic, and recognized, in the teachings of Zoroaster and the
cult of Mithras, the eternal battle between good and evil.
Many of the tribal groups produced warrior elites at one with
the dead and the wolves that prowled the European forests.
Bram Stoker was drawing on this mythology when Jonathan
Harker's horse-drawn coach rattles through the Borgo Pass on
its way to Castle Dracula:

> All at once the wolves began to howl as though the moonlight
> had had some peculiar effect on them. The horses jumped about
> and reared and looked helplessly around with eyes that rolled
> in a way painful to see; but the living ring of terror
> encompassed them on every side . . .

It is this ancient culture and the links between the dead, the
undead and the wolf that give us the lycanthropic vampire of
Eastern Europe. Names vary: in Slovenia, it is *vukodlak*; in
Poland, *wilkolak*; in Romania, *varcolac*; in Albania, *vurvolak*
and so on, but the origin is the same. *Velku dlaka* literally
translated means wolf-coat.

There are also vampires in the classical tradition, and this
helps to account for the obsession with succubi and incubi in
the late medieval Christian Church. Lamia was the queen of
Libya who was one of the many earthly conquests of Zeus,
king of the gods in Greek mythology. Long-suffering Hera,

Zeus' wife, tired of his constant infidelities, killed the children of the liaison. In despair, Lamia, made hideous by Hera's magic, prowled the night for other children to kill. Her name, in time, became the term for a demon. In the Hebrew tradition she became Lilith, the screech-owl, a Babylonian night-spirit and the first wife of Adam, and by the thirteenth century had been transformed into a vampire.

In 1214 Gervase of Tilbury[7] wrote in *Otia Imperialia* that the lamia 'disturbs the minds of sleepers and oppresses with weight', crushing their chests with a power intended to kill. A more likely scientific explanation of this is the comparatively common sleep apnoea, a condition in which sleepers literally stop breathing, until reduced oxygen tension in the tissues makes them wake with a gasping intake of breath. This oxygen starvation can also cause hallucinations, vivid dreams and night-terrors, tying in with the variously imagined visitations of the vampire. In the various accounts from folklore which we will examine shortly, those who experience such visitations invariably claimed that they were awake and that the vampire was therefore real. The same argument exists for 'death visitants', ghosts the Victorians believed appeared to people at the exact moment of their deaths. The 'appearance' of dead people is, of course, one way we keep them in our memories and they are usually doing, in our dreams, quite prosaic things. We often realise that they are dead but somehow their appearance is not frightening nor even particularly out of the ordinary.

Nicholaus of Cusa,[8] Professor of Theology at Prague and Heidelberg universities in the early fifteenth century, believed that lamiae were demons in the guise of old women (hence their general association with witches) who kidnapped children and roasted them over fires.

The infamous Bull of Pope Innocent VIII,[9] *Summis desideratus affectibus*, which appeared on 9 December 1484, gave the official seal of the Catholic Church to the Inquisition and unleashed a wave of terror which saw the deaths of thousands of innocent victims across Europe. Innocent wrote:

> It has lately come to Our ears, not without afflicting Us with
> bitter sorrow, that in some parts of Northern Germany ...
> many persons of both sexes, unmindful of their own salvation
> and straying from the Catholic Faith, have abandoned them-
> selves to devils, incubi and succubi ...[10]

He proceeds to list dozens of disasters that their infidelity has
caused. 'Our dear sons', Henry Kramer and James Sprenger,[11]
Professors of Theology of the Order of Friars Preacher, were
then unleashed onto an unsuspecting world. Between them,
they wrote *Malleus Maleficarum*, Hammer of the Witches,
over 500 pages in length which the gullible and terrified world
of the Reformation and Counter Reformation was all too
eager to accept as truth.

Although the witch craze as it developed in the sixteenth
century was largely a Western European phenomenon, creeping no further east than Nuremberg, the notion of incubi and
succubi is closely connected to the Eastern European belief in
vampires. 'Incubi' in Latin means to lie on, and this was
precisely what these night demons were believed to do. They
were linked with the familiars who were the devil's agents,
shape-shifters who fed on witches' blood. They were also
linked with the idea of the nightmare; they were demons that
had their origins in latent sexuality or even nocturnal
emissions. Shakespeare's plays and poetry are littered with
allegoric references to 'death' meaning orgasm. William
Caxton's *Chronicle* published in 1480 describes their activities:

> That fiend that goth a-night
> Women full oft to guile,
> Incubus is named by right;
> And guileth men other while,
> Succubus is that wight.[12]

The philosopher and friar Francisco-Maria Guazzo,[13] an
experienced judge in witch trials, produced his *Compendium
Maleficarum* (Handbook of Witches) in 1608. He wrote:

[The incubus] can assume either a male or female shape; sometimes he appears as a full-grown man, sometimes as a satyr . . .[14]

Thomas Aquinas,[15] writing nearly four centuries earlier (in *Summa Theologica*), was trying to work out the science of it all:

Nevertheless, if sometimes children are born from intercourse with demons, this is not because of the semen emitted by them, or from the bodies they have assumed, but through the semen taken from some man for the purpose, seeing that the same demon who acts as a succubus for a man becomes an incubus for a woman.

Not until the late seventeenth century was the existence of incubi and succubi, taken for so long to be scientific fact, challenged. De Saint Andre, physician to Louis XV of France, wrote:

The incubus is most frequently a chimera, which has no more basis than a dream, a perverted imagination and very often the invention of a woman . . . To conceal her sin, a woman, a girl, a nun in name only, a debauchee who affects the appearance of virtue, will palm off her lover for an incubus spirit which haunts her.[16]

Although De Saint Andre can be accused of much the same misogyny that characterizes the authors of *Malleus Maleficarum*, his jibes at least put the incubus issue into perspective. One obvious *difference* between the Western idea of witchcraft and the Central European and Eastern idea of a vampire is gender. In the Western tradition there were attested male witches (called warlocks) but the vast majority of witches were female. This suited the monks Kramer and Sprenger perfectly. Because Eve had effectively brought about the fall of man and his removal from Eden by allowing herself to be seduced by the serpent, *all* women were therefore tainted. Vampires on the other hand are almost exclusively male.

In Eastern Europe, where the Greek Orthodox rather than the Roman Catholic Church held sway, the vampire was treated differently, not as a demon in the conventional sense that Aquinas, Kramer, Sprenger and Pope Innocent VIII understood the term. James Dickie wrote in 1971:[17]

> Most mysterious and intriguing of all occult phenomena, the vampire, whatever his social status in life, becomes in death the expression of sadistic erotomania at its intensest. He is the hyphen between life and death: through his agency death poaches upon the reproductive function peculiar to the living. All the evidence amassed to prove the existence of the vampire contributes not an iota to his understanding, for in spite of all efforts, he remains an indecipherable hieroglyphic in the language of the Unseen.[18]

Nigel Jackson in *The Compleat Vampyre* lists no less than sixty-five variants of the vampire-werewolf that feature in European folklore. I have included here only those with relevance to the areas known to Vlad Ţepeş. 'There was once a time,' runs a Romanian folk tale, 'when Vampires were as common as blades of grass, or berries in a pail and they never kept still, but wandered round at night among the people.'[19] This wandering, nomadic quality is most usually found in gypsy folklore because the gypsies themselves are travellers. The attested vampire stories of the eighteenth century, although widespread, refer to individual villages or parishes. The wandering vampire was translated into fiction by, among others, Stoker. Count Dracula 'lives' in his castle but as long as he can lie in the Transylvanian earth of his coffin, he is able to wander the world and come ashore at Whitby.

South of the Danube where Vlad Ţepeş carried out his forays against the Turks in the summer of 1462, the Serbian *dhampir* was the offspring of a vampire and a living woman. With the psychic ability to detect vampires, the *dhampir* often took the role of *kresniki*, individuals born with a white caul which signified their ability to do good in the world. Babies born with a red caul, however, were probably predisposed to become vampires. Red is the colour, after all, of blood. Consciously or otherwise, Bram Stoker's hero, van Helsing, represents the *dhampir* role, although he is also blessed with scientific knowledge rather than pure folkloric skills. In the novel he states Dracula is:

> known everywhere that men have been . . . [in] the wake of the berserker Icelander, the devil-begotten Hun, the Slav, the Saxon, the Magyar . . .[20]

The Serbian *dhampir* fulfils the role of the 'cunning woman' in Western Europe, a devotee of white witchcraft whose skills were sought to ward off evil. There are examples of this happening in Serbia into the late 1950s.[21]

In Dracula's native Romania, the *dschuma* was a night-haunting hag whose appearance presaged a cholera epidemic; we will examine this important link later. Naked and wailing like the *leannan-sidhe* of Irish Gaelic folklore (see Chapter 3) with which Stoker would have been familiar, the *dschuma* could only be assuaged by the offering of a red shirt, again, the colour of blood, woven in silence in one night by seven old women and hung out before dawn for her to collect.

In Bulgaria, the first territory across the Bosphorus which the Ottoman Turks invaded in their Western conquests, the *krvoijac* was a vampire which rested in its grave for forty days. After that time, with magical powers enhanced, it broke free of its coffin and prowled the night in search of blood. We see here the traditional cross-referencing of Christianity and paganism. The 'magic' number in much of vampire mythology is nine, but in the biblical tradition, Noah sails his Ark for forty days and that is also the length of time that Christ wandered in the wilderness. Under Norman feudal law, forty days per year was the allotted time for knight service.

In Bosnia, the vampire variant known as a *vampir* was thought to be especially active in times of typhus epidemics. It may have been this type that Byron was writing about in *The Gaiour*, in that vampires returned from the grave to drink the blood and have sex with their still-living partners. Belief in the *vampir* was especially strong in the gypsies of Bosnia, irrespective of whether they were Orthodox Christian or Muslim. Nigel Jackson notes that as in many areas of the Balkans, ethnic genocide and war have recently combined to destroy many of the old myths. They have doubtless been replaced by new ones.

Westwards in Hungary, where János Hunyadi and Matthias Corvinus both sought to make their mark on Vlad Ţepeş' Wallachia, the vampire variant was the *kiderc nadaly* whose despatch was a nail driven through the temple.

South, in Albania, where, in the Impaler's time, the great Skanderbeg kept the Turks at bay, the vampire was called a *liougat* or *kulkutha*. The German traveller J.G. von Hann reported in *Albanesische Stuckein* in 1854 that *liougats* were 'dead Turks, with huge nails, who, wrapped up in their winding sheets, devour whatever they find and throttle men'.[22] The *liougat*'s enemy was the wolf, an idea commonly found among various Slavic gypsy groups, and a wound from one was fatal to the *liougat*, ending his night-prowling forever.

In Ţepeş' own Romania, the *moroii* were the undead, predatory vampires who stole blood, youth and beauty and also targeted chickens and bees; the Carpathians are famous for honey production. Oddly human and very like the witches of Western Europe, they were organized in covens and carried out necrophiliac orgies in graveyards. They could shape-shift and had powers over animals and the weather. They were easily distinguishable from ordinary people, however, by their chicken-clawed feet.

A variant in Vlad Ţepeş' Principality of Wallachia was the *murony*, able to change its shape, typically to that of a cat, toad, spider, hound or blood-sucking insect. Its physical appearance in its grave was repellent and was recreated by Murnau in the film *Nosferatu*. Its fingernails were long and blood seeped from its eyes, nose, mouth and ears. The only method of certain despatch was a stake of whitethorn or iron driven through the forehead.

Specific to Transylvania, 'the land beyond the forest' was the *nosferat* (plural, *nosferatu*). The folklorist Heinrich von Wlislocki described it over a hundred years ago:

> The Nosferat not only sucks the blood of sleeping people, but also does mischief as an incubus or succubus. The Nosferat is the still-born illegitimate of two people who are similarly illegitimate. It is hardly put under the earth before it awakes to life and leaves its grave never to return. It visits people by night in the form of a black cat, a black dog, a beetle, a butterfly or even a simple straw. When its sex is male, it visits women; when female, men. With young people it indulges in sexual orgies until they get ill and die of exhaustion . . . It often happens that women are impregnated by the creature and bear the children who can be recognized by their ugliness and by having hair all over the whole body. They then always become witches, usually Moronii. The Nosferat appears to bridegrooms and brides and makes them impotent and sterile.

Romania seems to have been at the centre of vampire beliefs in Eastern Europe. In 1845, at a time when folktales were being collected and printed for the first time, A. and A. Schott noted the wolf-coat tradition of the *prikolitsch*, a living man who attacked domestic animals in the guise of a black dog. Such animals have their echoes in Western European folklore too, the barguest of which Stoker wrote, Shriker and Black Shuck.[23]

The *streghoi* in Wallachia, *strigoii* in other parts of Romania, were those most closely associated with the lamiae of Greek and Roman mythology. As we have seen the word means 'screech owl', a bird long associated with magic and occult wisdom. It was claimed the *streghoi*'s favourite human targets were babies in their cradles. They were also vampire-shamans, often with auburn hair and blue eyes[24] and born with a caul. They were variously believed to have their left eyes open constantly in their graves and could also assume the appearance of lights like will-o'-the-wisps that floated over graveyards and forests. These lights are found in mythology universally,[25] but the name 'lamiae' itself probably reflects the Roman army's occupation of the area under the Emperor Trajan, during the two invasions that extended the Roman Empire in the first century. The vampire as mist occurs in both Hungarian and Chinese traditions, especially in connection with battlefields where the dead lay unburied. A chronic overcrowding of the dead in London's burial grounds before the 1850s gave rise to stories of a green miasma floating over coffins that jutted from the ground. Such places were genuinely unhealthy and became personified, as Montague Summers says, by the image of 'a ghostly creature who rides on the infected air and sucks the life from his victims'.[26]

Most terrifying of the Romanian vampires was the *varcolac*, the wolf-coat. The Romanian scholar G.F. Ciausanu describes them as follows:

> Varcolaci because their spirit is Varcolaci. They are recognized by their pale faces and dry skin and by the deep sleep into which they fall when they go to the moon to eat it ... The redness is the blood of the moon, escaping from the mouths of the Varcolaci and spreading over the moon.[27]

There was a tradition that the *varcolaci* were the souls of unbaptized children, and they took the shape of dogs, wolves and dragons (*drakul* in Romanian). Professor Cyprien Robert wrote:

The Voukodlak [*sic*] sleeps in his grave with open, staring eyes; his nails and hair grow to an excessive length, the warm blood pulses in his veins. When the moon is at her full, he issues forth to run his course, to suck the blood of living men by biting deep into their dorsal vein . . . [they] are especially eager to quaff the hot blood of young girls.[28]

The moon and the crossroads are images closely associated with the vampire in Eastern European cultures. In Romania, crossroads represented the *coloana ceriului*, the sky pillar that linked heaven and earth. Witches' gatherings, or sabbats, were held here and ghosts, too, haunted such sites. Long before ley lines came to dominate magic landscapes, the crossroads was a place of fear, especially after dark. And again, we have the cross-fertilization referred to in Chapter 3. Montague Summers wrote:

In Wales it was said that witches slept by day under any boulder that might be at a crossroad and when dusk had fallen, they crept forth to steal little children and feast upon their flesh. The gallows was often created at the crossroads and here the criminal hung in chains and, nourished by his rotting flesh, the mandrake[29] grew.[30]

What was the defence against the vampire? Such devices are called apotropaics, literally methods to turn away evil. Beginning with the corpse itself, if it was believed by his malevolent lifestyle that the dead man was likely to become a vampire, the body could be placed in the grave face down. This both prevents the body becoming a revenant and allows the soul to rest in peace. In the Greek island of Khios a crucifix of wax or cotton was placed on the lips of the corpse. In Prussia, a piece of pottery was inserted into the mouth to give the dead man something to chew on. The ancient Greek practice of placing a coin in the mouth or on the eyes to pay Charon the ferryman over the River Styx probably had the same origin. In some parts of Europe, the jaw was taped shut or held in place with a stone so that chewing could not take place at all.

Other grave goods, not intended for an afterlife but to prevent the dead from returning as the undead, included seeds, especially of the poppy for its narcotic properties. According to the Elizabethan poet John Fletcher, paraphrasing ancient Greek beliefs, there was a close affinity between sleep and the afterlife: 'Care charming sleep, thou easer of all woes, brother to death.' In northern Germany, nets or intricate knot designs were placed in the grave, the idea being that the corpse would be too busy untying them to return to pester the living. In Romania and some parts of Hungary, sickles were placed with the corpse so that as the revenant felt himself rising from his tomb, he would do the decent thing and hack his own head off.

Beyond the grave in some Eastern European countries, white garlic (*allium sativum*) had the necessary magic powers to protect the living. It was strewn around all entrances to buildings, doors, windows and chimneys and even, since night was the real danger-time, around a sleeper's bed. There is a long tradition of this. The Roman, Pliny the elder,[31] cavalry commander and admiral, wrote in his monumental thirty-seven books on natural history, that garlic was an antidote to snakebites; and snakes, like the dragon/serpent, have an affinity to the undead in many cultures. Fifteen centuries later, the German magician Heinrich Cornelius Agrippa believed garlic could ward off attacks by panthers.[32] And as we saw in the Stoke-on-Trent case (see Chapter 2), cloves of garlic were still considered beneficial in 1973. It is also documented that garlic cloves were sometimes stuffed in the mouths of corpses in the Banat region of Romania.

Romania was also the country where elaborate rituals for vampire detection were worked out. A teenaged virgin, male or female was irrelevant, rode an equally virginal white or black horse around a graveyard. If the animal hesitated or refused to pass a grave, that was deemed to be evidence enough of the existence of a vampire and the coffin was exhumed.

What followed will be familiar to all watchers of vampire films. As early as the fourteenth century, the English traveller Sir John Mandeville[33] wrote:

> Therefore hath the whitethorn many virtues, for he that beareth a branch on hym thereof, no thunder, ne, no manner of tempest may dere him, ne, in the house [that] is ynne may non evil ghost enter.[34]

So the whitethorn was the perfect wood with which to fashion a stake to be driven through the heart of the resting vampire. And it had to be a single stroke – more than one would merely revive the monster. There is a similar tale in *The Thousand and One Nights* where the hero hacks a ghoul in half with his scimitar. While the dying ghoul encourages Oman to hit him again, the young man's old blind friend advises, 'Smite not a second time, for then he will not die, but will live and destroy us.'[35] The ritual of death by the stake was very important and it is a recurrent theme, as we will see in the story of Vlad Ţepeş. Known as the 'Great Reparation' in Transylvania, it has echoes of the symbolic slaying of the dragon by St George, who in medieval art forms is depicted as a knight in full armour driving his lance into the monster's heart.

The legend of St George is an interesting meeting place of Christian and pagan beliefs. The eve of his day, traditionally 23 April, was a time in Eastern Europe for precautions to be taken against all forms of evil. We will discuss the myth of the dragon in a later chapter and it is a familiar symbol of all that is evil, primitive and terrifying. The man who was to become the unlikely patron saint of England was George of Cappadocia (modern Turkey), put to death by the Emperor Diocletian at Lydda on 23 April AD 303 although there are conflicting dates for his death and even the reasons for it.

George can also be identified with the *kresniki*, the vampire-killers of Eastern European folklore and the character of van Helsing in Stoker's novel. In the novel van Helsing describes the moment of 'execution' of Dracula in his 'journal':

Oh my friend John, but it was butcher work; had I not been nerved by thoughts of other dead, and of the living over whom hung such a pall of fear, I could not have gone on. I tremble and tremble even yet, though till all was over, God be thanked, my nerve did stand. Had I not seen the repose in the first face and the gladness that stole over it just ere the final dissolution came, as realization that the soul had been won, I could not have gone further with my butchery. I could not have endured the horrid screeching as the stake drove home; the plunging of the writhing form, and lips of bloody foam. I should have fled in terror and left my work undone . . . For, friend John, hardly had my knife severed the head of each, before the whole body began to melt away and crumble into its native dust, as though the death that should have come centuries agone had at last assert himself and say at once and loud 'I am here!'[36]

Stoker's destruction of Dracula by van Helsing does not actually accord either with folkloric beliefs or later literary and film interpretations. The staking of the vampire and its fascinating associations with the impalement obsession of Vlad Ţepeş was carried out in northern Europe with ash wood, presumably because it was easy to obtain. Further south, echoing de Mandeville, hawthorn or any kind of thorn bush was used, as vampires were believed to be particularly allergic to thorns. It is even possible that the famous crown of thorns ground onto Jesus' head prior to his crucifixion was not a cruel jibe at his alleged kingship but had a darker, more occult significance altogether.

We have already seen other examples of iron stakes being used (as we shall see in Vlad's treatment of the Turkish emissaries) and in some instances it is not the heart that is the target, but the stomach or head. Since such attacks would kill a living person it may be that this was folklore's way of making sure a corpse was actually dead.

Not content with staking the Count, van Helsing uses the other favourite folklore method of despatching a vampire: decapitation. This could be done with a ritual knife or even a spade but two things were vital. First, the vampire's blood was itself lethal, so staking and decapitation must happen at a sufficient distance for the *dhampir* not to get himself splashed. Second, the head can be reburied with the now harmless corpse, but not in a position where the corpse can reach it, otherwise, like the headless horseman of Washington Irving's short story *The Legend of Sleepy Hollow*, he will simply pop it back onto his shoulders. A ridge of earth must be constructed with the body on one side and the head on the other.

The Greeks, Serbs and Albanians disposed of their vampires by cremation, but since this was an acceptable form of body disposal in Bram Stoker's England, he probably did not consider it dramatic enough to be the end of the Count. Cutting out the vampire's heart might be sufficient. Paul Barber cites an example as recently as 1874 of a Romanian prince living in Paris who demanded this be done to him on the occasion of his death because his family had been driven out of their homeland on charges of vampirism.

Finally, and this is *highly* undramatic, the vampire of folklore could be rendered harmless by dumping the body in water or burying it on a high and remote mountain range where it cannot find its way back to haunt the living.

The use of all these methods has a very long history and almost certainly refers to a general fear of death and the supernatural. It is perhaps best expressed in a single British example from the first century AD: Lindow Man. In August 1984, a body was found in peat bogs at Lindow Moss below Saddleworth Moor near Manchester. The chemical action of the peat had preserved the corpse so well that experts could fix the time of the man's death, his approximate age, the last meal he ate and the cause of death itself. Archaeologist Anne Ross and chemist Don Robins believe that 'Pete Marsh' (the name the press gave to the body) died a triple death. He had suffered three cuts to the head, there were three knots in the animal gut with which he had been garrotted and there were three elements to the attack – bludgeoning which caved in his skull; strangulation; and throat slitting. It may be too fanciful to observe that all this adds up to nine – the vampire number – but it is clear that this method of execution was no simple murder. It was done deliberately as a ritual, almost certainly in accordance with ancient practice.

Whether 'Pete Marsh' and other bodies such as Grauballe Man and Tollund Man in the Danish peat fens were placed in their watery graves as sacrifices cannot definitely be decided, but in many cases the bodies show signs of being tied (in the case of Tollund man the noose is still around his neck) and that sharpened stakes were placed in the grave. There is no vampire tradition in Britain, but the idea of pinning a corpse to the ground so that his soul/spirit cannot rise would seem to be universal. Montague Summers ascribes the name *vampyr* to Danish and Swedish revenants, but a more precise creature is the *draugr*, literally death walker. Runic inscriptions have been found on old Norse graves designed to prevent the dead from wandering.

Why should Voltaire, in his cynical, enlightened eighteenth century, be amazed that people still believed in vampires? We are not talking about literature as the source. After all, Polidori, Rymer and Stoker were as yet unknown. What prompted Voltaire's outburst was the outbreak of a series of vampire epidemics that swept Europe in his own time. The vampire epidemic was not strictly new. The oldest use of the word – *upyr* – is found in Russian sources between 1047 and 1059. The Serbian term *volkodlak* dates from 1262 and the first official accounts can be found in Silesia (Germany) in

1591 where the revenant of a shoemaker from Breslau returned to plague the town following his suicide.

Described by Montague Summers, the Silesian shoemaker story is worth quoting in detail because it contains so many classic elements of the vampire myth. The unnamed cobbler cut his own throat in his garden early in the morning of Friday 20 September 1591. His widow and her sisters, anxious to keep the story under wraps in the Breslau area because of the taint of suicide, let it be known that he had died from a stroke. Visitors who called to pay their last respects were turned away with excuses as clearly a gaping throat wound would give the game away. A local woman was paid to stitch up the wound so that at least the burial could go ahead with a semblance of normality. The officiating priest certainly noticed nothing amiss and the Christian funeral and burial followed three days later.

But in a small community like Breslau rumours spread and the dead man's family now changed their story – he had fallen and hit his head on a rock, they claimed. The whole thing sounded suspicious enough for locals to put pressure on the town council to investigate. It was now that the haunting occurred. The ghost of the shoemaker appeared day and night:

> Often it came to their bed, often it actually lay down on it and was like to smother people. Indeed, it squeezed so hard that . . . people could see the marks left by its fingers.

By 18 April 1592 (eight months after burial) the council ordered exhumation. The entire governing body of Breslau was there, as well as priests and leading citizens. To their horror, they found the corpse swollen and bloated, the skin tight as a drum. The limbs were not stiff and the old skin had peeled back to reveal new, reddish skin underneath.

> As almost all sorcerers are marked in an out of the way place . . . so did he have on his big toe a mole like a rose.

The body itself did not smell although the winding sheet did and the wound in the throat gaped open. The corpse remained on a bier for twenty days while various locals came to gawp. The exhumation, however, made no difference to the apparitions and placing the body under the Breslau gallows only enraged the ghost still further.

Eventually the shoemaker's widow admitted the suicide to the town council and on 7 May the executioner hacked off the head, hands and feet of the corpse prior to disembowelling it and removing the heart. All the body parts were then collected and burned, the resulting ash shovelled into a sack and scattered in the river. After this the haunting stopped.

The Breslau tale is fascinating because so little of it is recognizable in the vampire of fiction. There is nothing aristocratic about the shoemaker. He appears in broad daylight – 'Sunlight is Stoker' (see footnote 45). In fact in some of the more obscure scholarly texts the vampire is referred to as *daemonium meridianum* – the noonday devil. His body is not pale, with blood around the lips, eyes, nose and ears, but bloated and red. He does not bite his victims – in fact there is no reference to teeth at all. The references are to suffocation or perhaps strangling. However the story does reflect other folkloric accounts. The shoemaker died, whether by his own hand or as a murder victim, before his time, a common vampire theme. The methods of bodily destruction – decapitation, removal of the heart, burning and drowning – are classic examples of overkill because of the over-riding need to make the corpse inert. Without its working parts, the corpse cannot continue to haunt as the undead. The reference to the sorcerer's mark is common to witchcraft too – the supernumerary nipple for feeding familiars often referred to as the witch's tit.

There are reports of vampirism from Bohemia and Moravia as early as 1618 and Poland six years later. Outbreaks occurred in Istria in 1672, spreading to East Prussia in 1710 and 1721, south to Serbia in 1727 and 1732, Prussia in 1750, Silesia in

1755, Romania in 1756 and Russia in 1772. Some of these areas were still at the time in the Ottoman Empire, although it was a declining force by the eighteenth century. The extraordinary military power against which Vlad Ţepeş fought, in the ascendancy in his day, was waning by the time of these vampiric outbreaks. Its government, the Sublime Porte, weak, ineffectual and riddled with corruption, could not prevent the eventual disintegration of the empire; into this chaotic scene of decay, the Habsburg and Romanov families sought to extend their own empires.

This fact is important because it almost certainly explains in part the apparent rash of outbreaks in this period. Folklore has an ancient pedigree and does not suddenly begin in the eighteenth century.[37] In other words, tales of the undead have been in existence for ever – almost certainly with a prehistoric origin – but were examined, reported and analysed for the first time in the eighteenth century. Surgeons with the army in Austria investigated cases of vampirism spreading 'like a pestilence through Salvia and Wallachia . . . causing numerous deaths and disturbing all the land with fear of the mysterious visitors against which no one felt himself secure'.[38] Writer and broadcaster Daniel Farson cites a number of examples from the Belgrade region in the 1730s, including many in which the vampire targeted members of his own family. In one case in present-day Croatia, a vampire killed a brother and three nieces. The investigating party sent by the authorities was closer to the witch hunters of the seventeenth century than to van Helsing's little band of heroes. It included a public prosecutor and civil and military officers who visited the vampire's grave and cut off his head with an axe, before reburying the body in quicklime.

In another case, reported to the Imperial Council of War in Vienna, a Hungarian soldier, Arnod Paole (the name was probably Pavel), was killed in a cart accident. Dead for thirty days, he returned and took four victims 'in the manner traditionally ascribed to vampires'. When his body was exhumed, according to surgeon Johann Fluckinger, it 'showed all the marks of an arch vampire. His body was flushed; his hair, nails and beard had grown and his veins were full of liquid blood which splashed all over the winding sheet.'[39] Since Paole had attacked animals and humans in his bloodlust, the epidemic broke out again five years later, with the recurrent contagion associated with the 'subspecies'.

The Paole case and its repercussions were written up extensively in *Visum Et Repertum* (Seen and Discovered) in 1732 by Fluckinger himself. Paole was said by superstitious villagers to have been plagued by a vampire during his own lifetime and that he had taken the extraordinary remedies of smearing himself with the vampire's blood and eating the earth from the vampire's grave as forms of protection. Paole's ghost was accused of killing four people at first and the subsequent exhumation produced a horrendous spectacle. Fresh blood flowed from his nose, ears, mouth and eyes. His skin had regrown, as had his finger- and toenails. When a stake was driven through his heart 'he gave an audible groan and bled copiously.'

A total of seventeen people died in Paole's village of Mednega near Belgrade and fourteen of them were examined. Twelve had not decomposed in the usual way. According to the surgeons, they were 'unmistakeably in the vampire condition'[40] and this accorded with the ritualistic excommunication of the Orthodox Church:

> Your place shall be with the devil and the traitor Judas and after that do not turn into ashes, but remain as undecayed as stone and iron.[41]

Officialdom in the form of the Catholic Church in Austria could offer no help. Whereas Pope Innocent VIII was quite prepared, in the 1480s, to issue orders for the destruction of the anti-Christian elementals the incubi and succubi, his successor in the mid-eighteenth century, Clement XII, was rather more circumspect, believing that vampirism was delusional. At the same time, the Vatican hedged its bets by recommending that suspected vampires be exhumed and burned.

Synonymous with the vampirism associated with Count Dracula is the symbolism of the bat, although the vampire bat (*desmodus rotundus*) is a native of Central and South America and is found nowhere in Europe. The animal lives on the blood of mammals, usually grazing cattle (which Arnod Paole was said to have attacked) although there are about half a dozen recorded cases each year of human hosts. The bat received its name from the Spanish Conquistadors of the sixteenth century, obviously using their own folkloric knowledge. It was probably the same animal listed by F. de Oviedo y Valdez in *Sumario de la Natural Historio de las Indias* in 1526. The only reference to Spanish vampirism that I have been able to find is the associated *lobombre*, literally wolfman, from the Pyrenees and Cantabrian Mountains, whose condition was created by drinking magical waters or eating certain flowers. The vampire bat was first catalogued by name by French naturalist Buffon in his *Natural History* in 1749, implying that the animal regularly attacked humans. The vampire tradition in Buffon's native France is connected with the *loup garou*, the werewolf, but it is interesting that he was writing at the time of the various vampire epidemics in Europe.

What was the cause of these extraordinary epidemics? There are rational explanations, but we are dealing with superstitious, uneducated societies into which the rationalists of the period found themselves thrown. In these illiterate peasant cultures the normal rules of evidence were ignored and we must sift through unsubstantiated rumour and exaggeration. A number of contemporaries commented on this problem. Archbishop Giuseppe Davanzati wrote in his *Dissertazione sopra I Vampiri* in 1744 that the whole thing was of the mind. Contrary to Stoker's elegant, cultured Count of the 1890s, Davanzati noted that vampires were never 'a scholar, a philosopher, a theologian, a landowner or a bishop', but always 'base-born plebians'. Those who believed in them were 'the half-witted and the ignorant'.[42]

Voltaire, as always, was even more scathing:

> We have never heard tell of Vampires in London, or even in Paris. I do admit that there were in both those cities speculators, brokers and businessmen who sucked the blood of the people in broad daylight, but although corrupted, they were not dead. Those true bloodsuckers lived not in cemeteries, but in the most congenial places.[43]

Much of the evidence used as 'proof' a person was a vampire was based on the corpse. However, what is striking about the eighteenth-century mid-European vampire reports is the complete lack of understanding of what happens to the human body after death. This was true even among men of education who governed whole districts. Today we are better informed. In 1981, the world's first 'body farm' was established in Knoxville, Tennessee to investigate the process of decomposition, an invaluable tool for police forces and forensic experts with murderers to catch. We now know the process by which the body decays although the speed at which this takes place depends on temperature and weather conditions generally. To be fair, the body farm, of course, has corpses rotting at ground level; research based on what takes place inside a coffin is less common.

Medieval depictions of the dead usually take the form of Death himself, the Grim Reaper. They show skeletons with the merest hint of skin stretched over the bone framework. Sometimes worms coil from mouths and eye sockets so the work of nature was well understood in that context. Long before the skeletal form comes into existence, however, preliminary changes which are all perfectly natural, take place. These changes in part gave rise to the vampire myth. The floppiness of limbs commented on by government officials in the eighteenth century is customary. It is rigor mortis, the stiffening of limbs, which is the aberration and it is a temporary phase, lasting no more than forty-eight hours in average conditions. Its onset is obvious some twelve hours after death, so if a body was to be buried *during* the rigor process, the living would probably assume that the condition was permanent.

The skin changes colour, turning green or dark brown depending on the part of the body it covers and blisters appear on the surface. Nails fall off and hair falls out, although shrinkage of the skin from nails can give the impression that nails are still growing post mortem. The skin itself flakes off, leaving the 'new' layer of the dermis visible beneath. A build-up of gases causes the abdomen and intestines to swell, giving a bloated, florid appearance to the corpse which the living body never had. It is even possible for blood to seep from nose and mouth and the so-called groan or even shriek reported by vampire chroniclers as issuing from the body as it was staked was no more than an outrush of air as the body cavity was punctured.

Paul Barber in his fascinating study skilfully demolishes all the unscientific folklore surrounding exhumations but he is prepared to accept the various eyewitness accounts as accurate. I doubt this. Given the highly charged graveside atmosphere, I think that government officials, even doctors, would tend to become infected by the hysteria of the locals and imagine that they saw something that simply was not there.

One obvious link that we need to explore lies between vampirism and disease. In two of Nigel Jackson's list of eighteen werewolf-vampire variants found in Eastern Europe, reference is made to specific physical epidemics: the *dschuma* of Romania is linked with cholera and the *nosferat* of the same region is associated with bubonic plague, the Black Death. One of the best attested eighteenth-century vampire accounts concerns Peter Plogojowitz, either a Hungarian or a Serb who died some time before 1725. The Imperial Provisor of Gradisk

District (a sort of magistrate cum police chief) described what happened to nine other people living in Plogojowitz's village of Kisilova. Within a week, all nine had died after a twenty-four hour illness and all had reported on their death beds that Plogojowitz had 'come to them in their sleep, laid himself on them and throttled them, so that they would have to give up the ghost'.[44]

In this case what we are probably witnessing is a man being the first in his village to die from a virulent infection and others following suit after a twenty-four-hour 'bug'. Since he was the first to die, it was believed that he must be the source – the bringer of death (or in the case of the vampire, undeath). Because of the narrowly defined limits of medical science, the disapproval of the Church and poor diagnosis, the vampire was thought to be a *cause* of the disease. In fact, the corollary was true; disease, especially frighteningly fatal epidemics, bred the belief in and fear of vampires. This notion may even be present, however subconsciously, in Bram Stoker. In 1832 the great cholera epidemic reached County Sligo in the West of Ireland. Charlotte, his mother, lived through this, but her house was attacked by looters, driven to desperation by the suddenness and inevitability of the disease. Horror stories about pallid corpses and panic-stricken regions were part of young Bram's childhood, together with wild tales of cannibalism during the famine of the 1840s.

Any number of diseases prevalent in Eastern Europe in the seventeenth and eighteenth centuries can explain the vampire outbreaks. Tuberculosis causes weight loss and extreme fatigue, symptoms associated with vampire victims. The coughing up of blood from infected lungs speaks for itself. Cholera causes a similar weight loss and dehydration; rabies (with its obvious links with the wolf-coats and lycanthropy) leads to convulsions and breathing problems with an apparent terror of water (which in some areas vampires were believed to be unable to cross). Rarer diseases and conditions, although not terrifyingly contagious, were still inexplicable and bizarre.

Albinos and porphyriacs are sensitive to light, giving rise to the vampiric fear of the sun.[45] In porphyriacs, the body cannot metabolise iron, so taking it in some digestible form, perhaps blood, becomes a craving. Garlic's 'magical' properties break down old blood cells, recovering iron that the body needs. Pernicious anaemia likewise exhibits a blood-craving and causes a shrivelling of the body. Tony Thorne hypothesises that some vampiric symptoms – exhaustion, lethargy, even paralysis – can be the result of shock, such as personal loss, the trauma of war or pestilence.

Another phenomenon may explain the vampire outbreak and that is the ancient problem of premature burial. In 1885, before Stoker wrote *Dracula*, the *British Medical Journal* claimed ruefully, 'It is true that hardly any one sign of death, short of putrefaction, can be relied upon as infallible.'[46] Scientists today are still arguing about the concept of brain death. Rather depressingly for those who put their faith in today's science, health expert Jessica Sachs contends that we are actually *further away* from accuracy now than at any time in the past.[47] We are able to keep people 'alive' on machines for years, so the concept of the irrevocable ending of life is still blurred. Edgar Allen Poe capitalized on the fear of premature burial in a number of his short stories in the 1840s and in 1851, Dr Herbert Mayo, Professor of Anatomy and Physiology at King's College, London, wrote:

> That the bodies which were found in the so-called Vampyr state, instead of being in a new or mystical condition, were simply alive in the common way, or had been so for some time subsequent to their interment; that, in short, they were the bodies of persons who had been buried alive, and whose life, where it yet lingered, was finally extinguished through the ignorance and barbarity of those who disinterred them.[48]

The condition known as catalepsy could easily be confused with actual death. The body is immobile and the pulse and heartbeat very difficult to detect. It is likely that an unknown number of people suffering this condition have been buried while still alive and in outbreak periods, where large numbers must be interred quickly, there is even more likelihood of this. According to Montague Summers, in 1900 it was computed that in the US, an average of not less than one case a week of premature burial was discovered and reported.[49]

Summers, as we have seen, was likely to swallow such stories hook, line and sinker, but he does quote contemporary examples to bolster his views. One of these is the case of a matron in one of America's largest orphanages who had been certified dead twice by doctors only to be resuscitated in the nick of time by friends: 'today [1927] she is an exceptionally active and energetic administratrix.'[50]

Washington Irving Bishop was what in America today might be called a mentalist. He put himself into a cataleptic state once too often, however, and an overhasty autopsy in 1858 probably killed him. Certainly his mother thought so and sued the doctors concerned, even having a photograph taken of her gazing sadly at her son in his coffin with the top of his skull removed. Early in the nineteenth century, according to Summers, two cardinals of the Catholic Church, Spinola and della Somaglia, were 'prepared for embalmment before life was extinct'.

During the mid-nineteenth century in particular many people became obsessed by the fear of premature burial and stories of such cases or near-misses abound all over Europe. Again, undoubtedly, the sheer terror of being walled up alive in a confined space fed the folkloric impulse, and stories circulated of loaded revolvers being placed in coffins so that anyone unfortunate enough to be buried alive could put an end to their own suffering. In England, Sir Henry Thompson, surgeon to Queen Victoria, argued in February 1874 that the best solution to the problem was cremation, although this filled most of his contemporaries with horror. In Russia in 1901, Count Karnicki invented a device which saved a potential victim from an appalling fate. A tube was inserted into the coffin through a hole drilled through the lid. At the end of the tube was a glass ball, resting on the 'deceased's' chest. Even the slightest movement of the thorax would break the glass, release a spring and above ground a flag would fly upwards from a box on top of the tube. Simultaneously, a bell would be rung and even an electric light would flash should the movement take place after dark. In Styria and other parts of Austria a century earlier, a simpler device merely linked a rope inside the coffin to a central churchyard bell. It is not known whether such devices were actually used.

There is, finally, a more prosaic explanation for the vampire outbreaks. Like the witch fever that gripped medieval Western Europe and even the anti-Communist hysteria of McCarthy's America, vampire outbreaks took place in a period of religious and social upheaval. During the maelstrom created by the Reformation and Counter-Reformation, devil-worship and similar nonsense was believed to reign unchecked. The ongoing struggle between the Catholic Church and the Orthodox resulted in anarchy in areas where both contended for peoples' souls. The fall of Byzantium in 1453 had a devastating effect on the Orthodox Church, commensurate with the effect of Martin Luther's attack on Rome,[51] and the focus of Orthodox power shifted north to Moscow. This clash of Christian Churches caused confusion, hatred and bigotry and the geographical watershed, torn between the Eastern and Western Churches, was Transylvania.

Here, in the late fifteenth century, Vlad Țepeș ruled three times. He was probably as superstitious as his people and believed in all the hobgoblins that haunted his mountains. It would take Bram Stoker to turn the man into the vampire, but by then the horror stories of the mass-murderer with a blood lust were well-established in Eastern Europe, and especially in Transylvania, 'the land beyond the forests'.

PART 2:
VLAD THE IMPALER: THE TRUE DRACULA

7

DRACULA'S PEOPLE

MEDIEVAL ROMANIA

In a large open space between the Capitol and the Palatine Hill in Rome, the architect Apollodorus built a superb esplanade. Made of red and yellow marble, 375 feet long and 350 feet wide, it was built to contain two vast libraries, one for Greek books, the other for Latin. Between these was a huge column, a monument to the man who ordered it to be made, the general and emperor Marcus Ulpinius Trajanus, known to us as Trajan.

The monument was unveiled on 15 May AD 113, a tribute to both emperor and architect and nothing like it had been seen before. Spiralling slightly up all its 110 feet, the column showed, carved in bas-relief, Trajan's campaigns in Dacia, which marked the most northerly of the provinces of the Roman Empire. The designs can be followed, unrolling on twenty-three drums of Persian marble extending, if laid end to end, to 600 feet and containing 2,500 'action' figures, originally brightly painted. They are building fortifications on the plains that would become medieval Wallachia, Vlad Țepeș' principality, crossing the treacherous Danube on a pontoon of war galleys, hurling missiles at Dacian strongholds. The art is realistic; no two faces are alike, and as a source of information for the military historian of the second century, the column is unparalleled.

Trajan himself was born near Seville about twenty years after his people crucified Christ. Distinguishing himself in wars of conquest in Parthia and Germania, he was made Consul in AD 91 and succeeded his colleague, the elected emperor Marcus Nerva, seven years later. He was then fifty-four, straight-talking, loyal, kind and tough and he won the hearts of his people. Ever a man of action, he rowed himself across the Danube and would swim the Euphrates at sixty. His object, both in commissioning the column and in undertaking the campaign that adorned it, was simple: to make Rome the greatest power on earth. To do this lesser states had to be subdued. It would be the same fourteen centuries later, when the Ottoman Sultan Mehmed II nursed similar ambitions and one of the states was the same too; Roman Dacia became medieval Wallachia – war was the only constant.

The first known inhabitants of what would become Trajan's province were the two tribes of the Getae and the Daciae, both of Thracian origin. The squint-eyed philosopher Strabo, whose seventeen volume *Geographica* has survived since the time of Christ, claimed that the Getae lived on the Danubian Plain and the Daciae further north in the Transylvanian region of the Carpathian Mountains.

One of the many authorities, several of them now lost to time, from whom Strabo quoted was the Greek historian Herodotus, the 'father of history', who travelled widely to the north of his birthplace in Helicarnassus. He called the Daciae 'the bravest and most law-abiding among the Thracians'[1] though the Thracians 'were a meanly-living and dim-witted folk'. He also mentions their god, Zalmoxis, a god of the sky and a god of the dead. The first known ruler of the Daciae was Burebista who died some forty years before Christ.

When Trajan set out in AD 101 to conquer southern Dacia before moving north, the Roman legions were second to none in military terms throughout Europe. Even so, the Dacian tribesmen, in their wolf-coats and carrying their wolf's-head standards, fought to the bitter end and the campaign lasted five years. The Dacians relied on the single, hectic charge in battle, accompanied by as much noise and speed as possible, hoping that the terror of their advance would unsettle the enemy and make them run. Years of training had taught the Romans to hold their lines, locked steady behind their shield walls, and had taught that this steadiness won victories. It is likely that the Dacians collected enemy heads as trophies, but the severed head may have had a shamanistic and spiritual significance now lost to time. Not for nothing were vampires' heads in folklore and reality hacked from their shoulders and not for nothing was the head of Vlad Ţepeş sent to the sultan in Constantinople.

Like many tribal chieftains who faced the disciplined conquest of Rome, the Dacian King Decebal, who ruled from AD 87–106, swallowed poison rather than submit to the humiliation of being dragged in chains through the streets of the empire's capital.

The Roman occupation of Dacia has left its mark for two millennia. Not only does modern Romania take its name from Trajan's legions, the veterans who settled and intermarried in the villages north of the Danube, but also its language is still curiously Latin-based, unlike that of the Slavonic states all around it. The urbane and widely travelled scholar Eneo Silvio Piccolomini who would be elected Pope Pius II during Dracula's reign wrote:

These people have a Roman language that has changed a great deal so that it is very difficult for someone from Italy to understand it.[2]

Despite the fact that, rather romantically, some Romanians today make a great play of this lineal descent from the legions, no country like Dacia could actually remain isolated, despite the protection of its mountains to the north, 'the horseshoe of the Carpathians' as Stoker called them. The anonymous author of *Slavs and Turks; the Borderlands of Islam in Europe*, written in the 1880s,[3] noted:

> [The Carpathians] have been the battlefield of nations; on their soil have contended in succession Scyths, Romans, Huns, Bulgarians, Hungarians, Poles and . . . Ottoman Turks.

The draw for these nomadic, warring peoples of Europe, apart from the inevitable fact that Dacia lay on the route to an even richer south as the Roman Empire crumbled, was the richness of its soil. The barbarians who drove the legions out in AD 271[4] knew that the Carpathians were rich in gold, silver, copper and iron, lead and mercury, bitumen and rocksalt. The forests of oak, beech and pine were prime providers of building materials, firewood and shelter and the flood plain of the Danube offered superb grazing land for sheep and cattle.

As Dacia ceased to be a name with the fall of Rome, the people who came to dominate the area were the Vlachs, the Magyars, the Szekely and the Cumans. All four tribal groups were nomadic, the Vlachs in particular taking refuge in the northern mountains which the Romans had called *trans silva*, the land beyond the forests. They followed their flocks to the extent that the word 'Vlach' became synonymous with shepherd, though in the harsh Transylvanian winters they came south with an altogether less pastoral intent to raid the trade caravans on the silk road to the East. These caravans, groaning with the expensive brocades of China, rumbled west via Constantinople before that great city began to produce silk of its own.

Christianity came to Dacia early in the fourth century, the Zalmoxian cult, already probably bastardized by the huge panoply of Roman gods, blending easily with the new faith.[5]

According to Herodotus, the Dacians believed that Zalmoxis was originally a man, imbued with Greek and Egyptian wisdom, who vanished:

> into a whirlpool chamber, where he lived for three years, the Thracians wishing him back and mourning him for dead; then in the fourth year, he appeared to the Thracians.

The parallel with the Jesus resurrection is clear as is Zalmoxis' hint of Heaven:

> [He] taught them that neither he nor [the Thracians] should ever die, but that they should go to a place where they would live forever and have all good things.

What is most intriguing about Zalmoxis – and in this respect is utterly unlike his Christian counterpart – is that clearly he was a god who demanded human sacrifice. Every five years, Herodotus tells us, the Dacians chose a man by lot to be a 'messenger' to be sent to Zalmoxis:

> and this is the manner of sending: three lances are held by men thereto appointed; others seize the messenger to Zalmoxis by his hands and feet and hurl him aloft on the spear-point.

A god who vanished beneath the earth? A god for whom his people longed? Are we talking about Vlad Ţepeş, the humanized Zalmoxis of his day? And what was the method of sending the messenger if it was not Dracula's favourite method of execution, impalement? The origin and use of impalement as a method of execution is discussed elsewhere and it may seem far-fetched to link the god Zalmoxis with all-too-human Vlad Ţepeş a thousand years later. The parallels, however, are too much of a coincidence to ignore.

The first visible sign of Christianity in what would become Wallachia was a bishopric at Constanta on the Black Sea, which survived into the time of the Magyar invasions. The Magyars under their warrior leader Arpad, a chieftain from the Caucasus, migrated west soon after their defeat by a neighbouring tribe, arriving in the late ninth century. Speaking a Turkic language and descended from Altaian nomads, they were related to the Huns who had driven the Romans out and settled in Pannonia, the vast plains to the east of Transylvania in the ninth century. Here they intermarried with the Dacians. In 997, Duke Stefan took the title of king, crowned by Pope Sylvester II and forced Christianity on his people, organizing the church and endowing monasteries, receiving canonization in 1083.

Within fifty years the Szekely established their settlements on the fringes of the Hungarian kingdom. The word itself means 'beyond the seat' and several anthropologists see them as the direct descendants of Attila the Hun's warriors. Their broad faces with high cheekbones, their sallow skin and black hair are perhaps a physical legacy of that descent. It was possibly a misreading of all this in the British Museum, or a misunderstanding of the history fed to him by Arminius Vambery, that led Bram Stoker in *Dracula* to claim that the Count was of Szekely descent.

The Cumans' base was the steppes of Poland and the Ukraine, but they were of Turkish origin from central Asia. They had spread west into the Carpathians and were fully Christian by the late twelfth century. The Cumans in turn fell to the Mongols, Khans of what became known as the Golden Horde.

These fierce nomadic peoples with their short-legged, fast ponies were the cavalry *par excellence* of the steppes. An army of 40,000 Cumans fled west before them in 1240 to the welcoming arms of Bela IV, King of Hungary. The Mongol leader Batu Khan wrote to Bela:

I have heard that you have taken the Cumans, who are my subjects, under your protection. I command you to send them away, for by taking my people away from me, you have become my enemy.[6]

Bela responded in a way similar to that of Vlad Ţepeş two and a half centuries later – he had Batu's envoys murdered. Hungary would be dissected by the whirlwind attacks of the great general Subedei Bat'atur of the Reindeer people. The Vlach leaders, nominally under the suzerainty of Byzantium, with their hard-riding cavalry and their spell-bound shamans, had no time to run to Pest, the Hungarian capital, for safety. Village after village fell until Bela's army, stiffened by Cuman cavalry, faced the Mongols at Nady Czeks on the banks of the River Sajo. There, on 10 April 1241, the vastly outnumbered Mongol army won a dazzling victory with their deadly archers and heavy cavalry. The road to Pest was littered with Hungarian and Cuman corpses, according to one source 'like stones in a quarry'. An estimated 60,000 had died.

As the original inhabitants of the area, the Vlachs had migrated north in the late thirteenth century to the safety of the Carpathians, to settle permanently in Muntenia, the land of the mountains, called today Tara Romanesca, the Romanian land. A second period of migration in the middle of the fourteenth century led to the colonization of Moldavia, the mountainous territory that stretched to the River Moldova, which by Vlad Ţepeş' time would be a separate province.

Victoria Clark, travelling in the area recently, forms an excellent snapshot:

Naturally bountiful, bucolic, woodsmoke-scented and hemmed in on all sides by a crown of the Carpathian mountains and the Transylvanian alps, the province sits like a bright, rough jewel in its mountain setting. A world apart, Transylvania is a Bruegelesque-cum-Grimms'-fairy-tale place, dotted with little villages – some Hungarian, some Romanian and a few Saxon German settlements dating back to the thirteenth century. Its Orthodox churches, fat-bellied and squatter than the taller, sharp-steepled Hungarian Catholic competition or the few, now sadly crumbling, Saxon church-fortresses, embellish the countryside. Silver-roofed and freshly painted, they gleam in the cleavages between rolling green hills.[7]

Wallachia, the land of the Vlachs, came into existence as a state in 1290, although the term requires some qualification. In Western Europe the feudal system with its vertical structure of lord and vassal was creating nation-states with a definite identity, bound by law, language and culture. There was no feudalism as such in Eastern Europe and the notion of a nation-state would have to wait until the fifteenth century to emerge. According to hero-hungry Romania today, it was Vlad Ţepeş who provided the focus for an independent Wallachia. The area was also very small, only 48,000 square miles, the size of New York State. Its population reached perhaps half a million (giving the lie to the alleged numbers of victims of Vlad Ţepeş) and this was scattered in the three thousand or so villages between the mountains and the Danube.

The legendary founder of Wallachia was Radu Negru (Rudolf the Black) and his immediate successor, in 1310, was Bessarab the Great, whose shield carried three blackamoors, black-faced dancers who may symbolize his victory over the 'dog-faced Tartars' (Mongols) at the turn of the thirteenth/ fourteenth century. His name has survived in Romanian folklore, but there is virtually no written evidence of him. His name implies Turkish origin and it may be that he was of Cuman stock. Thirty years after his death, however, Mircea the Old, often referred to as Mircea the Great or Wise, ruled Wallachia for an unprecedented thirty years. His grandson would become Vlad the Impaler.

Unlike Western Europe where the concept of primogeni-ture, the right of the firstborn, was by the Middle Ages well established, in Wallachia only the ruling family retained hereditary powers, not the individual. Neither was there the obsession with legitimacy which dominated the West. In Wallachia, it was the blood of the royal father that was important, not the noble or marital status of the mother. In other words, a prince could inherit even if his mother was merely his father's mistress and no marriage had taken place. There are interesting echoes here of the *nosferat*, defined in folklore as the still-born illegitimate child of two people who are similarly illegitimate. The *voivod* or prince was actually elected by the *boyars* or nobility and this led to a great deal of confusion in later years over Vlad Ţepeş' title. In John Polidori's time Vlad was referred to as 'the Wallachian boyard' thus reducing his status and may even explain why Bram Stoker gave his eponymous hero/villain the rank of Count. Medieval Wallachia was characterized by frequent changes of voivod and the bloody removal of any number of them. For instance, between 1418 and 1456 no less than seven different voivodes reigned. All charges of brutality against Vlad Ţepeş should be measured by this yardstick – 'nobody's virtue was overnice'.

The term 'voivod' is of Slavic origin and although it dominates the contemporary and neo-contemporary writings on the Impaler, Romanians preferred the term '*domnul*', from the Latin *dominus*, Lord. The power he wielded varied inevitably according to personality and popularity. The voivod effectively was the government. He was the highest judge in the land and alone had the right to mint coinage. He levied taxation and led his armies in time of war. Unlike the rulers of Spain and France for example, the voivod owed a particular debt to his boyars in the sense that he was merely *primus inter pares*, first among equals. He did not have to be the eldest son of the previous voivod to inherit the Wallachian throne; neither, as we have seen, did he have to be legitimate. What he did have to be was to be chosen by the Boyar Council and crowned by the Metropolitan of Ungro-Wallachia and Exarch of the Plains, the senior representative of the Ortho-dox Church.

The term 'boyar' is associated in the West with Tsarist Russia, the definition in the 2000 edition of the *Penguin English Dictionary* clarifying it still further as 'a member of the pre-imperial Russian aristocracy'.[8] The origin of Wallachian boyars is obscure, and they probably began rather as the *hetmen* of the Ukrainian Cossacks to the east, village elders rather than hereditary chivalric commanders of armies in the sense of the French *noblesse* or the Spanish *hidalgos*. There is disagreement among Romanian historians on the origin of the boyars. Some, like Peter Panaitescu, claim that linguistic evidence survives for the fact that these rulers were the Romanized Slavonic invaders from the Magyars, Pechenegs and Cumans. Others claim the native tradition as being more likely. In practice, however, they appeared little different from their counterparts in the West. One boyar might own vast estates with dozens of settlements and they acquired these exactly as the Western nobility did, through dynastic marriage, outright cash purchase or handouts from a paternalistic prince.

Rather as in England where certain families were developing a reputation for a specific kind of service to the king,[9] boyars, too, were recognized for services rendered with Byzantine titles and a complex hierarchy of power began to develop. Most of the power was centred on the voivod, so the odd symbiotic relationship continued: the voivod needed the election and at least nominal support of his boyars; they needed the occasional hand-out from him. The senior boyar, or *ban* was the governor of the province of Oltenia, through which the River Olt ran. Below him were two supporters, lesser nobility who governed provinces or commanded castles.

Far below the boyars in every sense were the peasants. Nominally free, these illiterate, superstitious people, so easily gripped by the night-terrors of the *varcolac* and the *strigoii* (see Chapter 6), actually lived as serfs on the estates of the boyars or the Orthodox Church. Ironically, just as the concept of feudalism, with its freemen and serfs, was disappearing in the

West in the rapid onset of a cash economy and mobile capitalism to become 'Bastard Feudalism', the idea was just becoming established in fifteenth century Wallachia. This was so partly because of the influence of Western ideas crossing the region via trade routes to the East and partly because of the increasing threat from the Ottoman Turks to the south-east.

The whole complex problem of Eastern European peasants and their relationship to their voivod and their boyars has been brilliantly researched by historian Kurt Treptow[10] who begins by redefining what feudalism actually was. Finding the lord–vassal vertical relationship definition too narrow, Treptow believes that the structure has two major elements. First, it contains the 'hegemony of small-scale individual production'[11] and second, 'the exploitative relationship between landowners and peasants in which the surplus beyond the subsistence [of the peasants] . . . is transformed under coercive sanction to [the landowners]'.[12]

This essentially parasitic relationship in purely economic terms was hit hard in the 'hurling time' of the fourteenth century by the holocaust caused by the spread of the plague and the upheavals of serious and prolonged warfare between rival states in Europe. Famine and fear in this most turbulent of centuries led to peasant risings which had always previously been small, intensely localized and easily crushed. For example, Wat Tyler's peasants, marching from Blackheath in the summer of 1381, tore down John of Gaunt's palace of the Savoy and held the City of London for four days before a kind of order was restored. In France the Jacquerie[13] spread terror in the spring of 1358, leaving perhaps 20,000 dead between the Seine and the Marne. As one chronicler wrote, 'cultivation ceased, commerce ceased, serenity was at an end.' When Vlad Ţepeş was six years old, the peasantry of Transylvania rose in revolt against an intolerable burden of boyar exploitation. The rising could only be crushed with help from Hungary. Other risings took place in the Balkan lands to the south of the Danube, especially in Albania between 1343 and 1405.

The Serbian ruler Stefan Dusan set out his famous laws in 1349. These were an attempt to control the peasantry, including Vlachs who by the mid century had drifted south into his territories in large numbers. In England, the 1351 Statute of Labourers tried to do the same thing and it is likely that both were in response to the crippling economic and demographic effects of the plague, although in Dusan's case it was also connected with the establishment of the Serbian state. On the positive side, Serbian peasants had the right to bypass potentially unjust and avaricious boyars by contacting Dusan's courts direct. On the negative side:

> If a serf flee anywhere from his lord's to another land . . . where his master find him, let him brand him and slit his nose and assure that he is again his.

Bandits were to be summarily hanged and any village sheltering them severely punished. Vlad Ţepeş would introduce a similar code over a century later.

There was virtually no middle class in medieval Wallachia. The three estates of Europe – *pugnare* (the boyars, literally those who fight); *orare* (the Orthodox Church, literally those who pray); and *laborare* (the peasants, literally those who work) – were fully represented. The difference was, whereas the bustling states of England, France, 'Germany', 'Italy' and the Low Countries were all providing native-bred merchants and artisans who bought, sold and manufactured in the increasingly capitalist pursuit of profit, the 'middling sort' in Wallachia was almost exclusively German.

The reason for the (almost totally urban) existence of these 'Saxons' in Transylvania and Wallachia is that they were imported as colonists by the Hungarians in the twelfth century. Still trickling in as late as fifty years before Vlad Ţepeş' birth, they actually came from all the myriad German states, not just Saxony. Some, in fact, came from as far west as the Rhineland and Luxembourg, bringing with them their different customs, fashions, language and culture. This may be the origin of Robert Browning's alien band in his poem, 'The Pied Piper of Hamelin'. Officially recognized as a 'nation', their wealth and Catholic (as opposed to Orthodox) religion at once set them apart from native Wallachians and were the source of continued friction. Even in 2001, Victoria Clark wrote:

> The two Christendoms have been rubbing and chafing for a thousand years here in Transylvania and there is still no disguising the rift between the minority population of Catholic ... Hungarians and the majority of Orthodox Romanians.[14]

They established towns which had German names: Sibiu was Hermannstadt,[15] Bod was Benkendorf and Braşov was Kronstadt in Burzenland, the richest and most densely populated of all. When I stayed in the town in 2007, during the making of a documentary on Vlad Ţepeş, the hotel was straight out of nineteenth-century Germany. It could also have been part of a vampire film set. The Saxons built fortifications to keep out the country's original inhabitants, solid walls with brattices and barbicans, and governed from within rather in the manner of the powerful city states of northern Italy, Venice, Milan and Genoa. Vlad's home town of Sigişhoara once had fourteen towers along its walls. The only one remaining which is open to the public is a huge, solid structure, designed to overawe passersby. The Saxons kept in regular touch with their homelands through family and trade and, as far as was possible under the voivod's overlordship, were a law unto themselves. Elsewhere in Europe, the Holy Roman Emperor Charles IV produced his Golden Bull in 1356 which was designed as a handbook for the princely election of emperors. It also so curtailed the power of the cities in the empire that they uniformly turned against him.

These Saxon cities could boast the finest craftsmen in Europe. Goldsmiths, tailors, shoemakers, silk weavers and metalworkers clattered and stitched side by side in the open-fronted workshops that thronged the cobbled streets. In Braşov and Sibiu they made bronze cannon, the new and terrible engines of war that would change the world forever, using the Carpathian ores of copper, gold and silver over which they had been granted a monopoly. Through the mountain passes of Bran and Turnu Roşu they carried on a trade that extended to the Danube delta on the Black Sea and to Constantinople, the ancient heart of Byzantium that would beat until the Turks stopped it in 1453. Bistriţa, on the northern, westward-facing route out of the 'horseshoe of the Carpathians' carried Transylvanian Saxon goods to Danzig and Hamburg, the ports of the Hanse, the most successful European trading venture before the Common Market in the twentieth century. At the Impaler's later capital of Tîrgovişte and the neighbouring Tîrgsor, large fairs were held where goods were on display and sale to an admiring population. Whether selling internally or externally, the Saxons paid duties to the voivod and in 1456 Vlad Ţepeş wrote to the Germans of Braşov describing them as 'honest men, brothers, friends and sincere neighbours'.[16]

Over all of Wallachia and Transylvania by the fifteenth century, though with less power here than nearer to Byzantium's heart at Constantinople, hovered the spectre of the Orthodox Church. The population of the Carpathians had nominally been converted to Christianity by missionaries during the ninth century, although various incursions by pagan Slavs and marauding Mongols had made this an unsteady and haphazard process. The Metropolitan of Ungro-Wallachia and Exarch of the Plains was the Orthodox Church's leader in Wallachia and Transylvania, acting on behalf of the Patriarch in Constantinople who officially recognized the Church in 1359. Based at Curtea de Argeş the Metropolitan presided over bishops and abbots who ruled estates as large as those of the boyars and whose monasteries, such as those at Tismana, Dealul and Snagov, were large and powerful centres of ecclesiastical wealth. In common with the Church in much of Europe, they paid no taxes unless pressed by the emergency of war. Traditionally, voivod and boyars alike hid treasure in their fortified vaults; everybody paid them lip service because they guarded men's souls and presided over their path to Heaven or Hell. Bessarab I was buried, like many other medieval rulers, in the church he built; his was at Cîmpulung.

An underlying concern of the Orthodox Church was the dualist Bogomil heresy which surfaced in the Balkans in the tenth century. Believing that the firstborn of God was a fallen angel, Satanael, the cult's leader, Bogomil, the 'beloved of God', thought that Satanael seduced Eve and that their son was the killer, Cain. Moses and John the Baptist were both Satanael's servants, although he himself was ultimately defeated by Christ's resurrection. The Bogomils, based largely in Bulgaria south of the Danube, resurfaced as an ascetic cult in the thirteenth century and were crushed by the Turkish onslaught in the 1390s. They despised marriage and condemned the eating of meat and drinking of wine. To them, the Church's rites of communion and baptism smacked of Satan. In purely religious terms, the heresy spread west to influence the much more serious stand taken by the Cathars and Albigensians.[17] Here, the word 'bugger', from Bulgaria where the sect had originated, crept into the French language by the thirteenth century, with all the smear of sexual deviancy the Catholic Church could muster.

The danger of Bogomilism for the ruling elites wherever the heresy spread was that, like most heresies, it had its insidious, political dimension. A priest called Cosmas wrote in the tenth century that the Bogomils:

> teach their own people not to obey their masters; they blaspheme the wealthy ... condemn the nobles, regard as vile in the sight of God those who serve the tsar [of Bulgaria] and forbid all slaves to obey their masters.[18]

We cannot know how many of the sect actually lived north of the Danube in the Impaler's principality, but their existence in large numbers south of the river certainly helps to explain why Serbia was destroyed by the Turks at the Field of Blackbirds in 1389. 'It is not our business to defend the king,' one of the Bogomils told Stephen of Bosnia, 'Let the nobles do it.'[19]

Outside the tiny state of Wallachia with its alien middle class, its avaricious boyars and its discontented peasantry was a world, far more powerful, waiting to swamp it.

In religious terms, what would become the Impaler's principality was still under the control of Byzantium, the Eastern Roman Empire whose native language was Greek. At the heart of this exotic and ailing white elephant lay Constantinople, the city of the Golden Horn, lying between two worlds. For just over eleven centuries, this place of magic and wonder guarded the approaches to the Black Sea and stood as what it considered itself to be, the rightful successor to ancient Rome. There still stands in today's Istanbul a marble column which marks with pride and assurance the city as the centre of the world.

Constantine the Great[20] chose Byzantium for his capital and renamed it as his – the City of Constantine – on 11 May AD 330. General decline in eastern Roman towns, exacerbated perhaps by Slav, Persian and Arab invasions, led to a shrinkage of the empire in which Constantinople stood out as the shining exception, the sun dazzling forever it seemed on the dome of Justinian's Sophia Hagia, the Church of Holy Wisdom and the last great Roman basilica ever built.

The sixth-century Byzantine historian Procopius wrote of this church:

> Within it is singularly full of light and sunshine; you would declare that the place is not lighted from without, but that the rays are produced within itself, such an abundance of light is poured into it. The gilded ceiling adds glory to its interior,

though the light reflected upon the gold from the marble surpasses it in beauty. Who can tell of the splendours of the columns and marbles with which the church is adorned? One would think that one had come upon a meadow full of flowers in bloom . . .[21]

The style of church building born in Byzantium spread throughout the Balkans in the seventh and eighth centuries, although here the churches and monasteries, like the Impaler's place of burial, Snagov, were rather more compact and modest. Everything about Constantinople was vast and designed to overawe. The Pantokrator monastery, for example, sanctified in 1136, had a leper-house, asylum and hospital. It employed 165 staff, including four permanent grave diggers and its land yielded nearly 10,400 tons of corn a year. Even today, modern Istanbul has not filled the old city walls.

Constantinople was just as much a fortified, armed camp as it was a religious centre. Its outlying villages provided regiments to defend the city, many of whom would die on the ramparts in May 1453 when the Turkish sultan, the Impaler's enemy Mehmed the Conqueror, ended not only an era, but a way of life. The city also had its own merchant fleet and war galleys, whose powerful oars and lateen sails were the envy of the marauding Turks who quickly copied them.

By 1204, Constantinople had grown even larger, the old walls of Constantine abandoned and the later ramparts of the Emperor Theodosius marking its south western boundary. The Golden Gate was the industrial quarter, with its over-crowded clutter of potters, tanners, wheelwrights and smiths. Beyond that stood the imperial barracks and parade ground of the men who would die under the Conqueror's guns. The city's water supply was poor, augmented in Roman times by a series of astonishing underground reservoirs, and the roads that stretched away across Bulgaria (ancient Thrace) merely dusty tracks.

In that year, Venetian crusaders took Constantinople on their way to the Fourth Crusade and from then the city lay awaiting a long and lingering death. The essential difference between 'Eastern' and 'Western' Rome was that at Constantinople the Emperor and the Patriarch of the Orthodox Church co-operated; indeed the secular power was paramount. Between 1204 and 1261 Constantinople was a Latin Kingdom under the control of Venice, although it reverted to Greek control after that.

When the Emperor Manuel II Palaeologus travelled west to attempt some sort of compromise with Rome, his reception was lukewarm, although the astonishingly successful flank attack by the 'Scythian shepherd' Timur-i-Leng halted for fifty years Turkish designs on the City of the Golden Horn. The West continued to treat Constantinople as a side-show at best and this serious rift between Greek and Roman Christianity left a power vacuum all too willingly filled by the Turks. As the English poet G.K. Chesterton would write 500 years later:

And Christian killeth Christian in a narrow dusty room,
And Christian hateth Christ who has a newer face of doom.[22]

So the Council of Florence signed in the presence of the Byzantine Emperor John VIII when Vlad Ţepeş was eight was boycotted by the Orthodox bishops of Wallachia and Russia, who could find little common kindred with Rome at all.

Against this background, it is hardly surprising that the calls for crusade by Eneo Silvio Piccolomini, Pius II, against a common threat from the Islamic Ottoman Empire in 1459 fell largely on deaf ears in the East.

The kingdom of Hungary to Wallachia's immediate west was to play a vital role in the life of Vlad Ţepeş. By 1301, the Arpad dynasty, which had reigned since the ninth century, had come to an end. In many ways, this was the most enlightened of the medieval kingdoms, with three diets (assemblies) representing aristocracy and gentry a full century before Simon de Montfort, Earl of Leicester, set up what is usually considered the first parliament at Lewes in England in 1264. Hungary's monarchy was also elective, because primogeniture was not established here and, under Louis the Great, a first step towards emancipation of the serfs was made in the Golden Bull of 1351. Louis' successor was his daughter, Mary, but only as long as she maintained the traditions of Salic Law by bizarrely styling herself 'King Mary'. The Salic Law was originally a Turkish code of the fifth century, its best known element being the banning of females from inheritance.

Further west still lay the scattered lands and widely differing cultures that called themselves the Holy Roman Empire. Voltaire, who had firm views on the vampire epidemics sweeping Europe in his eighteenth century, famously commented that it was 'neither Holy, nor Roman' and Napoleon Bonaparte took the concept further forty years later by destroying its existence as an empire. Some sixty years after the death of Vlad Ţepeş, the Emperor Charles V was allegedly to sum up the problems of ruling his vast dominions in the phrase, 'I speak Spanish to God, Italian to women, French to men and German to my horse.' The 'Germanies' (the single country was not welded together until 1871) comprised over 300 tiny states, with their own rulers, laws, customs, commerce, armies and dialects. As in Hungary, the Emperor was elected by three archbishops and four archdukes – the Electors – whose normal ploy was to choose an idiot who could be controlled by them. One bad choice from their point of view was Sigismund, son of Charles IV, who was crowned in 1411. Sigismund had married 'King Mary' in 1387 and assumed the role of King of Hungary too. When his half brother Wenceslas died in 1419, the Emperor also became King of Bohemia.

To the north of Wallachia, the most powerful state in Eastern Europe was Poland. The modern world has tended to treat this kingdom like a political football, wedged as it was between the twentieth-century 'superstates' of Germany and

Russia. The country had been badly ravaged by the Mongols in 1241, as part of the campaign which had destroyed Bela of Hungary's army, but Poland survived only to become a battleground between the Teutonic Knights of the Cross, one of the most formidable of the medieval orders of chivalry and the pagan Prussians further east.

Under King Casimir the Great, Poland became a united and important state, Casimir's laws of 1347 being the first complete legal code anywhere in Europe. He founded a university at Cracow in 1364 and, almost uniquely among Christian rulers, welcomed Jews into that city and others to develop trade and banking.[23] His nephew, Louis, was also King of Hungary and his daughter, the ten-year-old Jadwiga, married the pagan Duke Jagiello, who became baptized at the wedding and adopted the Christian name of Ladislas II. His son in turn would die in battle with the Turks, fighting alongside the elder brother of Vlad Ţepeş.

To Wallachia's north-east lay the Duchy of Muscovy. Eighteen years after Vlad the Impaler's death, its ruler Ivan III described himself as 'Tsar of all the Russias', yet two centuries earlier Muscovy was only one tiny city state along with the duchies of Tver, Riazan, Novgorod and Pskov. Easily defended and on the busy river network which made trade simple, the duchy grew inexorably in its defence against the Mongols, whose own internal divisions had led to weakness. In 1380 the Muscovite Duke Dmitri Donskoy smashed the Golden Horde at Kulikovo Polje and, despite a reversal two years later, the victory proved that the legendary Mongols could be beaten. In a series of dynastic marriages and open military attacks, the highly capable Ivan incorporated both Riazan and Tver into his duchy and then subdued Novgorod, its famous cathedral bell dragged to Moscow as a symbol of the defeated city's collapse.

Like Casimir in Poland, Ivan codified a *sudebnik*, a list of laws to govern his expanding territory. He sent envoys like Fedor Kuritsyn to the West to learn their secrets in an age of rapid change, inviting the best Italian architects to work at his palace-fortress of the Kremlin some time before the Impaler's death. In November 1472, he married Zoë, the niece of the last Byzantine Emperor. It was from the Roman legacy of Byzantium that Ivan chose the double eagle as his soon-to-be-imperial standard and from the old Roman title of Caesar that he took the term 'Tsar'.

Although geographically as far from Ţepeş' Wallachia as was Muscovy, the bustling city state of Venice was, by the fifteenth century, making a profound mark on the late medieval world. It faced the Balkans across a twenty-mile strip of the Adriatic and its arch trading rival, Genoa. It had outposts for commerce along the Black Sea coasts, the Crimea and Constantinople itself. Ragusa (today's Dubrovnik in Croatia) was Venice's principal city in the Balkans until it was won back from Venice by Louis of Hungary in the mid-fourteenth century.

Venice was an island, sheltered by a series of lagoons and protected by an army of grim-faced *condottieri* (mercenaries, literally contractors). It reached the height of its commercial success in the years immediately preceding Vlad Ţepeş' birth. The city's children were wrapped in swaddling bands to make their limbs grow straight; the brightest of them were schooled first in literacy, then in numeracy. Some drifted into law, where they clashed with other merchants' counsel. Some sailed on the armed merchant galleys themselves, supervising the arrival of silks and spices from the East, gold from Africa, jewels from Arabia and glass from Syria, dealing in wine, grain, dyes and alum, all in the name of profit. By the year of the Impaler's death, Venice had its own arsenal employing over 2,000 people, along with foundries, magazines, shipyards, chandlers and an army of sailors. All of Europe envied this city state and its rival Genoa. Venice's very name was synonymous with luxury and wealth. Not for nothing did Shakespeare, a century later, set one of the most tragic of his 'comedies' there. Officially, Jews such as Shylock had to wear

yellow hats to mark their 'racial affliction' and were only
allowed to engage in that most despicable of professions,
medicine. Over the city presided the Doge, an elected official
who had assumed the status of a prince, sailing out on the
lagoons each Ascension Day to bless the waters and give
thanks to God for the bounty of the money-bearing sea.

Further south, central Italy was the province of the Holy
Father, the Pope, with the Holy See of Rome at the heart of
the Papal States. In the year of Vlad Ţepeş' birth, a great
council of the Western Church was called at Basle to heal,
once and for all it was hoped, the great schism which had split
the Catholic Church in the previous century. It was then, in
1381, that Clement VII had retired to Avignon in southern
France, while his rival Urban VI had remained in Rome.
Inevitably, because the Pope was an 'Italian princeling', a
political figure as much as a religious one, the kingdoms of
Europe took sides. France, Spain and Scotland supported
Clement; England, the Italian states, the Holy Roman Empire
and Hungary backed Urban, even when the latter began
torturing recalcitrant cardinals to death. A series of councils
from Pisa in 1409 to Constance in 1414 were held to resolve
the split in the college of Cardinals from among whom popes
were elected. Between 1415 and 1418 no less than forty-five
assemblies were held with dozens of committee meetings and
no doubt hundreds of cloister-side chats. Scholars descended
from all over Europe, including representatives from the
Orthodox Church which had in theory been separated from
Rome since 1054. One pope was at last elected in 1417, but by
the time of the Basle conference, other issues had arisen and
exposed the papacy once again. The new pope, Eugene IV,
clashed with his cardinals and both sent envoys to Constantinople to effect some sort of reunion with the Eastern
Church. The whole enterprise collapsed under a welter of
bickering and animosity and by the end of the 1430s there was
even a schism of councils – one at Basle, one at Ferrara, then
Florence.

Even so, it was this papacy, petty and small-minded that alone had the power to call for a crusade. And alone of the rulers of Europe in 1462, it was Vlad the Impaler who actually took up the call.

The Europe of Vlad Ţepeş was a world that was turning. That most misunderstood of movements, the Renaissance, was already underway. Essentially an attempt to recreate the 'glory that was Greece and the grandeur that was Rome',[24] the movement in fact took men forward to an age of humanism, technology and science.

Leonardo da Vinci was ten when Ţepeş attacked the Turks along the Danube. He was eighteen and apprenticed to the sculptor-painter Verrochio by the time the Impaler was a prisoner of the Hungarian king Matthias Corvinus. Verrochio himself was already working with the goldsmith partner whose surname he adopted by the time Ţepeş took the throne of Wallachia for the first time. Donato di Niccolo di Betto Bardi (Donatello) was already carving his fame in marble in both Florence and Padua before Ţepeş was born and the future voivod was still a prisoner of the Turks and perhaps witnessing impalement at first hand when the artist cast the first life-size horse ever to be made in bronze – the mounted figure of the Venetian condottiere Erasmo da Narni, known as Gattamelata, the Honey Cat; it might have been a statue of the Impaler. Paolo di Dono Uccello, the Florentine goldsmith, was working with Ghiberti on the magnificent doors of Florence's baptistry when Vlad was still a boy in Sighişoara. The lumbering horses and dazzling heraldry of his painting, *The Battle of San Romano* could have been a painted snapshot of one of the Impaler's battles against the Turks.

Filippo Brunelleschi, the great architect, fascinated by straight lines and mathematical symmetry, had already established vanishing point perspective by the time Vlad was a boy and, by the decade of his death, the Italian explorer-adventurer Christoforo Colon (Christopher Columbus) knew that the earth was round. All he needed was the money, ships and men to prove it.

Where there were artists, sculptors and painters, there were patrons, powerful men who collected works of art and kept their makers busy with the designing of tombs to impress God and the weapons of war to kill His people. The Sforzas in Milan and the de Medici in Florence vied with each other for the accolade of the most influential scions of the arts, although the honour should probably go to the Impaler's contemporary, Lorenzo the Magnificent, who encouraged archaeological digs and archive-sifting as well as aspiring geniuses.

How much of this world of the Renaissance travelled east in Vlad Țepeș' time is difficult to gauge. Nicolas Copernicus, it is true, studied at the University of Crakow, but not in the Impaler's lifetime and the Copernican 'heresy' of the heliocentric universe belongs to another generation. Matthias Corvinus, the King of Hungary, was certainly a patron in the mould of the de Medicis. While Țepeș was under house arrest at Visegrád, Benedetto da Maiano, Giovanni Dalmata and Chimenti Camicia were all there and in Buda, working on the kings' castles and palaces. Visegrád itself was described by the ambassador of Pope Sixtus IV as a 'terrestrial paradise' and the extraordinary alabaster relief of Corvinus, made by Giancristoforo Romano thirteen years after the Impaler's death, is a wonderful example of Renaissance artistic skill.

But south of the River Danube, teeming with its rainbow trout, grayling, dace, sturgeon and Grecian carp, lay Bulgaria and the dangerous, creeping armed camp that was the Ottoman Empire of the Turks, the greatest military force on the edge of Europe. Here was a very different civilization, at once fatalistic and aggressive, poetic and barbarous. And against it stood the tiny mountain state of Wallachia, with its voivod, Vlad Țepeș, and his people.

8

'A WILD, BLOODTHIRSTY MAN . . .'
HISTORICAL SOURCES

In May 1484, a Silesian knight, Nicolas von Popplau, met King Richard III of England at his castle of Pontefract in Yorkshire. Von Popplau, emissary of the Holy Roman Emperor, Frederick III, was a giant of a man, known equally for his skills in the tilt as for his classical learning and diplomacy. The king told von Popplau, who later recorded it in his diary:

> I wish that my kingdom lay upon the confines of Turkey; with my own people alone and without the help of other princes I should like to drive away not only the Turks, but all my foes.[1]

The Silesian does not record what prompted the comment, but in all probability Richard III was talking about a man very much of his own stamp, a warrior-king whose reputation was destroyed, and distorted, by subsequent generations: Vlad Ţepeş, the Impaler.

Vlad ruled as voivod and Prince of Wallachia three times. The first reign, barely two months in 1448, was perhaps too brief to be worthy of anecdote and legend, but the second, between 1456 and 1462, produced scores of tales on which the man's reputation rests. He inherited a throne that was usually won and lost on the battlefield and came to rule a people whose hierarchy were fickle and untrustworthy. Intent on centralizing and consolidating his power, like so many of his contemporaries, Ţepeş was prepared to use harsh measures to achieve his ends. Above all, he took on a principality under threat – from the aggressive Hungarians to the west and the terrifying advance of the Ottoman Turks to the south. It is against this background that the stories of this 'wild, blood-thirsty man' must be set and against this background that he must be judged.

Apart from the official documentation from his court which will be discussed later, there are three broad sources for information on Vlad Ţepeş the man. The first, made possible partly by the Renaissance achievement of the printing press, comes from the Saxon community living in Wallachia but more especially Transylvania itself.

Europe did not actually invent printing. The earliest examples of printed texts come from Korea in the eighth century and the first example of movable type using individual letters is again Korean and dates from 1409. In the West however, it was Johann Gutenberg's great Bible of forty-two lines per page that lays claim to being the first printed book. Gutenberg called his printed Gothic letters 'artificial writing', nearly three million of them making up the 1,282 pages. He made perhaps 200 copies, when Vlad Ţepeş was in his twenties, of which a staggering thirty-eight still survive today.

The printing press caught on. By 1500, 250 towns had them, employing in each case dozens of specialist craftsmen to boil and wash linen rags to make paper or prepare vellum (calf-skin), to pour molten metal into tiny moulds and to file off rough 'flash'. The compositors laid out the letters to form the lines and paragraphs, the printers using ink made from lampblack or charcoal mixed with linseed oil. Mainz had been the first town to perfect this technique, possibly as early as 1455, but the technology spread to Leipzig, Stuttgart, Nuremberg and Augsburg within fifteen years. Crakow in Poland and Buda in Hungary had their own presses five years before William Caxton set up his at the sign of the Red Pale in Westminster Abbey in the year that Vlad Ţepeş died.

Inevitably, many of the earliest books, like Gutenberg's, were bibles, psalters or other religious works. But by 1463 the world saw one of its first political pamphlets. It was printed in Vienna, the Austrian capital, and its subject was Vlad Ţepeş, Voivod of Wallachia. Entitled *The Story of a Bloodthirsty Madman Called Dracula of Wallachia*, it was probably based on a poem penned the previous year by Michel Beheim, the court poet of the Holy Roman Emperor, Frederick III. Beheim was the son of a Bohemian weaver, born in Sulzbach, Württemberg in September 1416. He tried his hand at travel and the bloody trade of war before studying music and theology. The fifteenth century was an age of patrons and Beheim's first was Count Ulrich Cilli before the Italian was assassinated. By 1457 he was court poet to Ladislas V Habsburg and should correctly be regarded as a *minnesinger*, a court minstrel in the mould of the thirteenth-century troubadours. At the close of the 1450s, Beheim was flitting among patrons in Bohemia and Hungary and it was by chance that he met the itinerant preacher Brother Jacob at Wiener Neustadt, thirty miles south of Vienna, near Jacob's monastery of Melk. Jacob seems to have been the sole source for the *Story of a Bloodthirsty Madman Called Dracula of Wallachia*, which was probably completed in four months.

The 1,070-line work found its way in published form to the University of Heidelberg, and the Hungarian King Matthias Corvinus' scribes probably made an even more defamatory version for propaganda purposes late in 1463. The poem quickly became a favourite with the Emperor Frederick, who for the next two years insisted that Beheim regale important guests with it at banquets. There is no equivalent to the *minnesingers* today. Known in Wallachia as *guslars*, schools for such singers, where the apprenticeship was long and arduous, were set up throughout the Holy Roman Empire, but the earliest was probably at Mainz, followed by Augsburg in 1450. Whether Beheim ever set his Dracula poem to music is unknown; however, *minnesingers* were balladeers who took folk tales and even actual events, embellishing and changing them for particular audiences' tastes. For that reason as well as the bias of Brother Jacob, Beheim's source, we cannot rely on the poem as history. Beheim's poems about the Impaler were the direct forerunners, in one sense, of the works of Polidori, Stoker and all the celluloid fictions that followed.

The German or 'Saxon' stories were often accompanied by woodcuts of a particularly grisly kind. Some were mere representations of the Impaler as in the frontispiece of *Dracole Waida* printed at Nuremberg about twelve years after his death. The text begins, 'In the year of our Lord, 1456 Dracula did many dreadful and curious things.' The best known, printed by Ambrosius Huber, again at Nuremberg in 1499, shows the infamous blood feast. The text above the ghastly scene, in effect a sort of caption, reads:

Here begins a very cruel frightening story about a wild bloodthirsty man, Dracula the voivod. How he impaled people and roasted them and hacked them into pieces like a head of cabbage. He also roasted the children of mothers and they had to eat their children themselves. And many other horrible things are written in this tract and also in which land he ruled.[2]

The woodcut shows Ţepeş, a benign-looking Renaissance prince with full beard and civilian clothes, sitting at an open-air table with food and goblets in front of him. Several feet from him an underling is hacking the limbs off corpses with an axe and, behind the table, near-naked men and women are writhing in their death-throes, impaled on spikes. The event depicted refers to Ţepeş' attack on the Saxon city of Braşov, called by the Germans Kronstadt,[3] in April 1459. The pamphlet reads:

> And he led away all those whom he had captured within the city ... near the chapel of St Jacob. And at that time Dracula ... had the entire suburb burned. Also ... all those whom he had taken captive, men and women, young and old, children, he had impaled on the hill by the chapel and all around the hill and under them he proceeded to eat at table and enjoyed himself in that way.[4]

Most of the Saxon stories found their way into the monastery of St Gall in Switzerland or the cathedral at Lambach near Salzburg. The Lambach Papers, like Ţepeş' body and grave furniture, have disappeared. Today, St Gall is a canton, named after a seventh-century saint. The abbot of the monastery presided over the area until the nineteenth century. The fact that the paper trail of the Saxon stories of Ţepeş leads to Lambach and St Gall is important and explains a great deal about their bias. According to historical fact, the Impaler launched a series of raids against Saxon towns and churches in Transylvania between 1457 and 1460. The Saxon Catholic monks fled west, taking their horror stories with them. The Benedictines told their stories and anonymous scribes copied them down.

St Gall houses the bulk of the Saxon stories, thirty-two tales of terror written in *Plattdeutsch*, the low German dialect and can only have been intended for consumption by the monks themselves. Rather than translating, as most authorities do, all of the stories, this book attempts to categorize them according to type. Of the thirty-two, a possible ten can be verified by historical sources which, while not unimpeachable, at least have an air of authority. The first of these, numbered one in Manuscript No-806 in the St Gall Library, refers to the murder of Vlad's father, Dracul, and his brother, Mircea, by 'the former governor'. This must be János Hunyadi, the

'White Knight', whose name was legend among the crusaders of the late medieval period. His influence on Ţepeş and the effects of the murders are crucial to an understanding of the Impaler and will be discussed elsewhere.

The second tale relates Ţepeş' killing of Ladislaus Voda, the Vladislav II who was his rival and who ruled Wallachia for the eight years before his execution in 1456, the year in which, the St Gall tales remind us, 'this Dracula did and threatened to do terrible things in Wallachia, as well as in Hungary'.

The third describes Ţepeş' invasion of Transylvania, destroying castles, villages and towns including Beckendorf, which was either Bod or Benesti near Braşov, and the monasteries of Holtznundorff and Holtznetya. Prisoners and refugees from these raids were impaled, irrespective of age or sex. One translation of tale number seven[5] reads:

> He had a big family uprooted from the smallest to the largest, children, friends, brothers, sisters and he had them all impaled.

This family has been identified with that of the powerful boyar Albu cel Mare (Albert the Great), himself no stranger to rape and pillage, who had defected to Prince Dan III, another of the Impaler's rivals.

Dan himself came to a suitably sticky end for crossing Ţepeş, as tale nine relates.

> He [Ţepeş] also captured the young Darin [Dan]. Later on he allowed him to go through his priestly function and when he had completed it all, then he had him make a grave according to the custom of the Christians and he had his body slaughtered by the grave.

Other sources give us Dan's execution date in April or May 1460, probably at Tîrgsor.

Tale ten is typically repetitious and involves the imprisonment of emissaries sent by Matthias Corvinus, the King of

Hungary, who appear to have turned up with Saxon delegates from the various Transylvanian towns. Vlad held them for five weeks, mentally torturing them by setting up stakes in view of their cells as though for their impalement. He launched his attack on Transylvania, burning the fields around 'Kranstatt' (Braşov) and rounding up the populace 'near the chapel called St Jacob'. This was the infamous occasion when the Impaler reputedly sat down to dine al fresco within sight of his dying, twitching victims.

Tale number fourteen is a similar, if less gruesome, recital.

> there [in the towns of the seven fortresses at Siebenburgen and Talmetz] he had men hacked up like cabbage and he had those whom he took back . . . as captives cruelly and in various ways impaled.

In the story which Peter Painitescu describes as 'additions to the St Gall manuscript'[6] Ţepeş' attack on the village of Amlaş is told with particular relish:[7]

> In the year 1460, on St Bartholomew's Day [24 August] in the morning, Dracula crossed the forest with his servants and looked for all the Saxons, of both sexes, around the village of Amlaş and all those that he could gather together he ordered to be thrown, one on top of the other, like a hill and to slaughter them like cabbage, with swords and knives. And their chaplain and the others who he did not kill immediately, he took back to his country and there had them hanged. And he ordered that the village and everything in it, including the people, who numbered more than 30,000 to be burned.
>
> And then, from all the lands which are called Figaras, he took the people and brought them to Wallachia, men, women and children and he ordered that all of them be impaled.
>
> And then, he ordered that more of his boyars be decapitated and he took their heads and he used them to grow cabbage. After this, he invited their friends to his house and he gave them the cabbage to eat. And he said to them: 'Now you eat the heads

of your friends.' After this he ordered that all of them be impaled.

And then he ordered that some of his people be buried naked to the navel. After this he ordered that they be shot. He also had many roasted and the skin peeled off others.

In some translations, the final paragraph appears as a separate story, and it is one of a possible eleven which seem to have no purpose but to nauseate the reader and further blacken Ţepeş' reputation. Tale number six, which has echoes throughout history, concerns the murder, which seems to have no motive, of 'young boys and others from many lands' who were sent to Wallachia ostensibly 'to learn the language and other things'. Ţepeş 'brought them together and betrayed them. There were four hundred in the room.' Story number thirty is very similar. In this, the victims are 200 paupers lured to a feast provided by the Impaler.

As if bored by incessant impalement, Dracula experimented with other forms of torture. In story number thirteen:

he had a great pot made with two handles and over it a staging device with planks and through it he had holes made, so that men's heads would fall through them. Then he had a great fire made underneath it and had water poured into the pot and had men boiled in this way.

Tale number seventeen takes up this theme. A gypsy was caught stealing and the Impaler gave his own people the chance to hang him. When they said 'That is not our custom,' Ţepeş had the gypsy boiled in a pot and when he was cooked, he forced them to eat him, flesh and bone.

To see Vlad's singling out of a gypsy as well as his targeting of Saxons as examples of racism or xenophobia is to misunderstand the temper of the times. Wallachia was not yet a nation-state in the sense of modern Romania, but the fact that the gypsy was branded a thief has echoes throughout

Europe, where it was widely believed that the nomadic travellers stole children. Legend has it that Vlad Dracul, the Impaler's father, brought thousands of gypsies (*tiganes* in Romanian) as slaves to his principality, but in fact they were indigenous to the area long before reaching northern Europe by the end of the fourteenth century.

Tale number fifteen is particularly repellent:

> Once he had thought up terrifying and frightening and unspeakable tortures, so he had mothers impaled and nursing children, and he had one and two-year-old children impaled. He had children taken away from their mothers' breasts, the mothers separated from their children. He also had the mothers' breasts cut out and the children's heads pushed through the holes in their mothers' bodies and then he impaled them. And he caused many other sufferings and such great pain and tortures as all the blood-thirsty persecutors of Christendom, such as Herod, Nero, Diocletian and other pagans,[8] had never thought up or made such martyrs as did this bloodthirsty berserker.[9]

Tale number eighteen has a moralizing tone to it which is found in other Saxon stories relating to Ţepeş and is echoed in the other translations concerning him (see below). A surreal scene is conjured up in which the voivod and a boyar are strolling under rotting, impaled corpses 'as many as a great forest'. Ţepeş asks the nobleman if the smell offends him and when the answer is yes, 'Dracula immediately had him impaled and hoisted up high in the air, that he would not smell the stench.'

Among these quite random and repetitious stories of atrocities, there is a clear obsession with cannibalism. This aspect of the character of Vlad Ţepeş will be analysed later, but the constant reference to cabbages and relatives being forced to eat each other might tell us more about the clerical compiler of the tales rather than their subject. So, in number twenty-nine, 300 gypsies were forced to 'eat the others until there are none left'. In tale thirty-one, Țepeș 'had very young children roasted and forced their mothers to eat them. He cut the breasts off women and forced their husbands to eat them; after that,' the tale continues, with a certain inevitability, 'he had them impaled.'

Two stories in particular stand out and point perhaps to Țepeș' real character, which will be analysed in full elsewhere. Tale number twenty-one describes not the usual summary ordering of execution, but a hands-on murder directly committed by him. It provides, if true, a rare glimpse of a warped human being behind the mask of terror he showed to the world:

> He had a mistress who announced that she was pregnant, so he had her looked at [examined] by another woman, who could not comprehend how she could be pregnant. So he took the mistress and cut her up from under to her breast and said 'Let the world see where I have been and where my fruit lay.' He also had similar things cut or pierced and did other inhuman things which are said about him.

Tale sixteen takes us further into the dark soul of a madman.

> He had people impaled, usually indiscriminately, young and old, women and men. People tried to defend themselves with hands and feet and they twisted around and twitched like frogs. After that he had them impaled and spoke often in this language: 'Oh, what gracefulness they exhibit!' And they were pagans, Jews, Christians, heretics and Wallachians.

The point about the list of groups of victims is to show the Impaler's lack of discrimination. It is unlikely that the refugee monks fleeing to St Gall would be unduly perturbed by anything Vlad Țepeș chose to do to pagans, heretics and Jews, who were all fair game in their denial of God and Christ.[10] But to kill Christians, and Wallachian Christians at that, was truly unforgivable.

We know the names of some of those monks whose memories, reportage and embellishments form the crux of the thirty-two Saxon stories. The three referred to by Michel Beheim in his epic poem of 1463 are Brother Jacob, Brother Michel and Brother Hans the Porter, who may be based on, or actually be real characters, described to the *minnesinger* by the one, Jacob, who was undoubtedly a flesh and blood priest. The records of St Gall also record Blasius, who came from Bistriţa, one of the Impaler's target towns with its sawmills and tanneries and Johannes de Septum Castis (John of the Seven Fortresses, i.e. Siebenbergen, Transylvania).

It is the Saxon stories, with all their obvious bias, distortion and repetition, that formed the written kernel of the legend of the Impaler used by the Hungarian King Matthias Corvinus as propaganda against the voivod when it suited his political purpose. The lurid nature of the tales quickly made stationers (publishers) realize that here was a money-spinning spine-tingler that would run and run. The historians McNally and Florescu suggest the reasonable hypothesis that the Ţepeş pamphlet was the first non-religious bestseller and that probably only the Bible outsold him in the late fifteenth century. In 1488, three Dracula tales were printed at Nuremberg, and one at Lübeck. The stationer Hans Spörer produced another in Bamberg in 1491 and a fourth rolled off the presses of Martin Landsberg at Leipzig two years later. As the new century dawned, the stories travelled west. Matthias Hupfuff published in Strasbourg in 1500; Des Iegher produced a variant in Hamburg two years later. And they were still appearing in Nuremberg as late as 1521.

It was in these years, when the Ottoman Turks destroyed the flower of Hungarian chivalry at Mohácz (1526) and Martin Luther unleashed his torrent of protest against the Catholic Church, that Vlad Ţepeş first appeared in works of fiction far removed from the effects of Polidori, Rymer and

Stoker. He appeared in the satirical poem 'Floh Haz, Weiber Traz' by Johann Fischart in 1573. Thirteen years earlier, he is referred to in another poem, this time by the Hungarian priest Matthias Nagybanki. And the use of Ţepeş as a tyrant synonymous with pure evil extends through German and Hungarian literature well into Stoker's time.

The second set of sources for our knowledge of Vlad Dracula comes from the Russian narratives preserved in the Kirillov-Belozersky Monastery collection in the Saltykov-Schredin Public Library in St Petersburg. The 'sinner' monk Eufrosin probably wrote the manuscript and Fedor Kuritsyn, the envoy of Muscovy, met the Impaler's family at the Hungarian court and collected stories about him. Whereas the Saxon stories blacken the Impaler's reputation because he came down hard on them as foreigners and avaricious capitalists bleeding his own people, the Russian tales seem much more ready to accept that such violence was normal for the time and justified by what contemporary Englishmen called 'good governaunce'. There is a sense in which Vlad Ţepeş became a blueprint for later Russian governments, rather as Cesare Borgia, born in the year of the Impaler's death, was the model for Nicolo Machiavelli's *The Prince* written in 1515.

There are nineteen Russian tales from the Kirillov-Belozersky Monastery compiled about the year 1490, sixteen years after the Impaler's death:

> There lived in the Wallachian lands a Christian prince of the Greek [Orthodox] faith who was called Dracula in the Wallachian language, which means devil in our language, for he was as cruelly clever as was his name and so was his life.

Using the same criteria for categorization as in the Saxon stories, a different pattern emerges. Six are historical and can be verified, not only by reference to Saxon and Romanian versions, but independent documentary evidence. Of these, three refer to the Impaler's crusades against the Turks and will be dealt with elsewhere.

Three stories, however, exhibit a streak of morality totally missing from the Saxon tales. The first, number four, reads like a story from the *Arabian Nights*:

> Dracula so hated evil in his land that if someone committed a misdeed such as theft, robbery, lying or some injustice, he had no chance of staying alive. Whether he was a nobleman or a priest or a monk or a common man, or even if he had great wealth, he could not escape death. And he was so feared that in a certain place he had a source of water and a fountain where many travellers came from many lands and many of these people came to drink at the fountain and the source, because the water was cool and sweet. Dracula had put near this fountain in a deserted place a great cup wonderfully wrought in gold; and whoever wished to drink the water could use this cup and put it back in its place. And as long as this cup was there, no-one dared steal it.

Tale number six concerns two Hungarian monks who visited Wallachia. Dracula shows one of them his victims, 'countless people on stakes and spokes of wheels'. 'Have I done well?' the voivod asks the monk. 'No, lord,' comes the reply. 'You have done badly. You punish without mercy.' The second monk, however, has a very different perspective. 'You have been assigned by God as sovereign to punish those who do evil and to reward those who do good. Certainly they have done evil and have received what they deserved.' This cleric is given fifty gold ducats and safe conduct by carriage to the Hungarian border. The first is quizzed by Ţepeş as to why he has left his cell and wandered abroad when clearly he is so stupid. 'And he ordered that he be impaled from the bottom up.'

The next story in the sequence describes the arrival in Tîrgovişte of a Hungarian merchant who leaves his gold-laden carriage in the street outside the Impaler's palace. In the night someone steals 160 ducats from the vehicle and, not unreasonably, the merchant complains to the voivod. The Impaler orders a search for the thief, threatening destruction of the city if he is not found. In the meantime, Țepeş has the carriage loaded with 161 ducats and waits for morning. The merchant counts his money, extremely impressed and reports to the voivod that there is one extra coin. The thief is caught with the original haul and Țepeş delivers the moral of the tale himself: 'Go in peace. If you had not told me about the additional coin, I was ready to impale you, together with the thief.'[11]

Seven of the Russian stories are variations of the Saxon tales. In one of these it is Wuetzerland merchants whose headgear was nailed to their heads because they refused to uncover before the voivod. In the Russian story, we have the much more likely Turks:

> When they entered his palace and bowed to him, as was their custom, they did not take their caps [turbans] from their heads and Dracula asked them 'Why have you acted so? You ambassadors have come to a great sovereign and you have shamed me.' The ambassadors announced 'Such is the custom of our land and our sovereign.' And Dracula told them, 'Well, I want to strengthen you in your custom. Behave bravely.' And he ordered that their caps be nailed to their heads with small iron nails ... 'Go relate this to your sovereign, for he is accustomed to accepting such shame from you, but we are not.'

Tale number two follows on to claim that this insult to his ambassadors stung the sultan, Mehmed II, into an invasion of Wallachia. The truth, as always, is far more complicated.

A variant on this tale appears in story number twelve. Any ambassador who appears before Țepeş improperly dressed or unable to answer a question to the voivod's liking is likely to die, the blame for this lying squarely with the monarch who sent him. Vlad states: 'I am not guilty of your death, but your own sovereign.' Alternatively, it could be the fault of the emissary himself, 'because you are slow-witted and ... not properly versed ... then you yourself have committed suicide'.

Only two of the Russian stories appear to be examples of cruelty for its own sake and the first is widely found in folklore throughout the world, and so perhaps can be dismissed entirely. Ţepeş orders workmen to fill iron-hooped barrels with gold and bury them in a river-bed. He then has the men killed 'so that no one would know the crime committed by Dracula except for the devil whose name he bore'. The only glimmer of veracity here is any voivod's penchant for stashing valuables in monastic and church vaults. Could the lake at Snagov, Vlad's resting place, be one such hiding place?[12]

The other tale is a decidedly odd narrative concerning the Impaler's time under house arrest in Pest, across the river from Buda where he had been placed by King Matthias Corvinus some time in the mid 1470s. There is a hue and cry in the city, a felon hurtling through Ţepeş' courtyard in his desperation to flee the mob. Grabbed by the prefect (constable of the watch) the criminal suddenly finds himself free because Ţepeş has decapitated the officer with his sword. Taken to task by Corvinus' magistrates, the Impaler's reply is unabashed:

I did not commit a crime. He committed suicide. Anyone will perish in this way should he thievingly invade the house of a great sovereign.

The tale goes on to state that Corvinus is impressed with the voivod's courage and he laughs off the incident.

There is little doubt that Ţepeş' tales of terror struck a chord not only with Fedor Kuritsyn but the Russian psyche generally. And it manifested itself most obviously in the reign of Ivan III's grandson, called the Terrible. The Russian version of his nickname is actually *groznyi* which means awe-inspiring. Ivan carried out a grim regime of terror which might almost have taken as its blueprint the reign of Vlad Ţepeş. He reduced the power of his nobility, elevating humbler men whom he could trust. After the poisoning of his wife, Anastasia Romanova, in 1558, he turned on opponents with increasing cruelty. Unruly ambassadors who failed to show him respect, he punished by nailing their caps to their heads. He used impalement as a slow and excruciating form of execution, which had rarely if ever been used in Russia before his time. Many authorities, including Dracula experts, dismiss Ivan IV as insane, but are loathe to draw the same conclusion about the Impaler. The exhumation of Ivan the Terrible from his tomb in St Petersburg revealed that the impaler-tsar suffered from osteo-arthritis, an incurable condition that would have caused him almost constant pain and may explain at least some of his eccentric and vicious behaviour.

Did Ţepeş' philosophy and policies as relayed by Kuritsyn and Eufrosin survive the test of centuries? As recently as 1917, Tsarist officers who refused to submit to Bolshevik power by removing their epaulettes had them nailed to their shoulders.

The final strand of information on Vlad Ţepeş comes from the mangled memories of his own people. Of the eight Romanian folktales concerning Vlad usually listed in modern translations, seven of them also occur in the Russian texts and six in the Saxon versions. What is interesting is that several of them have two or three variations, reflecting their folkloric origin. So, for instance, the story of the merchant whose carriage is robbed in Tîrgovişte of 160 golden ducats has two further versions. In the first, the merchant calls to passersby at crossroads for help and the cash is in *lei*, Romanian currency. A local, described as 'a Christian' and 'a God-fearing man, as were the Romanians at the time of Prince Vlad the Impaler', finds the money bag, but it is short by 100 *lei*. The merchant takes the peasant to court, accusing him of helping himself to the money as a reward. Ţepeş presides as Solomon and decides that the merchant is the dishonest one: 'Master merchant, at my court people do not know what a lie is.' In the third variant, the tale begins: 'there reigned in Wallachia a Prince Dracula, also known as the Impaler. This prince was very severe, but also just. He would not tolerate thieves, liars and lazy people.' The travelling merchant is specifically from Florence and he goes to ask Țepeș for safe conduct through his land. Instead the voivod orders the merchant to leave his money in the square overnight insisting it would be safe until morning. And, in the usual pattern of morality tales and fairy stories, it is.

In the story of the man with the short shirt, whose wife had clearly neglected him, Țepeș orders her to be impaled despite her husband's protestations – 'She never leaves home and she is honest' – and provides him with another wife, whose sole duty is to work for the peasant. Tellingly, in this, as in other Romanian folktales, the story looks back nostalgically to a 'golden age' in which life was vastly better:

> It is just as well that Dracula does not rule our country today, for he would have had to expend many stakes, which might have eliminated from our land the innumerable drones who whither the very grass on which they sit.

The burning of the poor story, which occurs as Saxon tale number thirty and Russian number five, is treated as a cautionary tale of the type made popular throughout Europe in a later period.[13] The emphasis here is on the shiftlessness of Wallachian beggars, a view shared by the authorities of all European states concerning their own poor. As the Romanian tale says of such people, 'I am looking for a master, but God grant that I don't find one.' Țepeș' policy was to eradicate the poverty problem rather more swingeingly than other governments. He invites them to a feast in Tîrgoviște, the tables groaning with wine and fine food. When they are more than merry, the voivod orders the doors locked and the fire lit:

the blaze rose high like inflamed dragons. Shouts, shrieks and moans rose from the lips of all the poor enclosed there. But why should a fire be moved by the entreaties of men? They fell upon each other. They embraced each other. They sought help, but there was no human ear left to listen to them. They began to twist in the torments of the fire that was destroying them. The fire finally abated, there was no trace of any living soul.

The teller of the tale ruefully admits that Ţepeş' fire did not solve the problem: 'Beggars will cease to exist only with the end of the world.'

A tale in the Romanian collection found nowhere else relates to the voivod's attack on his boyars. In language reminiscent of his handling of the poor, he invites them to a banquet at his capital and in the course of the evening asks each of them, 'How many reigns have you, my loyal subjects, personally experienced in your lifetime?' There are a variety of answers, but one that probably annoys the Impaler most is, 'Since your grandfather, my liege, there have been no less than twenty princes. I have survived them all.' This is precisely the point. The answer is, in fact, wrong, but the moral is the issue. Such was the anarchy in Wallachia when Ţepeş assumed the throne in 1456 that he was faced with an oligarchy of self-servers prepared to condone and even commit murder to survive and to protect the status quo; any number of princes could come and go as long as the boyars continued to hold power. According to the tale, 500 boyars, their families and hangers-on are impaled on the spot.

Further stories continue the saga. According to other variants Ţepeş ambushed the boyars as they attended the Easter service with its famous words *'Hristos o-nviat'* – 'Christ is risen' – and the response *'Adevărat c-o-nviat'* – 'Truly, He is Risen.' The most recent research tends to confirm that this is historically possible, even probable.

Oral history is an infuriatingly vague minefield and when translated from a foreign language can sound a little naïve. The

problem with Țepeș stories in Romanian culture is that
the language itself did not develop into written form until the
sixteenth century. Church Slavonic was the language of
the Impaler's own court and we have no way of knowing
whether the Impaler himself understood the various dialects
of his principality or could even make himself understood
without an interpreter.[14] The story of the building of Țepeș'
castle at Poenari was first written down from Romanian
folklore by a writer called Constantine Cantacuzino in the
seventeenth century:

> He sent his retainers who, striking on Easter Day, apprehended
> the husbands and their wives, their sons and daughters in their
> gaudy clothes and took them to the castle of Poenari, where
> they toiled until their clothes fell off their backs.

The folk tales began to appear in print by stages after this time,
the castle-building saga being written up by the Metropolitan
Neofit in 1747, at a time when the Enlightenment was making
its presence felt in the wilder parts of Europe and vampire
epidemics were on the increase. The printer Petre Ispirescu
tackled the tales in Bucharest over fifty years after Neofit, but
he was no folklorist and much seems to have been lost in
translation. The teacher C. Radulescu-Codin did a better job,
and the Institute of Folklore under Mihai Pop has carried out
invaluable research on the tales. Much of this is still going on
in post-Ceaușescu Romania and the need is pressing. Under
the Conducator, there was a marked drift to the cities in search
of work because of the destruction of village life in order to
modernize. This has led to a breakdown of old cultures and
the folkloric tradition can be said to be under threat.

Vlad Țepeș emerged hesitantly in Romanian literature as a
folk hero along the lines of Spain's El Cid, Switzerland's
William Tell or England's Robin Hood. Whole books have
been written about these characters, at once men and legends,
in an attempt to find the truth. In the nineteenth century, the

age of nationalism, Romania was still under the rigid influences of the ailing Ottoman Empire on the one hand and the aggressive Russian Empire on the other. In 1848, the 'Year of Revolutions', Ţepeş assumed an Arthurian quality in Romania, a hero asleep and waiting for the trumpet call to waken him. The poet Mihai Eminescu imagined him sorting out the idiots who dominated the state:

> You must come, O dread Impaler, confound them to your care.
> Spilt them in two partitions, here the fools, the rascals there.[15]

The Saxons saw Ţepeş as a monster because he brought their rapacious capitalism to heel; the Russians, perhaps looking to echo the Impaler's centralized state, saw him as cruel, but just; the Romanians saw him as a hero on a white horse, at once delivering them from the corruption of the boyars and the Turkish onslaught on their borders. Where, in all this, lies the *real* Vlad Ţepeş? And what has he to do with the most famous vampire in history?

9

THE SIGN OF THE DRAGON
MIRCEA THE GREAT AND VLAD DRACUL

From the eighth to the seventeenth centuries the West experienced many attacks by Muslim forces: no coincidence, surely, that this period was the high plateau of the Devil's career in Christendom. Bearded, swarthy, impulsive, violent, deceitful and oversexed.[1]

We have only one signature known to be that of Vlad the Impaler. In a letter to the largely German citizens of Braşov dated 4 August 1475, he signs 'Wladislaus Dragwlya' – Vlad, son of the Dragon. In the as yet unwritten Wallachian language, however, Dracul meant devil as well as dragon and in this double sense it can be found elsewhere in Europe. A century after Vlad Dracula, the English seaman and pirate Francis Drake was called El Dracque by his Spanish enemies, as a pun on his name. '*Draco*' means dragon in Latin and, with the success of his raids on Spanish silver convoys and Cadiz, the Spanish thought he must, indeed, also be the devil.

In his book *The Flight of Dragons*, Peter Dickinson gives three views on the nature of dragons: they are legendary; they are secondhand sightings of real, exotic animals such as crocodiles or boa constrictors; they were once real. In the medieval mind, they were associated with fierce courage – in Britain, Arthur's battle standard traditionally depicted the dragon.

> The voice of the dragon is thunder, the trembling of the earthquakes his footfall, forest and heath fires are the heat of his breath . . .[2]

It is a destructive and dangerous power for the dragon hoards gold and strikes terror into its enemies. It was the Celtic tradition of the dragon as a symbol of sovereignty which probably explains the Arthur connection. The dragon was also associated with the serpent who seduced Eve in the Garden of Eden:

> Now the serpent was more subtil that any beast of the field . . . And he said unto the woman, Yea, hath God said Ye shall not eat of every tree of the garden?

Eve, tempted by the serpent, persuaded Adam to eat the fruit of the forbidden tree and God's vengeance was swift:

> And the Lord God said unto the serpent Because thou hast done this, thou art cursed above all cattle and above every beast of the field; upon thy belly shalt thou go and dust shalt thou eat all the days of thy life.[3]

Artistically, there was little to distinguish the dragon from the snake in medieval art, although the two creatures were distinguished in heraldry with the dragon a common device; the snake, rare. In art the serpent was always a symbol of evil as a result of the Fall. Often found at the feet of various medieval saints, the serpent crushed by a cross was a typical Byzantine motif. So the terms 'serpent' and 'dragon' were interchangeable and, probably because of the biblical curse, the dragon came to be associated with terrible events. For instance, the Anglo-Saxon Chronicle of AD 793 records:

> Here dire warnings were come over the land of the Northumbrians and sadly terrified the people. There were tremendous lightnings and fiery dragons were seen flying through the air.[4]

These were the ominous signs of the Viking raids on Lindisfarne and along the coast of north-east England. The imagery of the devil is associated with these marauders too: 'berserkers' chewing their shields in their battle-madness; the wolf-coats on the rampage. Terrified monks imagined their horns protruded through their headgear and the myth of the Viking horned helmet has survived until recent times. Peter Dickinson writes:

> The Devil, in Christianized art, became *the* dragon. We are so used to the identification that it is hard for us to see that it is not a very logical piece of symbolism, if everybody knew in their hearts that dragons were mythic monsters. Elsewhere, Christian symbols are very concrete, following the limitations of the parables of Christ. The souls of men are sheep; the Holy Ghost is a dove; sinners are goats; the enemies of the Church are wolves . . .[5]

Dragons are part of the folklore and mythology of many cultures world-wide, but in Europe they took a certain shape and are almost always associated with fire.[6] In the third century, the Greek philosopher Flavius Philostratus wrote knowledgably about the dragons of the mountains which:

> had yellow scales the colour of gold and [were] longer than the dragon of the plains, with a beard like the bristles of the swine

and very heavy eyelids and brows, giving a horrible appearance. When the dragon climbed and dragged itself across the land the scales on its stomach resounded like metal. And it would seem that these reddish creatures gave off sparks of fire.

In biblical references, which would have been known by Catholic and Orthodox priests alike, a dragon is equated with the primordial monster referred to in the Books of Job, Isaiah and Amos:

By his spirit he hath garnished the heavens; his hand hath formed the crooked serpent.[7]

In that day the Lord with his sore and great and strong sword shall punish Leviathan the piercing serpent, even Leviathan that crooked serpent; and he shall slay the dragon that is in the sea.[8]

... and though they be hid from my sight in the bottom of the sea, thence will I command the serpent and he shall bite them.

And he laid hold on the dragon, the old serpent, which is the Devil and Satan and bound him a thousand years ...[9]

And the great dragon was cast out ... which deceiveth the whole world: he was cast out into the earth ...[10]

The Apocalypse compares the dragon directly with the serpent of Eden and whenever dragons are found in pseudo-histories, the heroes who vanquish him are listed too: in Egyptian mythology, Anubis; in Greek, Apollo, Perseus, Hercules and Jason; in Christian, George, Michael and Margaret. In the last cases, typified by St George as an armoured knight piercing the dragon with a lance (an excellent example is the painting by Paolo Uccello completed during Vlad Ţepeş' lifetime), the representation is of good destroying evil. Impalement with the lance has fascinating echoes as we have seen both of Zalmoxian sacrifice in ancient Dacia (see Chapter 7) and of the execution methods of Vlad Ţepeş. It was the Impaler's father, as we shall see, who joined the Order of the Dragon, probably in the year of Vlad's birth, but among its many scions, only the rulers of Wallachia seem to have adopted the word as a sort of nickname, no doubt to drive terror into the hearts of their enemies.

Vlad Țepeș' grandfather was Mircea the Great, the nickname sometimes translated as the Wise or even the Old. Lord of Wallachia from 1386 to 1418, he ruled a country as large as modern Romania, with the Black Sea to the east and the Danube to the south. It included most of what is today Transylvania with a line of Marcher castles to keep out the aggressive Hungarians to the west and an island fortress at Giurgiu, on the Danube, guarding the south.

The river was important, not just as a source of trade, but also for defence. The longest in Europe at 1780 miles, the Danube rises in the Black Forest and was navigable by the ocean-going nefs or small boats of the Middle Ages as far inland as Ulm. Trajan built a stone bridge across the river to facilitate the Dacian campaign, the ruins of which still survive. In Țepeș' time there was no usable bridge, but a determined army could cross in rafts or boats, hence the strategic importance of Mircea's castle at Giurgiu. Brother Jacob's Benedictine monastery of Melk still frowns down from its 200-foot perch above the river and at Belgrade, where the Impaler's mentor and nemesis János Hunyadi died of the plague in 1465, it is a mile across and 40 feet deep. Further south, at Kazan, the Danube narrows to 160 yards with a depth of 150 feet. As it glides past the Wallachian plain, it reaches the Iron Gates near Orsova, rocks that block the river bed and make a crossing even easier. At its eastern end, the river flows into the Black Sea via channels, the Kilia, Tulcea, Suchia and St George, forming a delta teeming with its 110 species of fish and oozing with its post-Ceaușescu pollution.

This area, Dobriya, was taken in 1389 by Mircea who also built a delta stronghold at Chilia. He gave himself the rather grand title of 'God's anointed and Christ's loving autocrat

Ioan Mircea, Great Voivod and Prince, with God's help ruler over Ungro-Wallachia and parts of the country beyond the mountains, the Tartar lands, the duchies of Amlaş and Făgăraş, ruler of the Banat of Severin and of both banks of the Danube up to the Black Sea.'[11]

The reason for Mircea's obsession with the Danube is that beyond it lay Serbia, a land increasingly at the mercy of the Ottoman Turks pushing to gain territory from the south-east. This astonishing phenomenon, which terrified Central and Western Europe by its speed and success, will be evaluated fully in the next chapter, but between 1320 and 1390, the Turks had crossed the Dardanelles into Europe and were on the southern banks of the Danube. As historian Jason Goodwin says:[12]

> They moved so fast and so suddenly that they swerved beneath the eye of chroniclers and no single battle can be dated with precision before 15 June 1389, when they shattered the Serbs at Kosovo, on the Blackbird Field.

In all probability, there were Wallachians sent by Mircea to fight at Kosovo, a battle still observed today by the Serbs as a black day in their history. It was there that the sultan, Murad I, was killed, according to legend, in his tent. He was stabbed by a Serb assassin Milosh Obravitch, who was hacked to death before he could reach his horse to escape. Typical of a rising nation which had neither the time nor patience to cope with the contending rule of two sons, Murad's elder boy, Bayezid, known as Yilderim, the 'thunderbolt', had his brother executed either on the field or days later and assumed the throne. Jason Goodwin sums up the man who was to be an implacable enemy of the Christians:

> He dressed like a Greek, practised buggery like one, drank wine ... he seems to have enjoyed having enemies. 'For this was I born – to bear arms and to conquer whatever is before me.'

The concept of bearing arms and conquering was part of the creed of the Ottoman Turks. The Koran, in its first page, points the way:

> As to those who reject faith, it is the same to them whether thou warn them or do not warn them; they will not believe. Allah hath set a seal on their hearts and on their hearing and on their eyes is a great veil; great is the penalty they incur.[13]

Since the Arab conquests of the seventh century, European Christendom had good reason to fear the Muslim world. The songs of the *guslars* of the 1460s wailed:

> The Wallachian land is split apart, the people run to the mountains, to the valleys, away from the cruel Turks ... The old men cut down, they enslave the young ones, they rape the girls, they capture the youth and enlist them in their armies ... wherever they pass, they burn the villages.[14]

Two years after the death of the prophet Mohammed, Abu Bakr and his followers had conquered the Arabian peninsula. Driving their cavalry hard into the deserts of Egypt, Syria and Mesopotamia, they had besieged Constantinople by AD 669 and again between 673 and 678. The astonishing speed of their success can be attributed to much the same malaise in their opponents that existed in Vlad Ţepeş' time and explains the ultimate failure of the crusading ideal. Both the Byzantine and Persian empires were riven by internal feuds and, in an age before the coming of the nation-state, nationalist loyalty and its corollary, xenophobia, were not yet sufficiently potent forces to act as a rallying cry for anything approximating to collective security.

For their part, the Muslims used their faith like a weapon. Surprisingly tolerant of other faiths among the peoples they conquered, they insisted on no conversion to Islam, but for the Muslim warriors themselves to die for Allah and the prophet-promised paradise.[15] By the eighth century, they had spread west into southern France before being defeated by Charles the Hammer and his Franks at Poitiers in 732, and as far east as the Punjab beyond the mountains of the Hindu Kush.

The concept of the Muslim holy war, jihad, was echoed in the West by the crusade. Under their battle cry '*Deus Io Volt*' (God wills it) the crusaders first assembled under the banner of Pope Urban II in 1095, marching to the Holy Land with its shrines and Christian legacy, to free the holy places from the Infidel (a name for unbelievers used by both sides). The crusades were fought with bitter campaigns, pitched battles and wholesale slaughter. Neither did they live up to the chivalric ideal of the medieval knight epitomized in the Victorian view of Richard the Lionheart, who led the Third Crusade in 1199. It is possible to see Richard today as a psychopathic killer with a homosexual streak, a far cry from the fictionalized view of him in, for example, the Robin Hood stories. Ninety years earlier, Godfrey de Bouillon's Frenchmen had massacred men, women and children in Jerusalem, wading, according to one chronicler, up to their spurs in blood.

But it is important to see this in context, as we must the life of Vlad Ţepeş. The crusades were extraordinarily difficult, long-range military operations involving relatively small, sometimes multi-national armies travelling the length of Europe and beyond, by land and sea. After the First, which took Jerusalem in 1099, later crusades achieved less success, partly because of the disunity of the crusaders themselves. Godfrey de Bouillon's army was depleted seriously in numbers because his commanders Baldwin of Boulogne, Raymond of Toulouse and Bohemond of Taranto broke off to establish their own fiefdoms at Edessa and Antioch. In the Third Crusade, fierce bickering broke out between Richard of England, his cousin Philip Augustus of France and Duke Leopold V of Austria. According to legend, which, even if apocryphal, makes the point well enough, Richard ordered Leopold's eagle flag to be hauled down when he saw it flapping over the captured city of Acre and be used as a dishcloth.

Many histories of the crusades date the end of the movement as 1291 when the last Christian outpost fell in Palestine. The idea survived, however, depending on one's definition of crusade and with the appearance of the Ottoman threat in the fifteenth century, there was a renewed urgency about it.

Bayezid's advance was clearly not going to stop at Kosovo. If Serbia fell, Bulgaria would be next and Bulgaria was only across the Danube from Mircea's principality of Wallachia. For safety's sake, the voivod looked to friends in the West, most notably Sigismund of Luxembourg and Bohemia, the Margrave of Brandenburg who by virtue of his marriage to Mary, daughter of Louis the Great, had by now been elected King of Hungary. Sigismund did not love his new Magyar lands, but became grudgingly fonder of them as his reign continued. Shown in contemporary manuscripts as a wise man with a magnificent forked beard over his ermine robes and fine plate armour, Sigismund realized that he would need to check the Ottoman advance if the Turkish threat to the south was to be averted. The Balkan states were like a set of dominoes – if one fell, there was a risk to them all.

Accordingly, because it was mutually beneficial to them, Sigismund and Mircea signed an alliance some time in 1395, but there must have been an element of mistrust because Mircea had to send one of his sons, Vlad, as a hostage to ensure the Wallachian ruler's continued support.

We do not know the date of Vlad's birth, but it is likely that he was under ten when he was taken, essentially a political prisoner, to the court of Sigismund at Buda on the Danube. The notion of political hostages and noble sons growing up in other noble or even royal households is not as alien as it seems. Mircea would have wanted the boy to have the best education available and as Sigismund's court, in keeping with that of most European royalty, was endlessly peripatetic, the boy would have visited Prague, Nuremberg and Rome as well as the Hungarian and Transylvanian towns nearer to home. It is likely that Vlad would have learned Hungarian, Greek, Latin, Italian and perhaps French, because Sigismund's wife, Mary, was the daughter of a French prince.

Vlad's mother is unknown. Mircea's first wife was Maria, of the Hungarian house of Tolmay, and the couple's only surviving son was Mihail who would co-rule with his father for ten years after 1408. Vlad was the result of a liaison with an unknown mistress, but his claim to the throne of Wallachia was as strong as Mihail's under Wallachian law.

There are differing dates for the foundation of the Order of the Dragon with which Vlad and his son the Impaler would both be invested. It was possibly December 1387, the year in which Sigismund was elected to the throne of Hungary and it is likely that his wife Barbara (Barbola) was co-founder. It was not actually a knightly order, unlike the earlier crusader examples of the Templars and Hospitallers, but it served much the same purpose. The Society of the Dragon is an obscure organization and it is possible, according to D'Arcy Boulton of the University of Notre Dame, that it was founded before 1381. It makes no mention in its statutes reaffirmed in 1431, the year of Vlad Ţepeş' birth, of knighthood actually being a pre-requisite of membership.

The reason for the order's creation is likewise shrouded in mystery, but it is likely that Sigismund intended it to be all things to all men and a source of feudal power whose support he could count on in time of need. The fact was that his election to the throne of Hungary was not the peaceful event that it sounds. Sigismund had been betrothed to Maria, Louis the Great's daughter, as was the custom of the time, when she was eleven and he ten. On Louis' death however, Maria's mother ignored her late husband's will and married Maria to the younger brother of the French king, Louis of Valois-

Orleans. In August 1385, the seventeen-year-old Sigismund kidnapped the girl and forced her to marry him. Only the removal of a rival – Carlo di Durazzo – in February 1386 and the signing of a carefully worded agreement among the Electors allowed Sigismund to co-rule with Maria.

Sigismund's reign, however, was to be as troubled as the Impaler's. A rival clique of Hungarian nobility centring on the house of Horvathy backed the claims to the throne of Carlo's son, Ladislas, and Maria's death in the year of the treaty with Mircea left Sigismund with a weak claim to the throne.[16] It was now that young Vlad was probably sent to Buda, but at an inauspicious time.

Bayezid the Thunderbolt laid siege to the city of Constantinople in 1396, but news of Sigismund's crusade against him persuaded him to lift it and march north-west to meet his enemy. An army besieging a city attacked by a relieving force would be trapped and Bayezid was too wily an opponent to be caught that way. The crusade of 1396 began with an army of 6,000 French and Burgundians marching to free Constantinople. The capital of Byzantium had been besieged many times before, but there was a sense now that the city was vulnerable and if it fell, a way of life would be destroyed forever. In Buda, they joined forces with Sigismund's army of Teutonic and Hungarian knights, who, together with their peasant billmen and archers, probably numbered about 20,000. It must have been a colourful sight, the banners of Sigismund, Jean de Nevers, Frederick of Hohenzollern and, according to some sources, Henry Bolingbroke, Duke of Lancaster, the future King Henry IV of England, dancing at the head of the host.

The crusader army was caught napping on the hills overlooking the fortress of Nicopolis on the Danube on 25 September. There are conflicting explanations as to what happened, but the weakness, as ever, seems to be lack of cohesion among the crusaders. A rational explanation is that Bayezid sent out a feint, a weak force of *spahi*, heavy cavalry, knowing that the Christian tactic was the shock charge of armoured knights. Sigismund, perhaps advised by the more cautious Mircea who knew Turkish tactics well, advanced slowly with his Hungarian infantry. Someone, and it was probably Jean de Nevers, son of the Duke of Burgundy, ordered the charge of his 6,000 knights. These men were riding ham to knee up a hill, never a sensible ploy for cavalry, the *spahi* breaking before them as pre-arranged. The *destriers* (war-horses) of the fourteenth century weighed a ton and had a maximum speed of ten miles an hour, and, as they forged their way past the slogging foot soldiers and reached the ridge, they found themselves cut off and facing a force of Turkish janissaries (infantry) about ten times their strength. In a scene redolent of Vlad the Impaler, the Turkish horse-archers parted to reveal a row of sharpened wooden stakes angled into the ground. The terrified, rearing animals of the crusaders crashed into these, skewering themselves on the points. In the frantic hand-to-hand combat that followed, the janissaries closed in and hacked down those who still had fight in them.

Were the Hungarians too cautious? Were the French, notorious for their dash and fire, too impetuous? It looked to some as though Mircea had abandoned Sigismund to his fate, but he may simply have judged the battle lost and his troops melted away to the sheltering forests of the Carpathians.

On the field, the Thunderbolt ordered the execution of all but twenty-four of the best-armoured knights and a handful of baggage boys who would be trained as janissaries as was the Thunderbolt's custom. An estimated 10,000 died before dusk fell on that September night, although the exact method of their despatch is not recorded. A column of cavalry followed Mircea into Wallachia to carry out punitive raids on his villages; others struck west into Styria, taking thousands of prisoners. Back in Paris, the name Nicopolis was forbidden to be spoken at court and the stragglers of the French army returning over the coming months were threatened with the rope if they told what they knew.

The effects of Nicopolis could have been worse, but Sigismund was forced into exile for five years, having been toppled by his rivals, and he spent his days until 1408 contending with those rivals to win his throne back. In that year, to thank those who had stayed loyal to him, the Garai and Cilli families in particular, and to secure their continued support, he reinstated the Order of the Dragon. Its statutes, written on 13 December 1408, simply call it in Latin *Societas*, its members to be recognized by the *signum draconis*, the sign of the dragon, but it is called elsewhere *fraternatis draconem*, the dragon brotherhood. The statutes took the form of an agreement between Sigismund and Barbola and twenty-one *barones* (members of the nobility):

> in company with the prelates, barons and magnates of our kingdom, whom we invite to participate with us in this party, by reason of the sign and effigy of our pure inclination and intention to crush the pernicious deeds of the same perfidious enemy, and of the followers of the ancient Dragon; and ... of the pagan knights, schismatics and other nations of the Orthodox faith; and those envious of the Cross of Christ and of our kingdoms and of his holy and saving religion of faith.

The *signum draconis* was clearly described:

> the sign or effigy of the Dragon incurved into the form of a circle, its tail winding around its neck, divided through the middle of its back along its length from the top of its head right to the tip of its tail with blood [forming] a red cross, flowing out into the interior of the cleft by a white crack untouched by blood, just as and in the same way that those who fight under the banner of the glorious martyr St George are accustomed to bear a red cross on a white field ...[14]

Members of the order swore fealty to Sigismund and his wife and to their heirs as yet unborn and to defend them and their realm from actual attack or plot against them. They also swore to protect each other, coming to each other's aid and support wherever the need arose. In accordance with the feudal obligations on the wane in Western Europe, but only now strengthening in Eastern Europe, Sigismund and Barbola promised to defend the order's members, their families and property. Each member was to attend the funeral of a fellow member or, if that was not possible, to have thirty masses said for his soul and to dress in the black of mourning every Friday and to have five masses said for the five wounds of Christ and to wear the dragon.

In this respect, the Order of the Dragon was superficially similar to earlier monarchical orders of knighthood, but it was also different. There was no patron, despite references to St George. There was no headquarters and no regular meetings. Lastly, since no mention was made of knighthood, it may be that this was purely a political organization, the elements of which were essentially secret. True to his word, Sigismund granted lands and titles to his Draconists and they passed these among themselves, adding to their power so that in effect, the order, not the king, was the real power in Hungary by the time of Sigismund's death in 1437. Four years earlier, Sigismund, King of the Romans from 1410 and King of Bohemia by 1419, had the Dragon Order's statutes confirmed by Pope Eugenius IV when he was crowned Holy Roman Emperor in 1433.

Official documentation survives referring to the fact that the Order of the Dragon was not merely Hungarian, but international. Ernst 'the iron' of Austria was invested in 1409, the Marquis of Ancona (from northern Italy) in 1413, Vitautis, Grand Prince of Lithuania in 1429, and, in either January or February 1431, Vlad, son of Mircea, soon to be Prince Vlad II of Wallachia.

Since about 1395, Vlad had been with Sigismund's court wherever he went, some of that time, at least, out of his kingdom because of the years of political intrigue. Florescu and McNally conjecture that the boy became profoundly unhappy as he grew to manhood surrounded by the infighting and intrigue of an alien court. This is highly likely but the truth is we know almost nothing of Vlad's early life.

In these years Mircea's vulnerable principality was saved from Bayezid's continued advance by the timely arrival of another conqueror from the East, Timur-i-Leng. Born about 1346 near Samarkand, this Turkic Muslim hurtled west with a huge army bent on destruction of anything in their path. While Timur's protégé Toktamish swept north into Russia, burning Moscow in 1381 and slaughtering thousands of its inhabitants, Timur himself turned due west.

Here he was met by an extraordinary delegation in the spring of 1398. Ambassadors from Constantinople, emirs from Anatolia, emissaries of the merchant states of Venice and Genoa and from the King of France all called on the warrior to take on the Ottoman Empire. By this time, Bayezid's territory stretched to an incredible 267,000 square miles and he himself was unpopular. There was a sense that the Thunderbolt had over-reached himself.

Although Timur refused the Christian offer, it was perhaps inevitable that the Muslim–Tartar clash would happen anyway. He took the town of Sivas, executing Bayezid's son and burning 3,000 soldiers alive. With a fighting force twice the size of the Thunderbolt's, he met his army at Ankara on 28 July 1402. It was Bayezid's turn to be wrong-footed. Unaccountably setting out on a long hunt with 6,000 retainers when he should have been scouting the hills for the enemy, he returned to find his camp and the only water supply for miles in the hands of Timur. Deserted by his Anatolian emirs, Bayezid was outnumbered and outmanoeuvred by the Mongol cavalry on their sturdy little ponies. Timur even had elephants with him which must have struck terror into the Thunderbolt's janissaries, on foot as they were. By nightfall it was all over, Bayezid, chained in a cage and dragged in the dust behind Timur's conquering army. His favourite wife was made to serve naked at Timur's table, to the jeers of his troop commanders. Humiliated, the Thunderbolt smashed his brains out on the bars of his cage.

Everyone in Europe breathed a sigh of relief. Only the slaughter went on. Timur captured Izmir in Anatolia and made a ghastly pyramid from the heads of those he executed. In Ephesus, where the apostle Paul had wandered 1,400 years earlier, the children came out to greet Timur, singing and offering flowers. 'What is this noise?', he is reputed to have asked and rode them down with his cavalry. Luckily for Europe, he turned east to China and his own death.

Since 1408, Mircea had ruled in Wallachia with his only legitimate son, Mihail, but even before the death of the old man ten years later and of Mihail two years after that, old rivalries emerged in the principality rather as they had in Hungary. Dan, Mihail's nephew (Vlad's cousin), threw his hat into the ring to establish a feud that had echoes in just about every state in Europe. Vlad now began a throw of his own. Leaving Sigismund's court at Buda in the spring of 1423, he was apparently on his way north to the kingdom of Poland to seek support from Ladislas II of the Jagiellon family, a rival of Sigismund. Vlad's plan was discovered however and such treachery was rewarded by Sigismund confirming Dan as the second prince of that name of Wallachia. An odd relationship now existed between Vlad and the emperor which would be continued into the next generation. Vlad had been caught intriguing, his mission foiled, and he was for a while under observation by Sigismund's courtiers. On the other hand, he was entrusted as a diplomat for the emperor in the on-going negotiations between the Eastern and Western Churches. Specifically, Vlad travelled east to Constantinople to the court of the Emperor John Palaeologus, the representative of one of the two families who had ruled Byzantium for years. 'In those days,' recorded the Greek chronicler Michael Ducas, 'there appeared one of the many bastard sons of Mircea, the profligate voivod of Wallachia.'[18]

It may be that Vlad had ambitions of his own, perhaps to gain Byzantine support for his struggle in the complexities of Wallachian politics, perhaps to cement this with marriage to a Byzantine princess. But if this was in his mind, at some point Vlad abandoned the plan and stayed loyal to Sigismund.

Throughout the 1420s, the decade before Vlad Ţepeş' birth, Wallachia was in turmoil. After Nicopolis, Mircea had not licked his wounds for long before involving himself in the internecine struggle going on between the sons of Bayezid, the Thunderbolt. It was his bad luck perhaps that he backed Musa when the eventual survivor would be Mehmed, who, every inch the warrior his father was, captured Wallachian strong-holds and exacted an annual tribute of 3,000 ducats from the 'profligate voivod'. This was not the capitulation it seems on paper. A few thousand ducats was a small price for freedom of action and Mehmed was content to leave Mircea and his principality alone. The old king died and was buried at his monastery at Cozia on 4 February 1418.

His co-ruler and successor, his son Mihail, had none of his father's sense of balance and *realpolitik* and refused to pay Mehmed his tribute. He even joined Sigismund's army in raids on the Turks along the Danube in the late summer of 1419. Mehmed was occupied extending his empire elsewhere but he swung north for long enough to take Mircea's old castle of Giurgiu and demand back-payment of his tribute. In a move that would be grimly re-enacted in the next generation, he took Mihail's sons Mikhail and Radu as hostages.

Dan's challenge for the throne of Wallachia dates from 1420 when he engaged the help of the Turks. This action appalled Christendom and it certainly weakened Wallachia's chances in the future of keeping out of Turkish clutches. Inviting in a foreign power, no matter what the pretext, is never a good idea. During these clashes Mihail was killed and Dan took the Wallachian throne as Prince Dan II. As Mihail had his rival, so too did Dan, in the form of his cousin, Radu Praznaglava. Dan had the backing of the Turks, Radu of the Hungarians under Sigismund, setting the scene for Wallachian politics for the rest of the century. Another ally whom Radu enlisted was Alexander the Good, Prince of Moldavia, to the east of the Carpathians, but despite this Radu was killed along with his sons in 1427 and Dan held onto the throne.

By 1431, the likely year of Vlad Ţepeş' birth, there were two rivals for Dan's throne – the future Impaler's father and Alexandru Aldea, another of old Mircea's bastard sons. It was in that year, at Nuremberg on 8 February, that Vlad senior was invested in the Order of the Dragon and from that day, he styled himself 'Dracul', the Dragon. And the Order had been busy.

Jan of Husinetz, known as Hus, was born near Prachatitz in Bohemia probably in 1369, the son of a peasant. Even with this unlikely background, the brilliant young man took a master's degree at the University of Prague in 1396, the year of the debacle at Nicopolis, and had come under the influence of the philosophy of Englishman John Wycliffe. Six years later Hus was rector of the university but by 1408 was no longer allowed to officiate as a priest; the following year, an Inquisitorial investigation into his preachings led to a bull from Pope Alexander V ordering all his writings and those of Wycliffe to be burned. Hus himself was banned from preaching. His philosophy was deceptively simple – it emphasized purity and piety and stressed the importance of scripture. Everything else was a veneer – the doctrines of popes, cardinals and bishops that ran counter to the Bible could and should be ignored. Pilgrimages and false relics were so much 'hocus pocus'.

Hus continued to preach after the ban and was excommunicated in 1411. Now a popular hero, there were riots on his behalf in the streets of Prague, and the Bohemian king, Wenceslas, suggested he leave the city for his own safety. Hus ended up stating his case at the Council of Constance in November 1414, but talked himself into a public execution. This, despite the safe conduct guaranteed to him by

Sigismund, was carried out after a rigged trial on 6 July 1416. Controversy still rages over to what extent Hus was a heretic.

Important to the Order of the Dragon were the Hussite wars that followed in his name. There were many peasants and members of the nobility ready to use Hus' proto-Protestantism to strike a blow against the all-powerful Catholic Church and, in the case of Bohemia, to begin what many historians have seen as the birth pangs of Czech nationalism. The Hussites had a formidable general in Jan Žižka, a nobleman from Troczinov, brought up as a page in the court of King Wenceslas. A commander of vast experience, he had fought for the Teutonic Order against the Poles, for Sigismund's Austrians against the Turks and even the English against the French at Agincourt. Losing an eye at Tannenberg in 1410 fighting for Wenceslas, he became an ally of the Hussites at the king's court, orchestrating an outbreak of violence in Prague on 30 July 1419. Against him, Sigismund sent an army which included members of the *societas draconem*, but the wily Žižka defeated them in a series of battles culminating in his building of a fortress at Tabor, from which his followers came to be known as Taborites.

By this time, Žižka had lost the sight in his other eye, but his victories continued, largely due to Hussite zeal and his innovative use of the *wagenburg*, literally wagon fortresses, loaded with men, crossbows and (perhaps for the first time in southern Germany) firearms. Žižka used these to drive the horses to vital points on the field and disgorge men and firepower where they were most needed rather than allowing them to be locked into traditional battlefield formations. In a defensive circle, these wagons were virtually invincible. Mehmed II, the Impaler's enemy, would adopt their use to protect his camp while on the march. For the last three years of his life, Žižka invaded Hungary and south Germany before succumbing to that dread of all late medieval armies, the plague.

The Hussite rebellion continued however. Under 'Holy' Andrew Prokop, the priest-general who succeeded Žižka, they twice defeated Sigismund at Tachov and Domazlice. By 1429, the 'great raids' had reached as far north as Dresden before snaking south to Leipzig. At Nuremberg in 1430, Prokop insisted that Hus' famous Four Articles of Faith be read out in the town square. It was only the internal breakdown of discipline that led to the collapse of the movement and gave Sigismund and his Dragon Order a chance to relax once more, Prokop himself dying in battle with them at Lipan in 1433.

We do not know what, if any, part Vlad Dracul played in the wars against the Hussites. They were an embarrassment for Sigismund and for European tactical warfare an important turning point. What they establish however is an even more important point for the context of this book. If the Order of the Dragon took up arms against heretics, in accordance with its statutes, which spoke of the Orthodox Church as its enemy, then Vlad's 'education' at the peripatetic court of Sigismund must have meant that he was a Catholic. To be invited to join the Order as he was, this was a prerequisite. If his son Vlad Ţepeş was indeed despised by the Orthodox Church for his alleged lapse of faith and if this is why he was not buried near the altar at the monastery of Snagov (see Chapter 14), then this seems harsh in the extreme. The boy was merely continuing in his father's faith.

McNally and Florescu, perhaps a little over-anxious to prove the veracity of the yellow- and red-robed corpse in the Snagov grave, paint a vivid picture of Vlad wearing the colours of the Order and its curling dragon in gold and white. They picture him receiving the crown of Wallachia on the same day from Sigismund, swearing allegiance to him and clashing in the lists in the guttering flames of bonfires with bells ringing and crowds cheering. In reality, we know nothing of these entertainments and D'Arcy Boulton in his monumental work on medieval orders mentions no colours at all in connection with the robes of the Dragon. The civic sword of York, a broadsword of cruciform pattern, was given to the city by

Sigismund who was the father of Anne of Bohemia, the wife of the English king, Richard II. Along its crimson plush-covered scabbard are six metal dragons, each with its tail curled into a ring and each with a cross on its back. It is a fascinating example of the Dragon Order which has survived to our own time.

By that year of 1431, a treaty came to an end between Sigismund's Hungarians and the Ottoman Turks. The sultan now was Murad II, who had taken the throne only after the usual destruction of rivals who included his uncle and brother. The set-back at the hands of Timur the Lame had almost been redressed and the Ottoman Empire was once again straining at the leash to march north.

And by that same year, a baby was born in a house that still stands today (now a cafe), with thick yellow-ochre walls, high gables and small windows in the Wallachian town of Sighişoara. We do not know who the boy's mother was, but he was christened Vlad after his father, Dracul, the dragon, the devil.

10

THE CRESCENT ASCENDING
THE IMPALER'S APPRENTICESHIP

The Ottomans were frontier peoples, ever nomadic, ever pushing at their borders, born, as Bayezid had said, to bear arms. Expert horsemen, brilliant innovators, clever assimilators of ideas, they posed a permanent threat to Christian Europe. The founder of this phenomenon was Osman, the son of a border chief, born in Bithynia. His tiny state centred on Bursa, near the Sea of Marmara and historian Jason Goodwin paints a rugged portrait of the ragtail army that flocked to his early successes and saw him lord of much of Asia Minor by 1299. They were 'hard-bitten pastoralists, shepherds-in-arms, adventurers, Sufis [holy men], misfits, landless peasants, runaways'.[1] But, under Osman, they forged themselves into an army and a formidable one at that.

The eminent Ottoman expert Halil Inalcik[2] refers to the chieftain's son as Osman Gazi and '*gaza*' is the equivalent of jihad, holy war. Islam was intended to dominate the world: *darulislam* (the Islamic kingdom) would eclipse *darulharb* (the lands of the infidel) not by destruction, but by absorption.

In the early fourteenth century, as Osman's followers spread west, they settled in villages and small towns like Milas, Izmir and Manisa, creating mini-sultanates in what was actually Byzantine territory. Osman's son, Orhan, inherited this creeping kingdom on his father's death in 1326. The following year he had silver coins minted (always the mark of a stable and permanent state) at Bursa. Six years later, an Arab traveller, Ibu Battuti, found the place 'a great city with fine bazaars and broad streets'.[3]

Perhaps the most disastrous of the *gazi* advances from the Christian viewpoint saw Ottomans crossing the Dardanelles, the narrow straits that separated Asia from Europe. Even more disquieting was the fact that Bulgarian ferrymen were only too ready, for the usual haggled fee, to help them cross the Dardanelles. The straits were guarded by a Christian fortress at Gallipoli which acted as an outpost of Constantinople itself. In the early hours of 4 March 1356, the hand of Allah struck for Orhan's followers and an earthquake brought the castle crashing down. Similar rumblings would echo throughout the Balkans for the next two centuries.

The story of the early fifteenth century is as much one of Byzantine decline as it is of Ottoman ascendancy. On Christmas Day, 1400, King Henry IV of England, who according to some sources had fought, as Duke of Lancaster, at Nicopolis four years earlier, entertained the Emperor Manuel II Palaeologus. One of the guests, a lawyer named Adam of Usk, sat at a lower table from the Emperor and his king:

> I reflected how grievous it was that this great Christian prince should be driven by the Saracens from the furthest East to the furthest Western islands to seek aid against them. O God, what dost thou now, ancient glory of Rome?[4]

Manuel had come cap in hand to England because allies nearer to home were falling away. As early as the twelfth century, the advance of Islam had robbed Byzantium of its Anatolian cornfields and the traditional recruiting grounds for its armies. In earlier centuries, every male under forty had undergone conscription into the Byzantine army, which had once been 120,000 strong. Successive emperors, however, had to spend a fortune paying mercenaries to patrol their southern borders and became old and grey before their time attempting to co-operate with Islam and to play down any new wave of crusading zeal from the West. After the crusader attack on Constantinople in 1204, there seemed as if there might be a recovery under Michael Palaeologus, but the moment of greatness had gone.

Opposition to Byzantium did not just come from Islam, but also from the Christian West. Voivods in Wallachia and princes in Serbia and Bulgaria flexed their muscles, paying only nominal regard to Constantinople via the Orthodox Church. The Greek islands were heavily populated by Venetians, Genoese and even French merchants. Pera, across the Golden Horn's Sea of Marmara, was in Italian hands. As Jason Goodwin puts it, 'the nap had long gone on the velvet glove and there was no mailed fist underneath.'[5]

And in Constantinople, as in the moving capitals of the successors of Osman, as in Wallachia, internecine squabbles added to the chaos. John Palaeologus (1341–91) was removed from the throne three times, on each occasion by members of his own family. And the spread of bubonic plague, the Black Death, creeping west from China, took its toll on Byzantine towns and villages too.

In 1346 Orhan formed an alliance with Palaeologus' rival, his former chief minister John Cantacuzenos, cementing it with marriage to his daughter, Theodora. His son, Suleyman, ostensibly working for Cantacuzenos against the Serbs and Bulgars, occupied fortresses on the European side of the Dardanelles and refused to hand them back. Suleyman's death in 1357 barely slowed the advance as Murad, his younger brother, cut off the Byzantine supply lines and captured the Greek city of Adrianople, which now took its Turkish name, Edirne. What delayed the ultimate destruction of Constantinople itself was the arrival of Timur-i-Leng, but if Bayezid the Thunderbolt was stopped, there were plenty who would follow. By 1431, the year of Vlad Ţepeş' birth, the Ottoman Empire was as powerful and greedy as ever, and Byzantium was still in its death throes.

The house where the future Impaler was born in his father's fortress town of Sighişhoara was typical of the impressive merchant's houses that flanked it. The town itself was powerfully defended, with thick stone walls, 3,000 feet long, supporting fourteen huge towers, each one built at the expense of a town guild. It was a wealthy town, trading goods west into the German states, east to Constantinople and north into Poland. Travel writer Georgina Harding talks romantically of:

> the mystery of its stones and the gateways opening on to some other and secret place, on to an unexpected side of things. The slender, pointed iron banners which surmount the towers are silhouetted clearly against the sky, intrepid in the wind, fearless knights in the arena, waiting for the tourney and an unknown destiny.[6]

The house was probably new when Ţepeş was born, a solid, stone and timber construction of three storeys, large enough to house servants and a small body of armed retainers.

Prince of Wallachia Vlad Dracul may have been made by Sigismund, but it was politically in that intriguer's interests to maintain his relationship with Dracul's half-brother Alexandru Aldea and his ally Alexander the Good, Prince of Moldavia. Sigismund's common enemy in this particular piece of *realpolitik* was, Dragon brother notwithstanding, King Ladislas of Poland. For the moment, Dracul was merely voivod or governor of Transylvania with a watching brief to keep an eye on the Turks, trickling across the Danube now and again with the apparent blessing of Aldea, following, as did a number of local warlords, what was in effect a policy of appeasement.

We do not know if Vlad Dracul was present at the birth of his son because we do not know precisely when the future Impaler was born. Some historians posit a date as early as 1428,[7] others the autumn, 'under the sign of the scorpion', of 1431. We do not know the name of the boy's mother because of the low status in which Wallachian and Transylvanian women were held. It is possible that Dracul had married Cneajna, the eldest daughter of Alexander cel Bun (the Good) and that this ceremony took place about 1425. It would make dynastic sense were this to be the case and the legitimate result of the union was Mircea, born in 1428. Once the prince had been given the Order of the Dragon, all his sons – Mircea, Vlad and the youngest, Radu cel Frumos (the Handsome) born in 1435 – took the 'surname' Dracula.

It is equally likely that Vlad Țepeș' mother was one of the many mistresses the prince collected along the way. One, who later became a nun with the holy name Mother Eupraxia, was the daughter of a boyar from Transylvania and was called Cltuna before she entered religious orders. Her son was Vlad Caligarul, the Monk. In Wallachia there was no barrier to inheritance by an illegitimate son, so we may assume that Vlad Dracul would not ignore any of his sons born to mistresses.[8]

We do not know how Vlad Dracul's household was ordered. He would have had a steward to organize the servants, order the food and the wine and regulate the day. Umpteen skivvies would be employed to cook, clean and sew. The male children would have learned to give orders and adopt the airs and graces expected of men who would one day rule an entire country, however small by modern standards. Today, we bemoan the fact that our children grow up too quickly. In the late Middle Ages among this class they barely had a childhood at all.

Historians Florescu and McNally ponder the excitement that little Vlad would have known before the reality of his father's world impacted on him.

> There were ... the usual distractions that followed the feast days: puppet theatres ... ambulant artists, acrobats, minnesingers ... In summer there were ball games, running and jumping contests and games on quadrilateral swings made of red cloth and fastened in the form of a pyramid. In the winter, they hunted eagles with slingshots, slid down the Sighişoara slopes on primitive double-runner sleds, trapped hares ... [9]

The late summer harvest fairs were preceded in May by the festival of the Measurement of the Milk and countless Orthodox and Catholic saints' feasts.

When Ţepeş was still a small boy, his father received orders from Sigismund to do what was necessary to prepare for a potential Turkish advance. The Ottomans had defeated the Venetians at Salonika in 1430 and conquered southern Albania by 1432. In 1434, Dracul called up troops from the neighbouring fiefdoms of Făgăraş and Amlaş and paid the craftsmen of Sibiu for their elaborate and deadly cannon. The bronze cup given by the voivod to cannon-founder 'Master Leonardus' can still be found in the church at Sibiu today. What Dracul probably did not know is that other German gunsmiths were selling their wares to the Turks too.

Alexandru Aldea died of unknown, but natural, causes in the summer of 1436. It is difficult to empathize with this man and his lieutenant, the boyar Albu. Treading what was undoubtedly a difficult path between the Christian West and the Muslim East, Alexandru seems to have gone too far down the reconciliation road, paying a tribute to the sultan, Murad II, agreeing to back him militarily and sending political hostages to Edirne, now the gazi capital on the Ottoman fringes.

Dracul tried to take advantage of Aldea's duplicity before the man died, but found himself outnumbered by Albu and his Turkish allies before Sigismund decided to authorize Dracul to take what he needed from the towns of Transylvania. With this backing, the weapons of his gunsmiths and the billmen and archers of Amlaş, Dracul reached Tîrgovişte, Aldea's capital in December. His sons Mircea, Vlad and Radu joined him later.

Now, in the gigantic palace built by Mircea the Old, Vlad Ţepeş' apprenticeship to knighthood began. If it followed the Western pattern, and bearing in mind his father's recent acceptance into the Dragon Order it probably did, then training would have begun for the boy when he was seven. He would learn to ride, not perhaps as he already had on a pony at Sigişhoara, but on a palfrey, a saddle-horse used in campaigning and perhaps of the Hutul breed. Ultimately, by the time he was about fourteen, he would need to manage a destrier, the sixteen-hand warhorses bred for battle. He would need to ride with legs straight in the saddle, to balance sword and shield, and he would practice for war at the tilt. No doubt, as with most squires, he would ride at the ring or quintain, an ingenious device which swung on a pivot. If the tilter was too slow in galloping past, striking the dummy's shield with his blunted lance, a morning star mace with chain and ball would swing round and crunch into his back. No doubt Vlad received his share of bruises from this. He would learn to buckle on another knight's plate armour before he was given a suit of his own, probably of excellent German manufacture from Augsburg in Sigismund's Austrian provinces. He would learn to run errands, hold horses, carve meat and serve wine at his father's table, because the essence of medieval chivalry was the notion of service as well as *hauteur*. In that strange geographical hinterland between East and West in which Ţepeş lived and that strange cusp of time between the medieval and modern worlds, we cannot know how purely any of this code was taught.

It is likely that all the boys would have been taught together, perhaps by the tutor, a boyar, name unknown, who had fought at Nicopolis. Perhaps from him he learned Latin, some Greek, Hungarian, French and Italian. He would have been taught Church Slavonic and Cyrillic scripts as the formal languages of his father's court.

In the meantime, while the education of a future voivod was in hand, events moved swiftly. Sigismund died in 1437, and whether latterly *actual* power had slipped to the Dragon Order or not, effectively Dracul's patron had gone. In that year too, the peasant rising in Transylvania, brought on by the pressures of war, famine, plague and the much less tangible feudal crisis, was the most serious for years and could only be put down by a combination of Magyars, Szeklers from Transylvania and Saxons. With his new principality shaky and bereft of friends, Dracul found himself in the same position his predecessor Alexandru Aldea had been only two years earlier. And he had to deal with the crescent's ascending star, Murad II.

The sultan dressed soberly; at his own mother's funeral he had to be pointed out to guests who did not know him. According to the Greek chronicler Michael Ducas, he treated his slaves as brothers. The Burgundian traveller Bertrandon de la Brocquière had seen him in his palace at Edirne:

> He sat on this [a raised dais] in the manner of tailors when they are at work.[10]

Seven years later, Murad would build a magnificent stone bridge, nearly 400 yards long and with 174 arches over the River Ergene near this palace, with a cool resting place for travellers, a mosque for the good of their souls and a university for their intellects. During his reign, some of the finest minds in Islamic history were making names for themselves, usually far ahead of Christian scholars in their sophistication. Mullah Husrev wrote textbooks used extensively in Ottoman universities. Ali al-Fanari, a Koranic law expert, taught in Persia and Egypt. Samarkand was the centre of mathematical excellence under Murad's empire. His attitude to potential rebellion provides a classic comparison with the less enlightened approach in the West. While the Council of Constance burned Jan Hus (see Chapter 9) and Sigismund did his best to slap his followers down, Murad met a dervish peasant called Hacci Bayram, whose fanatical religious movement had neo-socialist undertones, and not only pardoned him, but exempted his followers from taxation. Unlike most Western rulers, who frowned on any kind of apostasy, Murad was fascinated by the Meulevis, the whirling dervishes, and founded a lodge specially for them at Edirne.

It is perhaps no credit to Vlad Dracul, but very much a sign of the times, that the August of 1438 saw him campaigning with Murad against the Transylvanians. The sultan crossed the Danube at Vidin and raided as far as Albu Iulia and Ţepeş' birthplace of Sigişhoara. He besieged Sibiu for eight days before pulling back and re-crossing the Danube at Nicopolis. Dracul was now in an appalling cleft stick. As a Catholic, as a Christian, as a member of the Dragon Order, he had a clear duty to defend fellow-Christians, yet here he was allying with the infidel, the enemy. The town of Sebeş surrendered to Murad on the condition that its people should not become Ottoman slaves. The chronicler 'brother George', styling himself a 'student of Sebeş', recorded that a great deal of loot and perhaps as many as 70,000 prisoners were taken.

The first written mention of Vlad Ţepeş can be found in a deed dated 20 January 1437 in which Dracul mentions his 'first born sons, Mircea and Vlad'. He appears again in August of the same year and by 2 August 1439, Radu is added to the list.[11]

The death of Sigismund saw the collapse of the powerful empire he had largely created by crafty politics and skilful determination. His son-in-law Albert of Habsburg, Archduke

of Austria, probably intended to become Emperor, but died
of dysentery in 1439, leaving his son Ladislas Posthumous (he
was born after his father's death) as his baby heir. Into the
breach – the advent of the boy-king inevitably spelling disaster
in kingdoms held together largely by force of personality –
stepped the man whom Albert had created governor of
Transylvania, the White Knight,[12] János Hunyadi.

Like Skanderbeg (see below) and Vlad Ţepeş himself,
Hunyadi has assumed legendary qualities over the centuries.
Ottoman mothers hushed their children into an uneasy sleep
with the whisper of his name. Born about 1387 in Wallachia
or Transylvania, the man with the distinctive high forehead
and powerful build was a self-made businessman, warrior and
a highly skilful dancer. He spoke Serb, Croat, Italian,
Hungarian and Romanian, despite a lack of formal education
and made himself indispensable to Sigismund by lending him
money. A page to Sigismund at first, based in Nuremberg,
Hunyadi was sent, as was the custom of the day, to learn the
art of war from a professional, in his case the condottiere
Filippo Visconti. In 1409, Hunyadi had been knighted and
given the castle of Hunedoara in Transylvania.

To the Wallachians, Hunyadi was Iancu de Hunedoara and
the great, brooding Gothic castle the most powerful in
Transylvania. Simon Marsden visited it in 1993, crossing on a
wooden bridge held up by 'precariously tall' stone pillars.

> I passed through the towering gates to find myself within a vast
> and intimidating courtyard, off which led a maze of galleries,
> spiral stairways, Gothic vaults, deep dungeons and dark halls
> . . . Everywhere pollution had added its ghastly stench and a
> layer of dust to the castle's aura of death.[13]

The well in the courtyard was dug by Turkish prisoners
with their bare hands to a depth of sixty feet. It took
them nine years and at the end of it, rather than receiving
the freedom Hunyadi had promised, they were thrown

from the castellations to drown in the 100 feet deep moat. Their names are still carved in the rock along with the inscription: 'You have water, but no soul.'[14]

More prosaically, the late Professor Allen Brown[15] points up Hunedoara's imposing position over its city and notes the same Teutonic influences in its architecture as in castles in Poland and Russia. But it is difficult to be prosaic about Hunyadi's power base. Its walls are immense, rising out of solid rock, with a combination of circular and square towers, fringed with an elaborate Gothic canopy under the pointed eaves that date from the reign of Hunyadi's son, Matthias Corvinus. Skeletons have been found in its recesses, including, in 1873, that of a woman whose skull had been split in two by a spike.

Murad II may have dressed soberly, he may have been tolerant of the wilder religions in his Sultanate, but he was a warrior and a shrewd one at that. His formidable spy network told him of Hunyadi's appointment in Transylvania and he struck first, taking the fortress of Smeredevo from the Serbian overlord George Branković in August 1439. The incestuous nature of this border warfare and the ease with which Christian and Muslim could co-operate for political purposes is shown by the fact that one of Murad's many wives in his harem was Mara, Branković's daughter. Her sons Gregor and Stefan were taken hostage by their new uncle.

In Wallachia, Vlad Dracul continued to play both ends against the middle. Creeping around the Hungarians after his role in Murad's raid into Transylvania, he welcomed Hunyadi on a state visit to Tîrgovişte sometime in 1441. By this time, with Ladislas Posthumous, the 'miracle child' rumoured to be the bastard result of his mother's flirtation with a courtier, the electors had chosen Ladislas III of Poland as King of Hungary. The boy was only sixteen, but he looked a better bet than the infant Posthumous and, for the time at least, had the support of men of ability and courage like Hunyadi. The White Knight and the Prince of Wallachia had met at

Nuremberg, probably in 1408–9, but there was no love lost between them. Apart from other considerations, Hunyadi would never compromise with Turks, whom he detested, and Dracul had just finished raiding his homeland. It must have been an uneasy meeting.

Perhaps because of guilt, perhaps because of Hunyadi's persuasiveness, Dracul did not join the next Ottoman raid into Wallachia in March 1442. This one, led by Murad's general Sihabeddin, Bey (Lord) of Rumelia, was allowed to reach the Carpathians before Hunyadi destroyed it.

Murad summoned Vlad Dracul, nominally his vassal, to meet him in the spring at his quarters in Gallipoli. He also summoned George Branković, but the Serb pulled up the drawbridges of his fortified city of Belgrade and refused to move. It is a little difficult to understand Dracul's trust that spring. True, he had fought alongside Murad against his own people, but his current leanings towards the always dangerous Hunyadi cannot have been missed by Murad, who was known to be a shrewd judge of men and to have spies everywhere. Perhaps out of a sense of maintaining a brave front, perhaps because he thought they were old enough to appear publicly in the world of *realpolitik*, his sons Vlad and Radu went with him. Serbian chronicles mention that Dracul put about a false rumour that Mircea, his eldest son, had been killed, so that he could not be sent as a hostage.

At Gallipoli they were shackled like slaves, the boys being taken to Anatolia, to the fortress of the 'crooked eyes' at Egrigöz in the principality of Caraman, the fiefdom of Ibrahim Bey, Murad's brother-in-law. Dracul was Murad's 'guest' at Edirne for nearly a year, before being released on certain conditions. Dracul took an oath on the Bible and the Koran not to take up arms against the Ottomans. He also promised an annual tribute of 10,000 gold ducats (inflation and having the whip hand had taken their toll since Old Mircea's day) and the *devşirme* was a new demand. This levy of boys was in some ways a renewal of the Turkish policy of taking slave prisoners dating back to the days of Osman. From each village in Wallachia, Dracul was to provide a certain number (figures differ from 1,000 to 3,000) of boys between the ages of eight and twenty. Urban children were exempt and in the case of an only child, the boy was not taken. The Turks' purpose was to train them as janissaries, the core of the Ottoman army.[16]

Vlad Ţepeş was probably twelve when he was ripped from his father's cohort and taken to Egrigöz. His handsome brother Radu was seven, 'no taller than a bouquet of flowers'.[17] We know nothing of the boys' time in this isolated town. It stands 1,000 feet above the sea in the Taslidag Mountains and is as heavily forested today as it probably was then with beech and oak and pine. Were Vlad and Radu held as prisoners, shackled in some dark dungeon? They did not speak the Turkish language and quite possibly, for all their father's double dealing, had never seen a Turk before. According to Constantin Rezachevici, Ţepeş was an 'intermittent' prisoner of the Turks between 1443 and 1448, but this gives a false impression. It is unlikely that he was actually confined in a cell (any more than he was later during his much longer captivity by Matthias Corvinus) but he could certainly not return home. Vlad Dracul wrote to the citizens of Braşov:

> Please understand that I have allowed my children to be butchered for the sake of the Christian peace, in order that both I and my country might continue to be vassals of the Holy Roman Emperor.[18]

It is unlikely that Dracul's motives were anything like as noble as this, but hostage-taking was a way of life in the fifteenth century and not just among the Turks. Vlad Dracul was certainly not above risking the boys' lives to play the great game of *realpolitik*. After all, he had not taken Mircea, his eldest son, with him to Gallipoli and the boy ruled Wallachia in his father's year-long absence, despite being only fifteen or sixteen years old.

From the Turks' viewpoint hostage-taking served a double purpose. The sophistication and allure of the Ottoman court created a mindset that some found difficult to shake off. Put simply, if the boys behaved, all well and good. If not . . . the sons of George Branković, suspected of plotting to escape, had red hot irons jabbed into their eyeballs on 8 May 1441 – and they were the sultan's nephews by marriage.

How long Vlad and Radu remained at Egrigöz is unknown, but they were taken next to Tokat, a far more civilized city on the trade routes to the East. In Vlad Țepeș' day, the Roman tombs were still standing to mark the legions' furthest reach eastwards and the boys were probably kept in the Byzantine castle that dominated the market square, with its leather-workers and coppersmiths. From there, following the sultan's travelling court via Manisa and Bursa, they came to Edirne.

The Greek city of Adrianople had fallen to the Turks in 1362. The city of Hadrian had an ancient history. Originally Uskudama, it was fortified by the Romans in the early second century and remained an important Byzantine city until its loss to Orhan's *gazi* warriors. Under the Turks, it thrived as never before, huge bazaars filling the cluttered tangle of streets, selling wine, opium, attar of roses, dyestuffs, leather, cotton, woollens and tapestries. Until the fall of Constantinople, Edirne was the Ottoman capital and here Murad built his palace.

Vlad and Radu were the sons of a prince and they were to be treated as such at Edirne, exposed to the full pressure of the Muslim way of life. One of the keys to Ottoman success was the way in which they *used* their enemies. They did not insist on conversion to Islam by the sword, knowing that that would only harden resistance and breed resentment. But the boys taken in the *devşirme* became some of the most fanatical and professional fighters for Islam via the gradual absorption of the Koranic code and the sensual pleasures of the East. With regard to the sons of Dracul, the idea was clearly to win them over, if not to full Islam, then at least to being true scions should the time ever come for either of them to rule Wallachia. They had a role model in someone whose name, like Ţepeş', has survived in the chronicles of Balkan heroism – George Kastrioti, widely known as Skanderbeg.

He was born between 1403 and 1405, the son of an Albanian prince and, like Dracul's boys, was taken as a hostage, this time by Bayezid, when he was seven. Brought up under Murad as a Muslim, Kastrioti would be given a generalship in the Ottoman army and the name Iskender Bey (Lord Alexander), a name given by Murad, who, like all medieval rulers in the East, was imbued with the folk-memory of Alexander the Great, who had conquered a third of the world by the time he was thirty.[19]

The education that Skanderbeg had received was given to Dracul's sons too, to the extent that the rumour persisted that one or both of them actually converted to Islam during their years of captivity. It was this duplicity of faith which has helped to damn the Impaler in the eyes of posterity – a boy raised probably as a Catholic converting to Islam, reconverting to the Orthodox Church and finally to Catholicism again, seems to be taking *realpolitik* a little far, even by fifteenth-century standards. The boys were exposed to the finest tutors the Ottoman court could provide – Iyas, a Serb convert, priests like Hamiduddin and Sinan, the Kurdish philosopher Ahmed Gurani. They learned logic, the Koran, the Ottoman language, spoken and written, and became proficient with the light, curved swords and the short-bows, fired with such deadly accuracy from the saddle of swift, sure-footed Arab horses. The training, Murad hoped, would be invaluable for future allies – it had worked, after all, with Skanderbeg. It would work with Radu; but not with his brother Vlad.

In the Inner Palace at Edirne, a smaller version of the one that Mehmed the Conqueror would build later in Constantinople, Murad II would spend his leisure hours with his viziers, his scholars, and his army of loyal slaves. It was a complex and highly structured regime which would reach its pinnacle under Suleiman the Magnificent a hundred years later and makes the structure of even the grandest Western court look quite primitive. The *Kapi Agasi*, the chief white eunuch, ran the palace like clockwork, hiring and firing, supervising the vast number of pages, administering punishments which could include death if the need arose. These eunuchs had been castrated as children so that backstairs liaisons with the sultan's harem (see below) would not be an issue.

Under the *Kapi Agasi* four chambers operated. The *Has Oda* (Privy Chamber) was responsible for Murad's clothes and weapons. The pages here stood guard on his door each night or by the fly of his tent when he was on the march. A whole hierarchy of officers carried the sultan's sword, held his stirrup as he mounted and wrote his letters. The chief of the chamber never left the sultan's side. Other chambers were the *Hazine*, the Treasury, which handled the expenses and accounts; the *Kiler*, the Larder, whose officers arranged Murad's food and the *Seferli Oda*, the campaign office, a reminder that the Ottoman dynasty was essentially a mobile war machine.

The officer known as the *Mir Alem* was responsible for Murad's regimental marches, and carried the horse-tail standard that, along with the crescent, was his symbol of authority. Under him a small army erected the sultan's tent at the centre of the vast circle camped under the stars on campaign. The *Kapici Basi* was the gate-keeper, responsible for the palace guard, safety and discipline. The *Mirahur* looked after the sultan's horses, making sure their coats were glossy and their tails dyed red, as was the custom. The sultan was carried even within the palace on litters maintained by this department. The chief falconers, the *Cakirci Basi*, kept the royal birds in their mews and Murad's team in the outlying provinces of the empire were exempt from taxation in exchange for training birds. Love of the hunt had wrecked the

Thunderbolt's chances of victory against Timur in 1402, so seriously did Ottoman sultans take their hunting. The *Casnigir Basi*, the chief taster, had a vast team of cooks to provide meals for the Imperial Council and was watchful of any poison that might find its way into Murad's food.

We do not have accurate figures for the size of Murad II's court. In the decade of Dracula's death, when Mehmed was sultan and based at Constantinople, the janissary corps of the army had 10,000 men. There were 100 gunners, 800 stable-boys, at least 120 cooks with 20 tasters, 200 tailors, 200 tent-pitchers, and 100 falconers. There were perhaps 400 door-keepers, 100 standard bearers and an unknown number making artillery for the cannoneers.[20]

The harem itself, which in 1476 numbered 650, was intensely private and access to it forbidden to strangers. Virtually all its members were slaves and they underwent a rigorous training to make them skilled in music, dancing, sewing and embroidery, puppetry and story-telling. Sultans only took four legal wives under Shari'a law – one of these for Murad was the Christian Mara Branković whose little brothers the Sultan had blinded. Unlike the misogyny becoming rampant in Christian society,[21] women were equal in the Koran and in the eyes of Allah as far as religious observance went. According to one *hadith* or Islamic tradition:

When a man looks upon his wife and she upon him, God looks mercifully upon them; when they join hands together their sins disappear in the interstices of their fingers. When he makes love with her the angels encircle the earth.[22]

The Burgundian Bertrandon de la Brocquière visited Murad's palace twenty years before Vlad Ţepeş' time there. He remarked:

We passed through the first gate. The door opened inwards and was guarded by about thirty slaves, all armed with staves.

Should any person wish to enter without permission, they warn him at once to withdraw; if he persists, they turn him back with their staves.[23]

The Greek chronicler Laonic (Nicolas) Chalkondyles, who was to write a vivid account of the fall of Constantinople and Ţepeş' war against Mehmed, hints that young Radu fell prey not only to the blandishments of Murad's court, but to the advances of Mehmed himself. Islamic tradition and law do not approve of homosexuality, although paradoxically, sodomy among the Turks was universal. Whether this was inherited from the Greeks and the Byzantine Empire they overthrew or whether it was already established as a native custom is difficult to say. Centuries of racial mistrust and slurs have blurred the truth, especially in the West, where the concept of 'buggery' was associated with Turkish Bulgaria and the Bogomil heresy. According to Chalkondyles, Radu's beauty seduced Mehmed Celebi, the sultan's son, who was a year younger than Ţepeş. While at first resisting, Radu eventually became a minion of Mehmed and did not leave Ottoman clutches until 1462 when the sultan put him as a puppet on the throne of Wallachia.

If Radu fell victim to the actual seduction of Mehmed and the cultural seduction of Murad's court and the Islamic way of life, Vlad almost certainly reacted the other way. Because we know nothing of the boy's temperament, we can only guess at the effect this way of life had on him. Did it explain, perhaps even create, a streak of cold cruelty which would come to the fore in his adult years? Did the tension in which he lived and the sense of betrayal from his father's actions at Gallipoli and the treachery of his little brother turn and harden a mind already warped? Above all, in the practical sense, did he witness the impaling and other tortures of Murad's enemies which gave him a blueprint for his own future?

Sources are surprisingly silent on this. Legend credits Sir John Tiptoft, the English Earl of Worcester, with using impalement as a means of execution and Florescu and McNally claim this is fact learned from the Turks and that he was executed 'for his crimes'.[24] Tiptoff was in fact the most renowned English scholar of his day, having studied at Rome, Venice, Florence and Padua in the decade of Dracula's birth. He was also a hard man and a staunch Yorkist. Given the post of Constable of England, his job was to execute enemies of the state and he did this assiduously during the 1460s. His execution was the result not of others' horror at his unnatural cruelty, but of the vagaries of fortune in the Wars of the Roses. He quietly asked the headsman in 1470 to use three strokes to remove his head 'in honour of the Trinity'.[25]

Writing with varying degrees of bias, J.A. MacGraham, the *Daily News* correspondent, reached Batik in Bulgaria in August 1876. He was reporting on the massacre of 12,000 Christians by the Turkish irregular cavalry, the *bashi-bazouks*:

> The number of children killed in these massacres is something enormous. They were often spitted on bayonets and we have several stories from eye-witnesses who saw little babies carried about the streets ... on the point of bayonets. The reason is simple. When a Mahametan has killed a certain number of infidels, he is sure of Paradise, no matter what his sins may be ... Here ... the Bashi-Bazouks, in order to swell the count, ripped open pregnant women and killed the unborn infants.[26]

When Charles Meryon, a surgeon, travelled in the entourage of the eccentric explorer Lady Hester Stanhope to Latakia, Syria in July 1813, he witnessed a ghastly sight:

> I was walking out of one of the gates of the town, about eight in the morning, when I came suddenly on a man who had been impaled an hour or two before, and was now dead, but still transfixed by the stake, which, as I saw on approaching him, came out about the sixth rib on the right side ... the stake was

planted upright, seemed scarcely to be sharp and was somewhat thicker that a hop-pole. I was told that it was forced up the body by repeated blows of a mallet, the malefactor having been bound on his face to a heavy pack-saddle and an incision being made with a razor to facilitate the entrance of the stake. The body, yet alive, was set upright in a rude manner, for the Turks preserve no decorum in executions . . . Jewish, Christian, Druze and Ansary criminals are alone subjected to this horrible punishment; Turks are beheaded.[27]

By 1440 the world had turned. Pope Eugenius IV, perhaps attempting to make work the flimsy reconciliation he had set up at the Council of Florence between the Eastern and Western Churches, had called for a crusade against the Ottoman Turks. This crusade was anxious not to repeat the disaster of Nicopolis and it was not until 1442 that an army numbering 20,000–25,000 marched east under the command of Ladislas III of Poland. Under him were the warlords János Hunyadi and George Branković, the latter no doubt distraught at Murad's blinding of his sons. The Pope was represented by Cardinal Guiliano Cesarini. And with them, a little half-heartedly perhaps, bearing in mind his brothers' predicament, was Mircea, the eldest son of Dracul. There were other Wallachians too, from Banat and Maramureş, but fighting under other banners. The cosmopolitan army of Germans, Austrians, Poles, Serbs and Wallachians did well, defeating the Turks at Niš in November 1443, recapturing Sofia in Bulgaria in December and driving the Ottomans back. A medieval army was always at the mercy of the weather and particularly heavy snows saw the crusaders falling back to Branković's Belgrade on the Danube by Christmas. Their food had all but run out and the provision carts were chopped up for firewood. Most of the horses had died.

Murad sued for peace. Cynically, it gave him time to concentrate on a crusade of his own, to be fought in the Morea. Branković's blind children were returned and, as things turned out, Murad was the only signatory of the treaty – the Peace of Seghedin – to keep his word. In the autumn of 1444, before any arrangements could be made to release Vlad and Radu Dracula, Ladislas launched another campaign season. This time the target was Varna on the Black Sea and would entail an ambitious amphibious operation involving Venice's renowned fleet.

Hunyadi summoned Vlad Dracul to join the *chevauchée*[28] at Nicopolis, but the Wallachian was unimpressed by Hunyadi's muster of less than 20,000 men. The German soldier of fortune Hans Mägest estimated the force at no more than 14,000, and Vlad Dracul may well have been warned by a soothsayer of the fruitlessness of the expedition. For all his Catholic leanings, Vlad Dracul was probably as superstitious as most Wallachians. Above all, his sons were still at Edirne and he knew the risk he was taking. In the event, he sent Mircea again with 4,000 cavalry, no doubt with instructions to keep his father's dragon banner discreetly furled.

The Varna campaign was as great a disaster as Nicopolis for the previous generation. It had begun well, with George Kastrioti, Skanderbeg, now on the side of the Christians and wreaking havoc among the Turks in northern Albania. Internal problems in the Ottoman Empire saw a rival claimant emerge to Murad's throne and, to cap it all, a fire at Edirne destroyed thousands of homes. The Venetian war galleys effectively closed the narrows of the Dardanelles and the White Knight was on his way to exact vengeance. Mircea seems to have swung away from the main army, taking the town of Petretz and using cannon for the first time in Wallachian history. With him was Hans Mägest, whose reminiscences would later provide the *minnesinger* Martin Beheim with the source of new songs.

Petretz was well defended with water-filled moats and Mircea's first instinct, to use siege ladders, failed. How many guns he had with him we do not know, but he breached the walls with these and found the exit to an underground tunnel escape route the terrified Turks were using. He had them cut down as they emerged. The fortress itself in the heart of the city was stronger, but most of the garrison surrendered and Mircea found himself with hundreds of Turkish prisoners claiming to be Christian. Those soldiers who had not surrendered were thrown into the moat.

All over Bulgaria as Hunyadi and Ladislas advanced, the population flocked to them, rejoicing in being liberated. This was, of course, nothing more than peasants hedging their bets (they welcomed any army in this way) but Turks as far away as Edirne and Gallipoli panicked and fled east.

Varna itself was a powerful port in an inlet of the Black Sea, specializing in leather goods, grain, cattle, wine and cloth. And it was defended in that November of 1444 by an Ottoman army perhaps three times the size of that of Hunyadi. The Venetian galleys may have been blocking the Dardanelles, but they had not rowed further north beyond the Golden Horn and were of no use to the crusaders on land. Murad himself led his cavalry into battle with the broken treaty document impaled on his lance. In the melee that followed, Ladislas of Poland was thrown from his horse by the crush of *spahis*. Before Hunyadi could reach him, he was hacked to death and his head impaled on a Turkish spear, hideously jiggled up and down in front of the demoralized Christians. Slowly and bitterly, the crusaders fell back, scattering to their homelands as Murad's vengeful cavalry pursued them. It was not until the next campaign season that Mircea and, this time, Dracul, would come upon the mutilated corpse of Cardinal Cesarini, the papal legate, ripped and naked in the hills near Varna, his eyes pecked out by crows. The body of Ladislas was never found and stories of sightings of him or his ghost spread through Europe for many years.

On that morning of 10 November, Mircea, who still cannot have been more than sixteen, is believed to have been in command of his Wallachians to the right of the centre. Hunyadi, whose thunderous counter-attack nearly worked, was on his right. Ladislas led the reserve, and, perhaps carried away by his youth or a belief in the invulnerability of his cavalry, charged through the centre, leaving both wings isolated.

The conduct of the Wallachians in battle was criticized at the time by the few observers who lived to tell the tale. The papal legate Andreas de Palatio said that they ran in all directions, yet it was they who actually saved his life. A local poet, Zofikos, claims that the Wallachians' only interest was grabbing what booty they could from Murad's coffer-tent. Since, on his own admission, Zofikos was hiding in a forest at the time, quaking with fear, *nothing* he says can be trusted.

As with Nicopolis, the Varna debacle left the crusaders in disarray and, as so often after such defeats, the losers turned to bickering among themselves. As Hunyadi made his way home across Wallachia, he found himself facing the halberds of Dracul's guard. The prince was furious that the Varna crusade had collapsed when he had expressly advised the Transylvanian voivod against it. In a charged meeting, probably at Tîrgovişte, each accused the other of treason and Dracul had his sword point at Hunyadi's throat when wiser council intervened and pulled the men apart. The White Knight was forced to pay 'a substantial ransom' for his freedom.

The 1445 campaign was better conceived than that of the previous year and was probably simply an attempt to find the body of Ladislas. The original protagonists seem to have been Dracul, Mircea and Jean de Wavrin, Lord of Forestel in Burgundy whose galleys were to row up the Danube with Wallachian troops (later augmented by Hunyadi's Hungarians) while Mircea followed on the north bank with his cavalry.

The fleet sailed from Brăila under the shadow of the cathedral of St Michael, past the warehouses with their grain, the workshops of the candle-makers and rope manufacturers, and on to Nicopolis. They took Turtucaia, raiding its grain stores and burning it down, Wavrin receiving a wound for his

pains and having to relinquish command to Renault de
Confide. The attack to recapture Mircea the Old's castle at
Giurgiu was far more important and it was achieved in
Hussite fashion, using war wagons to withstand the Turkish
assault. The garrison surrendered, but Mircea Dracula had the
prisoners hacked to death.

Either before the taking of Giurgiu or shortly after it,
Dracul arrived. Bulgarians now threw in their lot with him in
vast numbers, an endless column of refugees with bullock
carts and dogs, throwing themselves on the prince's mercy.
Five days from the difficult river crossing at Ruscgiuk, the
army reached Nicopolis, the scene of the disaster of 1396.
Dracul appears to have left them by this time, perhaps anxious
to try to safeguard Vlad and Radu, still at Edirne. After a siege
of several days and the loss of several Burgundian galleys, the
garrison surrendered, much to the crusaders' delight. Their
fathers had been avenged.

Winter closed in again. With dwindling food supplies, few
friendly ports and the risk of the Danube icing over, Hunyadi
and Wavrin had no choice but to pull back to Constantinople
and wait for spring.

Dracul signed a new treaty with Murad in the summer
of 1447, but he had to abandon the recently taken fortress of
Giurgiu on the Danube to do it and to promise the return
of the thousands of Bulgarians who had drifted north into his
safe-keeping after the fall of Nicopolis. In exchange, Wallachia
was to remain independent and his sons would be safe. As had
been the case in the past, the word of a Muslim carried more
weight than that of a Christian. János Hunyadi was doubly
suspicious of Dracul. He had refused to fight with him at
Varna and was clearly playing a double game. Dracul and
Mircea on the other hand still blamed Hunyadi for the Varna
disaster in that he had not taken the Wallachian prince's
advice.

In November 1447 Hunyadi launched an attack on Wallachia, with the intention of placing Vladislav of the Dăneşti

family on the throne at Tîrgovişte in place of Dracul. Faced with an attacking army, there seems to have been a boyar revolt in the capital and Mircea was captured trying to flee the city. He was tortured, blinded with red-hot iron stakes and, in a murder that would echo through vampire folklore, he was buried alive.

Dracul escaped, galloping east to the only ally he had left, the Turks. Somewhere in the Balteni marshes near Bucharest, the Dăneşti rebels caught and killed him, decapitating him with an axe. Legend has it that his body was buried in a wooden chapel where the monastery of Dealul now stands, but it has never been found. There is another legend that his body was taken to Snagov and buried there. If that is true, was this the headless corpse with the Dragon robes that Rosetti and Florescu found there in 1931? Dracul was a 'righteous and unconquerable hero,' wrote Antonio Bonfini, the Hungarian court chronicler, 'the mightiest and bravest in battle'. Jean de Wavrin, who had known him in the thick of the fight said that he was 'very famous for his bravery and for his wisdom'.[29]

But the righteous warlord, who had betrayed the West by allying with the Turks, who had betrayed his own sons by leaving them to the mercies of the Ottoman court, *had* been conquered. He left to Vlad Ţepeş, his eldest surviving son, his Toledo sword and his insignia of the Order of the Dragon. What he could not leave him, because at the time of his death he had lost it, was the principality of Wallachia.

11

VLAD VOIVOD
BATTLE FOR THE CROWN

Vlad Ţepeş ruled Wallachia three times. Most of the stories attributed to him in the Saxon, Russian and Romanian tales belong to the central period that lasted from 1456 to 1462. But in 1447, he was still a prisoner of Murad II and the Turks.

News of his father's and brother's deaths reached him by the end of the year. The story, according to one tradition, is that it was told to him by Mehmed, already by this time, more than his father's heir apparent. Another possibility is that the news was brought by a galloper, the boyar Cazan who had been Vlad Dracul's chancellor and that it was he who brought the boy his father's sword and dragon device. There is no doubt that in the complex, parasitical and rather 'big brother' relationship between the Ottoman Empire and Wallachia, the future Impaler's position now changed dramatically. He was heir to Wallachia; not simply a voivod, which implies a warlord governing for someone else, but a prince with all the hereditary status that that entailed. He was officially freed from his position as hostage and given a rank in the Turkish army, although exactly what is unclear. Given that Skanderbeg had held a similar place earlier and that the janissary corps were made up of 'foreigners', this made perfect sense.

The vacuum created by Vlad Dracul's death had already been filled. On 3 December 1447, János Hunyadi declared himself Prince of Wallachia, but this was merely to gain time to establish his protégé Vladislav II, son of Dan, in Dracul's place. In Wallachia, there was no law of primogeniture, so that contention for the throne was a free for all. Ţepeş, now seventeen and tired of being an exile in an alien land, waited for the opportunity to snatch the throne back.

The chance came in September 1448 when the White Knight crossed the Danube and marched through Turkish-held Serbia, to join forces with Skanderbeg to the south. With him slogged perhaps 9,000 Wallachians under Vladislav, the whole army looting and rioting in true crusader fashion among the villages they found. In an eerie repetition of history, Hunyadi's army met the Turks at Kosovo Polje, the Field of Blackbirds, the scene of the crusaders' defeat by Bayezid the Thunderbolt in 1389. The chronicler Chalkondyles wrote:

> On the left wing there was Dan [Vladislav II] who was [Hunyadi's] great friend whom he had brought to the throne of the land of the Dacians because of his animosity for Dracula . . .[1]

Unusually, for a medieval battle that normally lasted hours, the second Kosovo extended for three days, although it must have been in reality a series of engagements. Between 17 and 19 October, Christian and Muslim harried each other. Estimates of numbers vary, but it is likely that Hunyadi commanded a little over 20,000 men. Even so he was seriously outnumbered by Murad's 40,000. His German hand-gunners held the centre well but Hunyadi had not waited for Skanderbeg's forces as was the plan and one account says that the Wallachians deserted. The probable reason for the second defeat on the Field of Blackbirds was sheer numbers and only Skanderbeg's timely arrival to fight a brilliant rearguard action saved Hunyadi's life. The White Knight was taken prisoner by the Serbs under George Branković, who held him to account for his army's atrocities on the march south. For a while he languished in the fortress of Smeredevo.

The preoccupation of Vladislav and Hunyadi was a golden opportunity for Ţepeş. With the backing of the Turks in the form of cavalry and infantry from Varna and Nicopolis, the son of the Dragon invaded his own territory and took Tîrgovişte unopposed. Virtually no evidence exists for these, for Ţepeş, momentous weeks. The chronicler Chalkondyles implies that the Impaler only held the throne until Vladislav's return from Kosovo. This may have been as a little as two months. Ţepeş had not seen his father's capital for five years. And the boy had returned a man with vengeance on his mind.

It is from this period that the Impaler's first period of rule as Prince of Wallachia dates. On the one hand, it was a plain, old-fashioned military coup, one which had happened before and would happen time after time in the war-torn Balkans. Because of the presence of Turkish troops who had crossed the Danube despite repeated promises to the contrary, it could be interpreted as an act of open warfare – though hardly a surprising one considering that Vladislav and his Wallachians were currently fighting Murad in Serbia. To Ţepeş, it was a simple act to claim his rightful inheritance. Vlad Dracul and Mircea Dracula were dead – and Wallachia was his.

From the Saxon city of Braşov in Transylvania, Nicolae of Ocna, the area's vice-governor, voiced an inevitable concern and demanded an explanation for Ţepeş' actions. The prince's reply is the first documentation we have from the man who has gone down in history as a monster:

We give you the news that Mr Nicolae from Ocna of Sibiu writes to us [the royal we?] and asks us to be so kind as to come to him until John [Hunyadi] the Royal Governor of Hungary returns from the war. We are unable to do this because an emissary from Nicopolis came to us this past Tuesday [29 October] and said with great certainty that Murad, the Turkish sultan, made war for three days against [Hunyadi] the Governor and that on the last day [Hunyadi] formed a circle with his caravan [the Hussite-style war-wagons]. Then the sultan himself went down among the janissaries ... broke through the lines and defeated and killed them. If we come now to him, the Turks could come and kill both you and us. Therefore we ask you to have patience until we see what has happened to [Hunyadi]. We don't even know if he is alive. If he returns from the war, we will meet him and we will make peace with him. But if you will be our enemies now, and if something happens, you will have sinned and you will have to answer for it before God. Written at Tîrgovişte the day before All Saint's Day in the year of our Lord 1448.

It was signed, by a clerk on his behalf, 'Vlad, Voivod of Wallachia, your brother in all' and addressed to 'the officials of Braşov, our most loved brothers and friends'.[2]

No doubt vampire-lovers will see something sinister in the fact that the Impaler's first known letter was written on Halloween, but it is important because it gives us an insight into his psyche. It sounds a little naïve in places, perhaps because the boy was only seventeen, perhaps because the Latin or Church Slavonic of the original loses something in translation, but Ţepeş' position was difficult and he had to be careful. He was describing a battle that had happened a fortnight earlier in enough detail to make us believe that he had talked to survivors, or at least received good intelligence which may have come from Christian or Turkish sources (the emissary from Nicopolis). He was in Tîrgovişte with the support of Turkish troops, owed the sultan his freedom and could not, yet, afford to offend them. We do not know how much he knew of the circumstances of his father's and brother's deaths, but he must have known of the boyar revolt

and perhaps suspected the involvement of Vladislav and
Hunyadi. If both those men had died at Kosovo Polje, of
course, he would already be avenged. On the other hand, he
shows a shrewd grasp of *realpolitik* when he expresses a wish
to make peace with Hunyadi. Towards the end of the letter,
despite referring to the Braşov people as his 'brothers and
friends' he threatens them with God's wrath if they refuse to
accept him as Prince of Wallachia. On the one hand, this is
common 'medieval-speak', the natural belief in ruler and ruled
alike that God was the ultimate judge of sin. On the other,
perhaps Vlad Ţepeş really believed it and that the hand of God
guided all his actions.

What the Impaler may not have known is that Murad had
not followed up his victory at Kosovo. Perhaps because of
heavy casualties, perhaps because he had lost the heart for
slaughter[3] he ordered a three day rest while the dead were
buried. This gave Vladislav the chance not only to escape, but
to return to Wallachia to overthrow the young Ţepeş.

Eight years later, the 'son of the Devil' would simply have
batted the pretender aside. As it was, he was inexperienced and
lacked support among either the boyars or the peasantry. By
Christmas 1448 his troops were outnumbered by Vladislav's
forces, backed as they were by Petru II Bogdan, Prince of
Moldavia, and he abandoned Tîrgovişte to run east, to the life
he had known most recently, at Murad's court at Edirne. We
have no exact date for his exit but in all probability he had
ruled Wallachia for two months.

The years between Ţepeş' first and second reigns were spent
in the wilderness and for part of that time at least, he was a
fugitive. There is nothing like having to look over a shoulder
to make a man vengeful, distrustful and morose. From
December 1449 until October 1451, he lived at the court of his
uncle, Bogdan II of Moldavia, at his capital Suceava. Here, he
spent time and perhaps completed his education with his
cousin Stefan, who would become one of the most celebrated

rulers in Eastern Europe as Stefan cel Mare, the Great. Of an age, the princes became friends, pledging to support each other in time of need. Stefan's odd and uncharacteristic treachery against Țepeș in 1462 (described in Chapter 13) does not square with this oath but it probably only added to the already well-established sense of betrayal and mistrust that the prince-voivod felt throughout his life.

Moldavian politics, like that of Wallachia, was often brutal and nasty and the lives of its rulers short. Bogdan was murdered by a rival, Petru Aaron, his own brother, in October 1451, driving Țepeș and Stefan to escape to Wallachia through the Borgo Pass made famous four centuries later by Bram Stoker. They knew that, by this time, János Hunyadi had long since returned from his defeat at Kosovo. Stripped of his titles of governor of Transylvania and Hungary by the newly elected King Ladislas Posthumous of Hungary, he still held Hunedoara and other strongholds. By February 1452, Țepeș was in Brașov, relying on the tentative links he had made with the powerful city fathers four years earlier. He was still there in September despite Hunyadi's stern orders that the fugitive was to be handed over. Under pressure of some kind and perhaps fearing for his safety, Țepeș ran to Sibiu.

During 1451 and the following year, Hunyadi's relationship with Vladislav changed. There can be no doubt that the White Knight was ambitious and little doubt that Vladislav was very much the junior partner. Even so, Hunyadi's seizure of Amlaș and Făgăraș probably prompted the prince to open relations with Mehmed II, now sultan once again in place of Murad who died of a stroke on 3 February. In one sense, of course, Vladislav was simply carrying on the dangerous tightrope balance of his two predecessors. Vladislav's rather grand title on a deed of 28 March reads, 'Prince over all of Wallachia.' Weeks earlier, a document from Tîrgoviște had included 'and of the areas across the mountains on our borders, the duchies of Amlaș and Făgăraș'.[4] Obviously Vladislav was furious that Hunyadi had grabbed territory from him and a document from 1453 makes clear the extent of the rift:

> I, my boyars and my country have spilled our blood for the Holy Crown, for Hungary and for Christianity. No matter how much we have sworn, our father, [Hunyadi] voivod, does not care and he was not pleased with my work ... he acted badly towards me; and you can see that he broke the oaths and promises he made ...[5]

At some point during 1452 a reconciliation was effected between Hunyadi and Țepeș in a meeting at Hunedoara. We have no record of its substance or how sincerely Țepeș promised to serve the White Knight. We do know, however, that he attended the meeting of the Hungarian diet with Hunyadi and was present at Posthumous' coronation as King of Hungary the following year, at Buda, a city he would come to know all too well in the future. In a deal struck here, Țepeș was given the role of defender of Transylvania, with his headquarters at Sibiu. The long expected fall of Constantinople meant that an all-out Turkish attack north of the Danube was now more likely than ever. As Pope Nicholas V lamented in faraway Rome, 'The light of Christianity has suddenly gone out.'[6]

The Bishop of Sibiu, where Vlad Țepeș watched the borders, wrote to Oswald Wengel, the town's mayor:

> The Turks will subdue all of Christianity if God will allow it ... They will next conquer the lands of the despot George Branković of Serbia ... They also say that the city of Sibiu, which lies in their path, must be destroyed.[7]

While János Hunyadi prepared to defend Branković's strategic city of Belgrade on the Danube, Țepeș mobilized his own forces against his rival Vladislav, now in open union with Mehmed's Turks. In the middle of June 1456, he led his army through the Carpathians past the castle at Bran and caught Vladislav's army somewhere near Tîrgovişte. That month, a strange sight appeared in the night sky, 'as long as half the sky with two tails, one pointing west and the other east, coloured gold and looking like a flame in the distant horizon,' wrote the chronicler Antonio Bonfini. He was describing Halley's comet, which, to some, presaged victory and joy; to others, death.

At the end of July, Vladislav II, Prince of Wallachia, was hacked to death in hand-to-hand combat, according to legend, with Vlad Ţepeş. By 22 August, the Impaler was at Tîrgovişte, prince once more. One of the first things he did was to have a Braşov goldsmith strike a coin, the only one found from his reign. On the obverse was the Wallachian eagle displayed in all its heraldic glory; on the reverse, a crescent and a star with trailing wake.

Niccolo Modrussa, the Pope's legate to Buda, wrote a physical description of the new voivod around 1470:

> He was not very tall but very stocky and strong, with a cold and terrible appearance, a strong and aquiline nose, swollen nostrils, a thin and reddish face in which very long eyelashes framed large wide-open green eyes; the bushy black eyebrows made them appear threatening. His face and chin were shaven, but for a moustache. The swollen temples increased the bulk of his head. A bull's neck connected his head from which black curly locks hung on his wide-shouldered person.[8]

A number of portraits of Vlad Ţepeş exist, most of them showing a mature man of anything between twenty-five and fifty.[9] The woodcut from the 1488 Nuremberg edition called *Dracole Waida* is typical. It shows the long dark hair that Modrussa saw and the moustache is swept up and outwards at each end, typical of the time; portraits of János Hunyadi show a similar style. The eyes depicted in the woodcut are hard, focussed, the mouth grim and intense. There is a remarkable consistency in most of the Impaler portraits in terms of the headgear. They virtually all show a variant on the 'cap of estate' worn throughout Europe, decorated above the rim with a cluster of pearls around a central precious stone. The Leipzig version, *An Extraordinary and Shocking History of a Great Berserker called Prince Dracula*, from 1493 is far wider of the mark. The curly hair is short, the eyes rather more melancholy than intense and the cleft chin very pronounced. The Strasbourg edition of 1500 shows the famous banquet scene with a bearded Ţepeş with long, flowing locks gazing up with a mildly interested look at his victims on their stakes.

There is a further interesting painting which may show Vlad Ţepeş. It was discovered by accident in 1970 and was previously known to hang in the Belvedere Palace in Vienna. It is a fifteenth-century oil on canvas work showing the martyrdom of St Andrew, whose mummified head was one of the few relics to survive the fall of Constantinople. Legend has it that the saint, one of the fishermen disciples of Christ, was crucified on a saltire cross at Patra in about AD 70. A number of his relics, including the cross on which he died, were taken to Constantinople and supposedly to Scotland by the eighth century. He was the patron saint of the Saxons from Transylvania which accounts for the presence of Ţepeş, hovering at the left of the canvas and supervising the lashing of Andrew in place on the cross.

Another likeness was discovered even more recently, in 1989, by Dr Virgil Candea and is on display in the library of Wurtenberg, in Stuttgart. On a circular plaque with the legend 'Vladislaus Dracula, Wallachiae Weywoden' it shows a slightly portly voivod with high gilt-encrusted collar and fur-edged robes. The eyes are small and weaselly, but the nose and hair are exactly as Modrussa described them.

It is likely that all three portraits and possibly others now lost to time are copies of the version that hangs in Ambras Castle near Innsbruck in the Tyrol. It is on display in a bizarre gallery once owned by Ferdinand II, Archduke of the Tyrol in the sixteenth century, who specialized in collecting artefacts of the macabre. Many of the portraits are taken from life, such as the Munich wolfman, Petrus Gonsalvus (Pedro Gonzalez), whose painting, along with those of his children, is a reminder of the past's fascination for freaks.[10] There is also a likeness of poor Gregor Baxi, who suffered the same fate as Henri II of France in having his head pierced by a lance. The portrait shows him with the lance-head protruding from his eye socket, months before the wound's infection killed him.

And next to Baxi is the famous portrait of Vlad the Impaler. This one is a sixteenth-century copy from an original probably painted at either Buda or Visegrád during Dracula's imprisonment by Matthias Corvinus. Various reproductions distort the colour of the Ambras version and add sinister lights to what is actually a standard fifteenth-century portrait. The eyes *are* very large and the famous crimson velvet cap is augmented with rows of pearls, a gold star and an upright ostrich-feather plume. The hair, hanging in heavy curls, is very long, well below the shoulders. How much of this is artistic licence by the anonymous artist is impossible to say.

Vlad Ţepeş was twenty-five-years-old when he took the throne of Wallachia for the second time. He inherited a political structure from the time of his grandfather Mircea the Old which comprised a council, the *Sfatul Domnesc*, which increasingly was made up of the leading boyars and which doubled as a civil service. The structure was essentially Byzantine although it has its parallels in the Ottoman sultan's court and the *Curia Regis* (household) of Western kings. Among the documents relating to the Impaler's time as prince, the word '*Jupan*' refers to any lord who was a member of the Council. There were two *Vornici* at the Impaler's capital of Tîrgovişte, one more senior than the other, whose responsibility was the judiciary. The *Logofat* headed Ţepeş' chancellery, charged with correspondence and retention of court papers. Every surviving document from Ţepeş would have been handwritten by a clerk at this court. The *Spatar* was a military commander, usually, because of its knightly linkage, of cavalry. He was not technically commander-in-chief of the army; the prince himself assumed this role. The *Stolnic*, first mentioned in a document in 1392, was the prince's food taster and responsible for the court victuals, while the *Paharnic* was responsible for wine. The prince's horses were the particular remit of the *Comis* who also saw to the payment of the cash tribute and the boy levy to the Turks. The *Vistiers* kept the prince's wardrobe as well as being his treasurer, keeping records of the taxes paid by the 222 villages and towns in Wallachia. The *Stratornic*, also called *Postelnic*, was in charge of the prince's private quarters.[11]

Ţepeş had been crowned 'Prince Vlad, son of Vlad the Great, sovereign and ruler of Ungro-Wallachia and of the duchies of Amlaş and Făgăraş' in the Biserica Domnesca, the great cathedral at Tîrgovişte, probably in September 1456. How far he had planned his domestic and foreign policy and how far he was merely reacting to events is difficult to gauge, but in the six years of his reign, there does seem to be a consistency and a new dynamism altogether missing from the rule of his father, grandfather and their Dăneşti rivals.

In domestic policy, the paramount problem was that of the boyars. Some of these men had openly taken up arms on behalf of Vladislav II (often referred to as Dan, his family name, in contemporary literature) and had been responsible, probably with Hunyadi's backing, for both the beheading of Vlad Dracul and the burial alive of Mircea. The Impaler's treatment of the boyars must be seen in the light of this. The boyars as a class pre-dated the principality of Wallachia and had been used to garnering wealth and power for some time. Temporarily conciliating the two 'super-powers' on his western and southern frontiers, the Hungarians and the Turks, Ţepeş began a systematic purge of his boyars with Stalinesque efficiency. The famous coup against them probably took place in the first Easter of his reign, arguably on Sunday 17 April 1457. The horror stories attributed to Ţepeş which form Chapter 8 of this book can now be seen against an historical framework. The boyars were feasting in the hall of the prince's palace at Tîrgovişte, still, for many modern visitors, a place of death. The Easter rituals in the Chapel of the Holy Spirit were over and Ţepeş asked the nobles how many princes had ruled Wallachia in their lifetime. Whatever they told him was the wrong answer. By this time, he had already found Mircea's grave and the tell-tale clawmarks on the coffin lid where his desperate brother had fought for air in his dying agony. According to some accounts, 500 of the boyars and their families were impaled in the palace courtyard. In reality, the whole party cannot have included more than 200 and the place of execution, the ruins of which still stand today, is only large enough to house about 40. Tîrgovişte today is an isolated cluster of low walls and cellars. Only the chapel and the Impaler's Chindia watch tower, restored in the nineteenth century, show any shadow of their former glory.

The survivors who were not impaled were shackled together and dragged north for two days up the river Argeş, fifty miles away. Here, they worked as a chain gang restoring the castle at Poenari – the original of Bram Stoker's Castle Dracula – as a mountain stronghold for the prince. It is debatable how much actual use these captives could have been in the rebuilding programme. The children, women and old men would have been too weak to last long and the stories say that they worked on the stone-carrying until their fine clothes fell off their backs. However, the building of Poenari by a previously exalted and privileged elite was a powerful lesson in humility and the power of a prince, and probably has no parallel in European history.

Poenari, now a dramatic, ivy-clad ruin high above the Argeş, once had five cylindrical towers with platforms for cannon and angles for crossfire. Its walls, double-reinforced with stone and brick, were built to withstand a possible Turkish bombardment. A well provided the castle with its own water-supply and there was possibly an underground tunnel that led to the river for escape and the smuggling in of supplies. A series of earthquakes, rather than Turkish or Hungarian guns, eventually destroyed it.

How complete was Dracula's destruction of the boyar class? It may have been decimated. Kurt Treptow has analysed the names of the members of the council between 16 April 1457 (the day before the palace coup) and 10 February 1461. At Easter 1457, Marea Udriste heads the list, but he has gone by March 1458 and Dragomir Tacal is in his place. Only one *Vornic* (Chief Justice) is listed. This is Codrea and his name is missing too by the following March. It would be tedious to recite them all and we cannot know the specific reasons for their removal in each case. Suffice it to say that out of thirteen 'departments' of the council, only two remain unchanged over the five year period. Voico Dobrita, *Vornic* in 1458 and clearly senior boyar by 1461; and Iova, at first *Comis* (Master of the Horse) and later *Vistier* (Treasurer), survived. The others have gone and it is reasonable to suppose that most of them perished in the Easter coup.

Treptow believes that the removal of the boyars was neither as vicious nor as sudden as the folk tales tell. Individuals are listed again in the council under Ţepeş' brother Radu after 1462, implying that they were either out of favour or out of the country during the Impaler's reign, not rotting at the top of a stake.

There was one boyar, however, whom Ţepeş particularly singled out for punishment and that was Albu cel Mare. His death, and that of his family, is number seven in the Saxon stories: 'He had a big family uprooted, from the smallest to the largest, children, friends, brothers, sisters and he had them all impaled.' The fact that Albu called himself cel Mare, the Great, may say it all. He saw himself as a king-maker, an over-mighty subject. A document dated 1 April 1551 in the reign of Prince Mircea Ciobanul puts his end in context:

> In the time of Vlad Voivod Ţepeş, there was a boyar called Albu cel Mare, who took the ... villages [Glodul and Hintea] by

> force and devastated the holy monastery [of Govora] . . . In the
> days of Vlad Voivod Ţepeş, this boyar . . . tried to take the
> throne from him . . .

Whether Albu's attempt was an organized boyar resistance
against the Impaler's centralist policy and his emasculation of
the class or whether he was simply another Dăneşti rival, the
result was the same. Albu himself, his relatives, his friends, all
died in the same vengeful 'wipe-out'. His children would have
grown to be adult rivals; his sisters would have bred those
children. Everybody had to die.

There are conflicting theories as to Ţepeş' treatment of the
boyars as a group. He clearly did not eliminate them all, either
by impalement or castle-building. Neither is the situation
regarding the replacement of the class clear-cut. One view is
that, having removed the boyars, Ţepeş brought in his own
relatively humble men whom he could trust. There was
inevitably an element of this, the usual nepotism and cronyism
which is the hallmark of many governmental structures, past
and present. Whereas Ţepeş might not have wished to reduce
the feudal powers of the boyars (powers which were in fact
relatively new since feudalism was only now establishing itself
in Wallachia), he certainly introduced new men, some of them
from the ranks of the *Mosneni*, the small-holding peasantry.
The debate focuses on the speed and scale with which this was
done.

Particularly sinister in the light of the voivod's reputation
was his creation of new hirelings. The *Vitesji*, in effect an
officer corps for his army, was recruited not from the boyars,
who had their own agenda, but from the *Mosneni*. Such men
could be used to hold a border castle against the Turks or
crush an internal revolt – it was all one. It also gave rise to the
notion that the Wallachian army was a peasant one, which,
while not altogether accurate, has a certain basis in fact. The
Armas were the rough equivalent of a secret police today –
Ceauşescu's Securitate of the 1980s would have recognized

their role. Many of them were foreigners, probably because they would be most likely to carry out atrocities on Wallachians, if ordered, with less conscience than native troops. Gypsies, Hungarians, Tartars, Serbs, they carried out the prince's executions and tortures. In a letter written to the ruler of Braşov, probably in 1458, Ţepeş refers to his former wine-provider Stoica as *Armasul*, 'stake-master', but the stake-master was not included in the Council until 1478, by which time the Impaler was dead.

Much has been made of Ţepeş' relationship with the Church. His own personal faith is a closed book. His father, by virtue of the Dragon fraternity, had to be Catholic. The Impaler may have taken up the Islamic religion during his time in Edirne and this could explain his position as an officer in the Turkish army. We know, after all, that George Kastrioti, Skanderbeg, did the same. The Serbs, however, were regarded as a rather more pagan society within the Balkans; the Wallachians were more firmly rooted in the Orthodox Church.

Like most medieval rulers, Ţepeş was a staunch builder and patron of the Church. At Tîrgsov, in the Church of St Nicholas, stands the inscription, 'By the Grace of God, I, voivod, ruler of Ungro-Wallachia, the son of the great Prince Vlad, have built and completed this church on 24 June 1461.' This may have been in atonement for the killing of Vladislav II, which legend says happened nearby, or in celebration of the event. If so, that too was standard medieval practice. Ţepeş founded a monastery at Comana, gave grants of land and tax exemptions to others at Tismana, Cozia and Govora and greatly extended the island monastery at Snagov. He also gave large donations to Mount Athos in Greece, the spiritual centre of the Eastern Orthodox Church outside Russia.

Foreign policy at once had an influence on the Wallachian Church. The Metropolitan who ran it was appointed before 1453 by the Patriarch of Constantinople, but the fall of the Byzantine capital in that year brought about a change. To the west, the creeping encroachment of Hungary, under the charge first of János Hunyadi, then of his son Matthias Corvinus, meant that Catholicism was seeping into the Impaler's principality. Many of the horror stories found in Saxon, Russian and Romanian versions deal with Ţepeş' clashes with Catholic monks – Brother Jacob from Melk may well have been a survivor – and they speak volumes for the anti-Catholic and therefore anti-Hungarian stance that the voivod took. It was under Vlad Ţepeş that the first Wallachian, Abbot Iosif, was made Metropolitan in April 1457. Previous incumbents, appointed by Constantinople, had been outsiders. All this is very much in keeping with the Impaler's centralizing policy. Church and state went hand in glove in Wallachia, as in the rest of Europe. As he appointed his own boyars and officials, so he began to appoint his own Church hierarchy, especially in the spiritual wilderness in which the collapse of Constantinople had left him.

The other element in Ţepeş' reign is the substance of the Saxon horror stories relating to Transylvania: 'In the year of our Lord 1456 Dracula did many dreadful and curious things.' The documents tell us that the voivod's targets here were particularly Braşov (referred to by the German name of Kronstadt or Burzenland) and Sibiu (Siebenburgen, the seven cities). Both these towns were in the Amlaş and Făgăraş duchies which Hunyadi and Vladislav II had taken from Vlad Dracul. Transylvania by the 1450s was wholly dominated by the 'alien' German or Hungarian merchants and landowners; the Romanians themselves were purely peasant in the sense of barely subsisting and having no rights. Early in his reign, Ţepeş was at pains to continue the cordial relationship with the Saxon towns that he had briefly enjoyed in 1448. On 10 September 1456, styling himself 'Vlad, Prince of Wallachia and ruler of Făgăraş, your brother and friend in all,' he wrote to the elders of Braşov:

You brethren, friends and neighbours who are truly loved . . .

Certainly, Ţepeş was asking for help, but he was also trying to unite the Transylvanians with his own people in a great cause. What he wanted was a show of strength to give the Turks pause in what appeared to be a renewal of hostilities against both Wallachia and Transylvania.

In the previous month, Sultan Mehmed advanced along the Danube to take Dar-ne-jihad, the battlefield of Holy War, George Branković's city of Belgrade, the white city. Built on high ground where the Danube and the Sava meet, it was a vitally strategic point south of the Hungarian plain and leading north via undulating valleys where a large, predatory army could never be stopped. Made aware of Mehmed's advance by scouts and spies, János Hunyadi hurried to defend the five-gated walls of its island fortress. Either by accident or design, the janissaries were allowed to break through the breaches their cannon had made and began to ransack and loot the town with its ramshackle houses and twisting lanes. They were suddenly attacked by an organized band of citizens led by Hunyadi, using muskets against the Turks who by this stage expected civilian submission.

The janissaries broke in panic, the braying of their regimental bands and the screaming of their generals failing to hold them. Mehmed, never the gentleman his father was, hacked with his scimitar at his flying troops.

Twenty days later and a bare fortnight before Ţepeş was writing to Braşov, János Hunyadi died. Whether it was the plague or dysentery, those haunters of medieval armies, that cut him down, the White Knight had gone. And the Balkans had need of new warlords.

Ţepeş asked Braşov for 200 men, fifty if that was all they could manage. There was nothing odd about this request. Constantinople unsuccessfully, Belgrade successfully, had seen its citizens man the walls. Medieval towns had walls for that purpose. Ţepeş wanted the Braşovians to move fast. His letter was dated 'the Friday after St Mary's Day' and he wanted the troops by the next Sunday – nine days away. There is no record of whether this contingent was sent, but presumably it was because it was soon after this that the Impaler signed an agreement with the city promising aid against the Turks and giving their merchants rights to trade freely in his Wallachian cities of Tîrgovişte, Tîrgsov and Rucăr. He was to be given asylum in Braşov should the need arise. It is likely that similar arrangements were made with other cities like Sibiu.

So what went wrong? How did this ostensibly friendly relationship end? Romanians believe that, in keeping with their view of Vlad Ţepeş as a national hero, he was protecting Wallachian interests against the avariciousness of the foreigners. In that these foreigners were members of the merchant class and generally wealthy, there is even an element of class warfare in all this, 500 years before Nicolae Ceauşescu issued commemorative postage stamps of the Impaler,[12] portraying Ţepeş as a class warrior. It is true that the first punitive measures against the Saxons were economic, but that was merely because Ţepeş wanted to hit them where he knew it would hurt most, in their purses. The impalements would come later. The real reason for the voivod's actions against the Saxon cities which earned him the reputation 'berserker' and 'bloodthirsty madman' is that he suspected those areas, quite rightly, of plotting with his rival, the future prince Basarab Laiota.

The position was complicated by affairs in Hungary, which had suffered for years an ongoing feud similar to that of the rival Draculeşti and Dăneşti families in Wallachia. On the one hand were the Hunyadis, László and Matthias, the sons of János, the elder boy carrying on his late father's role as commander of the Hungarian armies. On the other was the Habsburg king, Ladislas Posthumous and the Cilli family to whom he was related. The murder of Count Ulrich Cilli in László's city of Belgrade had led to the execution of László and the imprisonment of Matthias in March 1457. Their torch had been taken up by the in-laws of János Hunyadi, his widow Erzsebet and her brother Mihaly Szilágy.

Vlad Ţepeş was in the cleft stick found so commonly in the Balkans and in feudal Europe generally of having sworn fealty to one side – the Habsburgs – and owing allegiance to the other – the Hunyadis – for helping him to the throne. This link with the Hunyadis is rather difficult to grasp. After all, János was in the background at least over the deaths of Vlad Dracul and Mircea, but the new voivod seems either to be unaware of this or happy enough to forgive and forget. Whatever the truth, the lines were drawn. The Holy Roman Emperor, Frederick III, supported Ladislas and so did the Saxon towns in Transylvania.

The first spark of open trouble came in the summer of 1457 when the citizens of Bistriţa revolted against Szilágy over alleged misappropriation of funds. This has a very modern ring to it and it may be that the townspeople had simply had enough of the warlord's high-handed rule. Backed by Ţepeş, Szilágy sacked the town and burned the houses of the ringleaders. The other Saxon cities rallied together after Bistriţa and received support from the Szekler leader Count Oswald of Rozgony, anxious to prove his worth as Ladislas Posthumous' new commander in the Carpathians.

Braşov backed Ţepeş' Dăneşti rival Dan III, whose brother the Impaler had killed at Tîrgsov. He was even crowned in the Orthodox cathedral outside Braşov with all the panoply of state and using the exact title that Ţepeş already possessed. Dan's temporary capital was outside the city walls on a hill that would become notorious in the Impaler legend – Timpa.

Sibiu, for reasons that are unclear, did not join Braşov in supporting Dan but backed another claimant, 'a priest of the Romanians who calls himself a prince's son'. This was almost certainly Vlad Calugarul, the monk, Ţepeş' half brother by the Wallachian peasant woman Caltuna. Calugarul set himself up at Amlaş and gained support from disaffected boyars and Saxon merchants, furious that Ţepeş had dropped the trading concessions he had given them the previous year.

So by 1457, the Impaler was faced with no less than three rivals – Dan III, Vlad the monk and Basarab Laiota. At first, he tried diplomacy, sending boyars from the Council to both Sibiu and Braşov. There was no reply. The result was Ţepeş' first devastating raid on the Saxons in the spring of 1458. The villages of Satul Nou, Hosman and Casolts were burned to the ground by his cavalry and the supporters of Vlad the monk were butchered. Bod was totally destroyed, Talmes left blazing and its people hacked 'like cabbage' in the town square. Merchants were now expected to sell their wares at the specified towns of Tîrgovişte, Tîrgsov and Cîmpulung at below the market value. Any who refused were rounded up for non-compliance and impaled by the roadside or boiled in cauldrons, according to the Saxon accounts. The young men whom it was claimed had been sent to Wallachia to learn the language were likewise executed, quite simply because they were clearly spies.

The international chess game of politics moved on. On 9 December 1457 Ladislas Posthumous, shown in contemporary portraits as a rather effeminate young man with flowing blonde curls, was suddenly taken ill and died the same day, probably poisoned. His place was taken by the election of Matthias Hunyadi, the remaining son of the White Knight who now took the surname Corvinus, 'the crow', and the great black bird bedecked his shield and banners. Mihail Szilágy, the new king's uncle, now brokered a deal between Ţepeş and the Saxon towns and an uneasy peace ensued. Matthias Corvinus sent his ambassador Benedict de Boithar to open negotiations with the Impaler, while Szilágy signed a treaty with Braşov. The deal was that Ţepeş should restore the town's trading rights in exchange for the surrender of the pretender Dan III and his boyar followers. 'Know that I shall keep the word ordered by my brother and lord Mihail Szilágy,' Ţepeş wrote on 1 December 1458.[13]

By the winter of 1459, this promising new start had collapsed. Dan and his boyars were not forthcoming and

Corvinus, keen to stamp his own imprint on his kingdom, dismissed Szilágy as commander in Transylvania. As well as threatening to skewer de Boithar on the highest stake he had, Țepeș hit the Brașov suburbs like a whirlwind. Attacking at night, his cavalry clattered across the wooden bridge and burned the stockade that gave flimsy protection to Dan III's enclave on Timpa Hill. It was here that the inhabitants were impaled in large numbers as the Chapel of St Jacob burned to the ground. According to the poet Michael Beheim, the Impaler sat at a table in the open air and mopped up from his plate the blood of his writhing victims. The boyar who complained of the foul stench was impaled higher than the rest.

He followed up his attack with another on Brașov itself, looting and burning the Church of St Bartholomew and carrying away its holy relics. But Dan and his supporters were long gone, armed with plenty of propaganda against his rival. On 2 March 1460, Dan wrote to the burghers of the damaged city, sympathizing with the fact that they had been victims of:

> untold abuses, damage hardly reparable, sad murders, mutila-
> tions, sorrows, being grieved, mercilessly killed, destroyed,
> maimed and tortured . . . by the unfaithful cruel tyrant Dracula,
> who calls himself Vlad, prince of that country . . . He did this
> following the teaching of the Devil . . .[14]

Probably hoping to emulate Hunyadi's success in 1448, Dan launched a counter-offensive against Țepeș later that month, taking the often-fought over Amlaș and Făgăraș on the way. The clash with the Impaler, probably near Rucăr, was a failure, however; only seven of Dan's boyars scrabbled to safety. Dan himself was forced to dig his own grave and a mass for the dead was said while he was still alive. According to Beheim at least, Țepeș hacked off his rival's head himself.

With their claimant dead, Brașov now sent a fifty-five-man embassy to the Impaler, led by Johann Gereb of Vingard.

Ţepeş held them at Tîrgovişte and set out to eliminate his second rival, his own half brother, Vlad Calugarul. On 24 August 1460, St Bartholomew's Day, the Impaler burned the corn standing in the fields beyond the walls of Amlaş and slaughtered, according to the Saxon tradition, 30,000 inhabitants. Şercaia, the territory of the rebellious boyar Bogdan Doboca, was devastated, the villagers being hanged on hooks and pitchforks. Beaten down by the Impaler's brutality, Braşov took the hint and concluded a treaty with Ţepeş on 1 October. By its terms, there was to be an exchange of prisoners: the voivod would release Gereb's embassy; Braşov would hand over rebel boyars and merchants. Full trading rights were to be restored. Ţepeş would be paid for the cost of a standing army of 4,000 men to 'guard' the Seven Fortresses. And he would pay the town for war damage.

Curbing the power of the boyars and bringing the German merchant class to heel as he did has led many Romanians to see Vlad Ţepeş as a Robin Hood, a man of the people. This is to misread medieval history. The peasantry in Wallachia may have constituted nearly 90 per cent of the population, and there were times, as in the Bogomil disturbances of the 1430s, when they could be troublesome. They also constituted, as in all other medieval states, the numerical bulk of the voivod's army. But in all respects, they were cannon fodder. They died on the ramparts of castles that they themselves had built. They grew the grain which was the food supply of the state. They cleared forests for the voivod and built the monasteries he endowed. The peasantry were an accepted fact of everyday life to a prince. Deferential by nature, they pulled off their caps and knelt in his presence, overawed by the God-given role that he played. He was their lord in every sense. He could read and write. He could buy any one of them a thousand times over. He could outride and outfight any of them. And he had the power of life and death over them all.

Ţepeş had no need to curry favour with these people any more than any ruler did. Murad II may have regarded his slaves as his brothers, but they were still technically slaves and he showed no inclination to set them free. If Ţepeş elevated such men to positions of authority it was for his own purposes, to out-manoeuvre recalcitrant or rebellious boyars. If he refused, as he did, to send the boy tribute to the Turks, that was not because he cared for the boys and their families; it was because he wanted to offend the Turks. If he meted out punishment for wrongdoing equally to boyar and peasant alike, it was because he expected absolute obedience to his will from everyone.

One story, found in the Saxon, Romanian and Russian chronicles that relates specifically to the peasants is the tale of the old, the lame and the sick who were invited to dine in a great hall at Ţepeş' capital of Tîrgovişte. Having fed them and got them drunk, the Impaler's attendants locked the doors and set the house alight. In the folk tales, Ţepeş justified his actions: 'These men live off the sweat of others, so they are useless to humanity. It is a form of thievery ... They are worse than robbers. May such men be eliminated from my land.'[15] Romanian historians from the Ceauşescu era, anxious to find in the Impaler a hero on a white horse, have posited that his intention here was to wipe out bubonic plague, the ever-prevalent Black Death which had probably claimed Hunyadi and was a constant source of fear. We know that victims of *pestilencia* throughout Europe were treated with appalling cruelty, whipped out of settlements, stoned, walled-up alive. We know too that burning the clothes and bodies of the infected was tried, as one of many desperate remedies, at various places where the disease raged. Even so, the theory seems a little far-fetched. No one would have allowed plague victims to enter a major town, especially the voivod's capital, because the belief – and the reality, depending on the strain of the disease – was that the plague was highly infectious.

Another theory follows the reasoning that is attributed to Ţepeş in the folk tales: he committed the crime to eradicate poverty in Wallachia. If so, this seems draconian[16] in the extreme. All medieval (and many modern) states were faced with poverty on a massive scale and some sought ways to control it. In Wallachia, according to the theory, the way was mass murder.

Ţepeş' foreign policy was always going to take into consideration the Ottoman Turks. He had spent years with them; his family had fought them. And for the time being he needed to keep them at arm's length. Accordingly, between 1456 and 1459 he sent his emissaries to Mehmed's court, now at Constantinople, and probably sent his *Comis* personally to pay the tribute. In 1460 it suited both men to conclude a treaty. Nine articles covered the essentials of their relationship.

In the first, the Turks were not allowed to enter Wallachia, except for diplomatic missions specifically allowed by Ţepeş. The payment of the tribute – 'totalling 10,000 *galbens* from our treasury' – was to be paid at Tîrgovişte from then on and the Turkish ambassador responsible for its collection was to be escorted from Giurgiu to the capital and back again, a receipt being issued for the money as it left the country. The second article gave the voivod total independence, allowing him to make war with his neighbours and giving him 'the power of life and death over his subjects'. Article Three insisted that any Wallachians adopting Islam when south of the Danube should revert to Christianity on their return to avoid friction. This may tell us a lot about Ţepeş' personal views on religion. The fourth article allowed Wallachian travellers in the Ottoman Empire to be exempt from Turkish taxation and to be allowed to wear their own dress. The 'horror' stories of the Impaler, of course, record that the voivod himself was a stickler for protocol of this type, nailing heads and torturing people who were improperly attired. 'The prince,' said Article Five, 'shall be chosen by the Metropolitan, the bishops and the boyars.'[17] This was in marked contrast to what would follow two years later when, effectively, Ţepeş' younger brother Radu was placed on the Wallachian throne by Mehmed. Should there be a dispute between a Turk and a Wallachian, Article Six contended, the case should be tried by the prince himself. Turkish merchants' rights were carefully controlled by Article Seven. They could cross the Danube and sell only in specific places and leave again quickly. There was to be no 'sight-seeing'. Article Eight added that those merchants could not take Wallachians with them when they left, nor would they be given a special place for prayer. Lastly, the sultan's government did not have the right to act against any of the Impaler's people or take that person out of Wallachia.

The whole thing seems heavily weighted in Ţepeş' favour, but it was assumed that the cash tribute and boy levy would go on as before and Mehmed needed a quiescent European frontier because he was about to make war in Asia. He concluded a similar treaty with Skanderbeg in Albania.

We know almost nothing of Vlad Ţepeş' private life but by the time of the Turkish treaty he was probably married to his first wife. Her name is unknown. She was probably Wallachian or Transylvanian and may have been a noblewoman who committed suicide in 1462. Fedor Kuritsyn, who met members of the Impaler's family at Mathias Corvinus' court at Buda in 1480, is probably right when he says the pair were not married. Under Wallachian law, as we have seen, a son of a liaison had equal inheritance rights with a legitimate child. Mihail was the son born of this relationship and would follow his father in almost every particular. Raising rebellious boyar armies against Dracula's successors he took the Wallachian throne in 1508 and held it for less than two years. He received almost as bad a press as the Impaler. Known as 'the evil one', it is said that he:

took all the boyars captive, worked them hard, cruelly confiscated their property and even slept with their wives in their presence. He cut off the noses and lips of some, others he hanged and still others drowned.[18]

By this time of course, the horror stories of his father were already international bestsellers and it is likely that Mihail was happy to bask in the notoriety, in that it usually got results. He was stabbed to death by an assassin in 1510. The direct descendants of this branch of the family died out in 1632.

The story of Dracula's second marriage to Matthias Corvinus' cousin Ilona Szilágy will be dealt with in the next chapter but Kuritsyn wrote of the family:

the king [Corvinus] took his sister [Dracula's widow] with her two sons to Buda in Hungary. One of these sons is still in the retinue of the king, the other, who was residing with the Bishop of Oradea [in Transylvania] died in our presence. I saw a third son, named Micahel [Mihail] here in Buda. He had fled from the Sultan to the Hungarian king. Dracula begot him on a young lady when he was not married.[19]

We cannot know how many mistresses the Impaler took to his bed. Hopefully, they were not all as unlucky as the one whose body he ripped open to disprove her pregnancy.

By 1462, Vlad Ţepeş had centralized power in his own hands at Tîrgovişte, although increasingly he began to favour the more southerly town of Bucharest. He had controlled his boyars and regulated trade with the Saxons in Transylvania, bringing them to heel. He had executed one rival to his throne and terrified the others. Allying with Mihail Szilágy and through him King Matthias Corvinus of Hungary, he had protected his western frontiers. But to the south, despite the treaty of 1460 which both its signatories knew was no more than a temporary truce, the situation was unresolved. There, poised on the Danube, waited Mehmed the Conqueror.

12

ENEMIES OF THE CROSS OF CHRIST
THE FALL OF CONSTANTINOPLE

In the early hours of Thursday 29 May 1453 – the feast day of Saint Theodosia – a way of life came to an end. It was the last of Byzantium and the shock waves reverberated throughout the civilized world, the end of an empire which had lasted almost exactly 1,100 years. Since 2 April, a vast Ottoman army, perhaps numbering as many as 100,000 including camp followers and led by Sultan Mehmed II, had been camped on the landward side of the great city of Constantinople. Prowling the Sea of Marmara and the Golden Horn were the war galleys of the Admiral Hamsa Bey, blocking escape routes by sea and ready to tangle with the Venetian warships which were part of the city's defences.

Those defences were still impressive. There was an inner and outer wall built to facilitate artillery fire, with a deep moat between the two. The inner wall had ninety-six towers, each of which could be held independently of the wall below it. There were eight major gates and a number of posterns which could be used as sallyports for the defenders to reach out and strike the attackers. The perimeter of the city's walls was twenty-eight miles long (the longest in Europe), and the wall itself was enormously thick at the most likely attack points.

There was to be no reprieve for Byzantium. And in many senses, the fall in 1453 was inevitable. The split with Rome in the eleventh century had caused an irretrievable isolation for the city which no poorly attended and half-hearted councils of reconciliation could repair. Almost the only 'Western' nation to defend Constantinople was Venice and its war galleys were penned in by the May of 1453 by the brilliant transportations of Turkish vessels overland on rollers to the Golden Horn. One of the reasons for Turkish military superiority in this period was their capacity to adapt. Already a formidable land force, they copied the style of Venetian warships and created an equally formidable navy that would not be checked until Lepanto in 1571.

Attacks on 12 and 17 May had been beaten back, but the defenders of the city, under the Emperor Constantine Palaeologus and the Genoese condottiere Giovanni Giustiniani, could not have numbered more than seven thousand. When the attack began about half past one in the morning of 29 May, the churches of the city rang their bells, partially as a siren to the inhabitants, partially as a cry to God for salvation. Old men, women and children hurried to the walls, to plug holes with timber and stones, *anything* to keep the invaders out. On the ramparts, all able-bodied men waited in silence as the deafening roar of the Ottoman attack echoed and re-echoed around the moonlit walls. They saw the waves of *bashi-bazouks*, the ragtail mercenaries, Germans, Hungarians, Slavs, Italians, anxious to earn the sultan's promise of a great prize by being the first into the central stockade. Beyond them, a solid line of military police whipped on the first wave with thongs and maces.

For nearly two hours this attack went on, scaling ladders clattering against masonry, culverins and matchlocks roaring in the darkness, guttering torches sailing through the air to ignite thatched roofs and dry timbers. Mehmed pulled back his first wave and sent in his steady Anatolian troops to attack the Gate of Saint Romanus. Their drums and trumpets bellowed and screamed as this disciplined, instinctive force lodged its ladders on Constantinople's walls. By now the Ottoman artillery was having its effects on the inner as well as the outer wall. A giant cannon rocked back on its huge carriage on the ridge of Rumeli Hisar, the Fortress of Europe. It had been dragged there by sixty oxen and fired cannon balls weighing twelve hundredweight for a range of over a mile. The irony was that it had been built by a Hungarian gunsmith named Urban who had offered his services first to the emperor. Constantine, strapped for cash, had turned him down.

Still, the walls held. The emperor himself led a determined counter-attack that drove the Anatolians back from a breach the guns had made. Now Mehmed sent in his janissaries, the elite backbone of his army, fresh troops who would crash through the gaps in the stonework against an exhausted force who had been fighting now for four hours. The condottiere Giustiniani, of whom Mehmed had muttered, 'What would I not give to have that man in my service?',[1] fell back, his breastplate and ribs shattered by a musket ball. Even the emperor's urging could not make him stay and he let his Genoese mercenaries carry him down to a waiting ship, deserting the city as the sheer weight and determination of the janissaries, anxious to find Paradise, forced the defenders to waver.

Like Horatius over the Tiber 'in the brave days of old', Constantine, his cousin Theophilus and comrades Francisco of Toledo and John Dalmata stood in the path of the oncoming hordes. The emperor tore off his eagle insignia and the mob swallowed them all.

Crescents and horsetails now fluttered over the city in the red-gold of a May dawn and Mehmed unleashed his troops for

the customary three days of looting. They killed anyone on
the ramparts or in the streets, hacking down men, women and
children indiscriminately. The blood ran down the steep
cobbled streets that led from Petra to the Golden Horn. No
one made an accurate count of the dead. Women and children
were cut down where they huddled, praying to St Theodosia
even at this late hour to save them. Some were literally torn
apart by *bashi-bazouks* and Anatolians fighting over them like
the spoils of war they were.

Countless icons and relics were smashed and burned, to us
the priceless artefacts of history, to the victorious Turks alien
trinkets without worth. The holiest of all were said to be
hidden in the warren-riddled walls of the Cathedral of the
Holy Wisdom, against the day when Christian Constantinople comes again to Muslim Istanbul. In that Church of
Hagia Sophia, with the sunlight streaming in through its
astonishing glass dome, Mehmed, soon to be styled the
Conqueror, walked to the high altar. He threw a handful of
dust over his turban in humility before Allah for giving him
this victory. He quietly pondered the handful of cowering
priests hiding behind pillars and faced Mecca while an *ulema*,
a Muslim scholar, intoned that there was no God but Allah
and that Mohamed was his prophet.

The head of Constantine Palaeologus was brought to the
sultan's tent. Washed and embalmed, it was placed first on a
pole in the Forum of Augustus in the city, then taken as a prize
around the courts of Islam. The head of Vlad Ţepeş would be
sent to Mehmed's palace twenty-four years later.

The portrait of Mehmed II by Gentile Bellini shows a
sophisticated man with a sharp, aquiline nose, soft brown eyes
and a receding chin disguised by a full, pointed beard. As a
child he had been wayward and idle, his lessons driven home
with the whip. At the age of twelve, he was made regent in
Rumelia while Murad, his father, was fighting enemies in
Karamania. The janissaries despised the child, perhaps because

they saw in him a streak of viciousness wholly missing in his father. As a teenager, he appears to have developed homosexual leanings and one of his targets was Radu Dracula, the hostage brother of the future Impaler. Five days after the fall of Constantinople, he demanded that Constantine's chief minister or *megadux* Lucas Notarus surrender his pretty fourteen-year-old son to the sultan, along with the equally attractive child of Andronicus Cantacuzenius, the Emperor's chief steward. When Notarus refused, Mehmed had both boys decapitated in front of him and then executed him too. Likewise, the son of the chronicler George Phrantzes died because he refused to bend to the sultan's will.

Mehmed had become sultan in the winter of 1451 when Murad died. Spurred on by a god-given belief in his superiority and realizing that Constantinople was actually more bluff than substance, he launched his attack on the city with great preparation, and its capture turned him into the most popular of the Ottoman rulers. There is no doubt that Mehmed was the real founder of the Ottoman Empire. He called himself the 'Sovereign of Two Lands', Rumelia and Anatolia, 'and of the Two Seas', the Mediterranean and the Black. As Jason Goodwin says in *Lords of the Horizons*:

> Turnstile of the continents, seal of empires, geomantic paradise, Constantinople was a place of absolutes. It was either very hot or very cold. Here Europe and Asia met.[2]

After May 1453, the city did not immediately become Istanbul, but Konstantiniyye, and by 1455 Mehmed had completed his astonishing new palace in the old Tauri forum within its walls on the site of an abandoned monastery. He did not like it and began four years later on a new one overlooking the Sea of Marmara that would become the legendary Topkapi on a hill of olive groves, the Palace of Felicity, a paradise on earth. Today, thousands of tourists wait in patient lines to see the jewels, the clothes, the kitchens and the courtyards of the sultans. A military band plays and the palace is home to hundreds of beautiful, well-fed cats.

Vlad Țepeș was in Sibiu when he heard of Constantinople's fall. He probably heard it from Venetian sailors struggling home via the mountain pass at Turnu Roșu. He would have learnt how Hamsa Bey, the Turkish admiral, had sunk their galleys, how Mehmed had ordered the impaling of their captain, Antonio Rizzo, and had his body displayed on a stake in full view of the city walls.

Mehmed *el fatih*, the conqueror, would fail to take either Belgrade or Rhodes in the years ahead before Vlad Țepeș, Voivod of Wallachia and Lord of Amlaș and Făgăraș, decided to attack him along the Danube. In 1459, the humanist Pope Pius II, who as Eneo de Piccolomini had already a reputation as a traveller, scholar, writer and man-about-many-towns, launched a new crusade. It was a singularly bad omen that on 1 June, when his congress opened at Mantua, not a single delegate turned up. The fresco in the Cathedral of Siena, showing a less-than-rapt papal audience, is based on events four months later, by which time some of Europe's leaders had sent their emissaries. The point was that crusading as an ideal of chivalry, on a par with the quest for the grail, was dead. There was no Peter the Hermit now to lead the dewy-eyed Christians across lands longing to be free and to be part of the kingdom of Christ. Everyone now knew that the Red Sea would not part for them, as the strange, mania-driven children of the crusade of 1212 had naively believed. In most states of Europe, nationalism was fast becoming reality – Christendom was as vague and obsolete a term as the Flood.

What many of these self-absorbed rulers chose to ignore, however, was that ultimately the Ottoman threat was a threat to them all. Was it only Pius who had noticed that Mehmed the Conqueror was now calling himself the Eastern Roman Emperor because he worshipped in the mosque of Hagia Sophia? His war fleet of nearly eighty galleys commanded the

Black Sea, forcing tribute from the Genoese colonies on its shores and from the kingdom of Trebizond and the Romanian principality of Moldavia. His white-helmeted janissaries had smashed their way into Smeredevo, the last Christian Serbian stronghold and all the lands south of the Danube were in Ottoman hands like a great stain spreading west. Pius warned:

> Every victory for [Mehmed] will be a stepping-stone to another, until after subjecting all the Christians of the west, he will have destroyed the Gospel of Christ and imposed that of his false prophet over the entire world.[3]

The delegates who heard him, from Hungary, Burgundy, Milan, shuffled in embarrassment, their 'elsewhere' faces apparent in the Siena fresco. The Holy Roman Emperor, Frederick III, promised 32,000 foot soldiers and 10,000 horses. They were never forthcoming. Gregor von Heimburg from 'the Germanies' muttered about internal unrest. Alfonso the Magnanimous of Spain, who might have been earnest in support, had died the previous June while planning an attack on Genoa. His illegitimate son Ferrante was embroiled in a succession squabble over Naples with Charles VII of France, who in turn was pinned down keeping his obnoxious son Louis off the throne of France. The English, torn by the Wars of the Roses that would decimate their nobility, sent no one at all. Sigismundo Malatesta, the condottiere from Rimini, summed up the feeling of most of the Italian states when he said, 'I serve him who pays me more.'[4] In the following year he was paid to fight the Pope himself and Pius excommunicated him.

Of the Western powers, only Venice, already threatened and damaged by the Turks, offered a genuine force – 8,000 sailors for their galleys, 50,000 horses and 20,000 foot soldiers. The catch was that they demanded money from the papal coffers to meet the cost of all this. And Pius' coffers were empty. George Poděbradý, the Hussite King of Bohemia, had his own internal troubles to sort out and, in view of his faith, his relations with Rome were strained; Pius' successor, Paul II, would excommunicate him in 1464. Nearer to Wallachia, Casimir the Great, King of Poland, was embroiled in war with the Teutonic Order, driving its knights west across Prussia in the previous year. Ivan III, the Grand Duke of Muscovy, had his hands full with religious dissent and the Tartar tribes still raiding his eastern frontier. Stefan of Moldavia, the cousin whom Ţepeş had helped to the throne two years earlier, was going head to head with Matthias Corvinus over the Hungarian king's support of those who had murdered his father.

It must have struck Pius with great irony that Eastern Muslims, as appalled by the warlike Ottomans as he was, should have been the most enthusiastic to join his crusade. Mehmed's brother-in-law Uzun Hazan, of the White Sheep Uzbeks of Iran, promised Pius 5,000 battle-hardened troops. Dadian Liprait, King of Mingrelia on the Black Sea, offered men. The Lord of Karaman in Trebizond spoke of 40,000. The irony is of course that if all three offers had become reality, then Mehmed would have faced a force three times the size of his own and, as with Bayezid the Thunderbolt and Timur-i-Leng, the Ottoman subjugation of the Balkans would have come to a crunching full stop.

At Mantua, in January 1460, Pius declared a three year crusade. Anyone who took the cross would have his sins pardoned. He would be a warrior for Christ. A hundred thousand gold ducats would be raised somehow and, like the Dragon Society, the Order of St Mary of Bethlehem was inaugurated to give the whole venture holy substance.

The Morea, the last Byzantine stronghold outside Constantinople, fell to the Turks in March 1461. By that time, not a single gun had been limbered, not a single sword sharpened. A number of potential crusaders, including Matthias Corvinus, had accepted Pius' gold and they were doing precisely nothing. Alone of the Christian leaders, Vlad Ţepeş went to war.

Romanian historians have explained the Impaler's motives in 1462 as a genuine crusading urge, upholding the oath he inherited via his father from the statutes of the Dragon Order to defeat the 'enemies of the cross of Christ'. The truth is that Ţepeş was a realist. Despite the treaty with the Turks two years earlier, geography and history combined to tell the voivod that Mehmed was a megalomaniac who would never be content to have his horizons limited by the Danube. Beyond the Danube lay Wallachia. And Ţepeş knew that his army was a fraction of the size of the Conqueror's. Unsure, as he was, of Hungarian help from Matthias Corvinus, his only hope was to strike first and strike hard.

Several historians have assumed that Mehmed's aim was to make Wallachia a *pashalik* or province of his empire. But this does not seem to have been the case. Technically, Ţepeş was already a vassal of the Conqueror and should have continued to pay him an annual tribute of 10,000 galben and 500 boys under the *devşirme* system. The voivod, perhaps genuinely busy with subjugation of the boyars and the Saxon cities, had paid nothing since 1459 and flatly refused to send any Wallachian children. The point was that, alone of the Christian rulers, Ţepeş knew Mehmed personally. He knew his vanity, his ambition and knew exactly how to provoke him to a fight. In November 1461, he sent a letter to the Conqueror explaining that he could not pay the tribute, neither could he pay it in person at Constantinople as had been the custom. The dust was still settling over his Transylvanian dispute; the time was not right:

> for if I should leave my country my political opponents would invite the Hungarian king to rule over my domains.[5]

Tursun Bey, secretary to the sultan's council and subsequently historian to Mehmed's successor, Bayezid II, explained:

> He [Ţepeş] said he had no more resources to pay the tribute, for the Hungarian army was strong and represented an obstacle

in his way. He also said the Sublime Porte [Constantinople] was
too far for him to come and that he had spent everything he had
in battles that year ... He neither came nor paid the tribute.
Then he had to be punished and destroyed.[6]

Ţepeş had visited the Turks on a diplomatic mission before, to
Varna when he was eleven years old, with his father. Those
years may well have warped his life and he was not going back.
With Mehmed at Constantinople and no doubt whispering in
the sultan's ear in the councils of the Inner Palace was Radu
cel Frumos, Ţepeş' younger brother, now twenty-six and
probably as ambitious and proud as the Impaler he had not
seen for twelve years.

   Konstantin Mihailović, a janissary who had entered the
sultan's service under the boy-levy, wrote:

We marched forward to the Wallachian land after Dracula; and
his brother ahead of us.[7]

In an extraordinary duel of wits Ţepeş allowed himself to be
lured to the fortress of Giurgiu on the Danube, which his
grandfather had built and the Turks had captured, in order to
show his good faith to Mehmed to whom he had promised, in
the fullness of time 'many children and horses ... and I will
also ... add gifts of my own'.[8] This was in accord with Article
One of the treaty of 1460 but in fact he was well aware that
the sultan's emissaries, the admiral at the Siege of Constantinople and now his chief falconer, Hamsa Bey and Thomas
Catavolinos, a Byzantine renegade, were planning to take him
prisoner. He explained what happened in a letter to Matthias
Corvinus, whose aid he still desperately wanted, on 11
February 1462:

... the Turks, the most cruel enemies of the Cross of Christ,
have sent their highest ranking messengers to convince us not
to keep the peace and the agreements that we made with your

Majesty ... By the grace of God, while we were going to that border [the Danube] we found out about their deceit and trickery and it was us who captured Hamza-Bey ... near the fortress that is called Giurgiu ...⁹

With him, the voivod had brought a cavalry force, evidently in Turkish armour because they were able to intermingle with the crowd in the fortress and take it: 'The Turks opened the gates of the fortress at the shouts of our men ...' Ţepeş burned Giurgiu, one of the most important of the Ottoman strongholds on the river, as it had been his grandfather's.

And we killed the men and women, old and young, who lived from Oblucita and Novoselo, where the Danube flows into the sea, to Rahova, which is near Chilia, down to the villages of Samovit and Ghighen, 23,884 Turks and Bulgarians in all, not including those who were burned in their houses and whose heads were not presented to our officials.¹⁰

The Impaler's attack along the Danube took place in a winter that was bitterly cold. The sluggish river was frozen for much of the 800 miles his cavalry covered in two weeks, so that the horsemen could strike at bridgeheads and crossing places and ports like Turnu and cross into the forests of the Wallachian plain before the Turks could organize their defence. Mehmed himself together with the bulk of his army was tied up by the White Sheep Uzbeks in the east and Ţepeş for now had time on his side. His letter to Corvinus went on:

First, in the places called Oblucita and Novoselo there were killed 1350; and 6,840 at Darstor, Cartal and Dridopotrom; likewise 343 at Orsova and 840 were killed at Vectrem; 630 were killed at Turtucaia; likewise 210 were killed at Marotin; 6,414 were killed at Giurgiu on both sides of the river and the fortress on the Danube was conquered and taken. The commander of the fortress was killed ... and the commander of Nicopolis, the son of Firuz-Beg was also captured and beheaded; and of the

Turks stationed at Nicopolis, all the most important were killed with him. Likewise 384 were killed at Turnu, Batin and Novigrad; at Sistov and in two other villages near it, 410 were killed; likewise, the crossing point at Nicopolis was burned and completely destroyed; the same at Samovit; and at Ghighen 1,138 were killed; at Rahova 1,460 ... and the crossing point was completely burned ...[11]

With what may be an example of Dracula's black humour and what may be the greatest example of understatement in medieval history, he concluded:

Therefore, your Majesty should know that we have broken our peace with [the Turks].[12]

Hamsa Bey and Thomas Catavolinos were marched in shackles back to Tîrgovişte and impaled on especially high stakes.

Ţepeş knew that his action would whip Mehmed into a fury and that full-scale retaliation would only be a matter of time. His letter to Corvinus made the position clear:

When the weather permits, that is to say in the spring, they will come with evil intentions and with all their power.[13]

The voivod's suggestion was that Corvinus should send his army (he was not expecting the king's presence in person) to reach Transylvania by St George's Day (23 April). If that was impossible, then the troops and arsenals from the Saxon cities would be a help:

And if, God forbid, it ends badly for us, and our little country is lost ... it will be a loss for all Christianity.

One of his most trusted lieutenants, Radu Farma, galloped through the snow-drifted passes as best he could to reach Buda.

Europe was ablaze. The half-hearted crusaders could not believe the Impaler's nerve. The man was getting results. Pietro Tommasi, Venetian ambassador to the Hungarian court at Buda wrote home on 4 March, 'The Hungarian king will do all he can to help Dracula.' Travelling home to England from his elongated 'grand tour', the pilgrim William of Wey wrote that in Rhodes:

the military men ... upon hearing of Dracula's campaign, had Te Deums sung to the praise and honour of God who had granted such victories ...[14]

But Ţepeş needed halberdiers, pikemen, arquebusiers and light cavalry, not te deums. He sent emissaries to the Tartars of the Crimea, to Armenia and Georgia, all of whom lay in the potential path of Ottoman expansion.

But it was Corvinus he really wanted. Sadly, the son of the White Knight was no crusader. Cautious and clever, Corvinus made procrastination an art. He had been elected king four years earlier, but without the famous crown of St Stephen his role was neither fully legal nor sanctioned by God. And that crown was in the hands of the Emperor, Frederick III. Much of the cash that the hopeful Pius had sent to Buda for crusading purposes would be spent on buying it – and the emperor did not come cheap. For the time being, the only Hungarians at Ţepeş' disposal were those in the garrison at Chilia on the Danube delta, and their presence there would cost the voivod a valuable ally.

The size of the army that Mehmed the Conqueror led against the Impaler can never be known with any accuracy. The Greek Laonic Chalkondyles, commenting on the invasion of Wallachia in the early Mohamedan spring, wrote:

People say that this army was very large, second only to the one the Emperor took against Byzantium. This camp is said to have been more beautiful than other camps and to have been well supplied with weapons and equipment, the army being as large as two hundred and fifty thousand men.[15]

Tursun Bey, better informed perhaps and closer to the action, wrote years later:

> When the spring of the year 866 [1462] came, the colours of triumph waved on their way to Wallachia. An army of almost thirty tümen (300,000) crossed the Danube; the land of Wallachia shone in the presence of the Sultan . . . The whole sky seemed to move. The army looked like powerful waves on the sea.[16]

Unfortunately for us, of course, Tursun Bey was in the propaganda, not to say the poetry, business and the educated guess of Tomassi, the Venetian ambassador at Buda, of 90,000 is probably more realistic. Even this conservative estimate, however, gave the Turks three times the Impaler's strength.

One who knew this army well shortly before Vlad Ţepeş became its hostage as a child was Georgius de Hungaria:

> When recruiting for the army is begun, they gather with such readiness and speed you might think they are invited to a wedding and not to war. They gather within a month in the order they are summoned [Matthias Corvinus's crusaders took nearly a year], the infantrymen separately from the cavalrymen, all of them with their appointed chiefs, in the same order which they use at encampments and when preparing for battle . . . with such enthusiasm that men put themselves forward in place of their neighbours and those left at home feel that an injustice has been done to them. They claim they will be happier if they die on the battlefield among the spears and arrows of the enemy than at home among the tears and slavering of the old women. Those who die like this are not mourned, but are hailed as saints and victors . . .[17]

A detailed estimate of the size and structure of Mehmed's army comes from 1475, the year in which Vlad Ţepeş was unleashed against them for a second time. Then there were 6,000 janissaries, 3,000 *kapikuli* (the sultan's personal cavalry), 22,000 European cavalry and 17,000 Anatolian *sipahi*. By the time of Suleiman the Magnificent and his defeat of Hungary at Mohacs in 1526, the size of the Ottoman army had doubled.

At the heart of Mehmed's army were the janissaries, a highly trained and efficient body of infantry whose origins may lie in the reign of Orhan, the son of Osman who founded the Ottoman state. These men were co-opted by means of the *devşirme*, the boy levy, and their rigid education, which would be criticised as brainwashing today, made them eager to accept the Koran and the sultan's orders. Tolerant and sympathetic to other faiths in the areas they conquered, the Turks welcomed 'Christian' renegades into their service – Bogomil heretics from Serbia; refugees from Constantinople; even Jews who found a greater acceptance from the followers of Allah than from Christians. Boys selected for the *Acemi Oglan* or military service were chosen for their bearing and strength. Honesty, loyalty and good manners were their watchwords and they learned riding, wrestling, archery and sword-play exactly as the Dracula brothers had learned it at Edirne under Murad II. The better class here were groomed for the sultan's personal cavalry, the *kapikuli*, which had parallels in various households of the kings of Western Europe.[18] Those who had not qualified were given specialist training as armourers, gunners and drivers. Even the 'ordinary' janissaries completed a six-year training that included mathematics.

The ritual of joining the janissary corps was deeply symbolic. Graduates, every bit as proud and well trained as those at Sandhurst or West Point today, lined up in front of their company officer and were given the tall, distinctive white cap of their corps. Each man would kiss the officer's hand, saluting him as 'travelling companion'.

The janissaries were organized into companies known as *artas*, consisting of about fifty men, and the officer ranks had curiously culinary titles. The sultan was 'the father who feeds us', the colonel was 'the soup maker', the major 'the master cook'. The junior officers were 'head scullions'. There were 'barrack-room chiefs' and 'heads of water distribution'.[19]

The janissaries on the march must have been an incredible sight. At their head was carried the *Imam Azam*, the white silk banner of the faith. Inscribed in gilt curling letters was the legend, 'We give you victory and a sparkling victory. It is God who helps us and His help is effective. Oh, Mohammed, you have brought joyful news to the Believers.' Other banners depicted stars, crescents, moons, hands, boots, spearheads and animals. Traditionally, a day ahead of the army marched the carriers of the *tug*, the horsetail banner. One wonders if the Impaler cut them down in the Danube's reeds.

Bertrandon de la Brocquière saw these men in action. They wore:

> two or three thin, ankle-length cotton robes one over the other, for a coat they wear a felt robe called a *capinat*. It is light and very water-proof ... They wear knee-high boots and wide breeches ... into which they stuff all their robes so that they will not get in the way when they are fighting or travelling ...[20]

The *capinat* was woven in wool by Jews from Thesalonika; the *bork* or white cap was fronted by a spoon, another culinary symbol. Officers' jackets were trimmed with fur of the fox, sable, lynx or squirrel. Boots were always of red leather, except for the senior officers who wore yellow.

The weaponry of the janissaries varied enormously and reflects their ability to learn fast from their enemies. For long distance killing the curved short-bow was carried by infantry and cavalry alike. The superb drawing of a seated officer by the Italian artist Gentile Bellini, who painted Mehmed, shows just such a weapon, with quiver and arrows slung from a waist belt. At close quarters, the curved sabre, with a sharp point and single-edged blade was the favourite, but daggers, either straight or curved, were also carried. Ram's head maces and murderous-looking battle-axes could crunch through sallet (helmet) and skull of a Wallachian and any one of a variety of pole-axes like the glaive or halberd could rip a fully-armoured boyar out of the saddle and disembowel him in seconds. Mail shirts were worn when pitched battle was likely, with reinforcing plates of iron on the chest, back and arms. Most impressive of all was the janissaries' rapid assimilation of firearms. They probably first saw them in use by Hunyadi at Varna in 1444 and called them blowpipes. They were the clumsy forerunners of the matchlock, the first recorded use of which is in 1475. But Europeans marvelled at the janissaries' aim with these 'inventions of the devil'.

The other units of Mehmed's army, his cavalry and the outriders of Anatolia, were less disciplined and reliable perhaps, but good soldiers for all that. They had the advantage over European armies of the best horses in the world – the small, fast and patient Arabs. The cavalrymen were skilled archers, firing from the saddle at the gallop, wearing mail shirts and conical copper helmets with adjustable nasals. Known as *sipahi*, they wore animal skins over their armour, probably as much to reduce the heat on the metal as to appear fierce in sight of the enemy. Most of them hoped to be *timar* holders, owners of plots of land similar to the feudum or fief of Western feudalism. 'Take a Turk from the saddle,' ran an old saying, 'and he becomes a bureaucrat.' De la Brocquière described Turkish soldiers as follows:

> They are diligent and get up early in the morning. They are frugal when on the road and live on only a little food, a little badly baked bread and some raw meat, dried a little in the sun, or some curdled or otherwise prepared milk, some cheese or honey or grapes or fruit or grass, or a handful of flour, from which they make porridge for six or eight men a day.[21]

With the soldiers, no doubt at a respectful distance, came the camp followers that dogged any medieval army. In fact, they were the essential 'support services' of the army, the sword-cutlers, bowyers, blacksmiths, silk merchants, pharmacists, bakers and tailors without whom the military effort would soon grind to a halt.

A vital service was provided by the Ottoman equivalent of regimental bands, the *Mehterhane*. Using drums, cymbals, trumpets and clarinets, they stood on the field of battle in a semi-circle around the seated kettle-drummer. Cavalry units had mounted bands, some of these with the drums slung across the humps of Mehmed's dromedaries. Most of the instrumentalists were Greek, but the volume had an important psychological role. Evliya Celebi, writing two centuries after Ţepeş, stated:

> Five hundred trumpeters raised such a sound that the planet
> Venus began to dance and the skies reverberated . . .[22]

We know the names of Mehmed's troop commanders who crossed the Danube in late September 1462. There was the Grand Vizier Mahmud and with him Evrenos Ali, Tura-hanoglu Omer, Nesuh of Albania, Delioglu Umur of Janina and, most chillingly of all perhaps, in his borrowed Eastern armour, Radu cel Frumos, Dracula the Handsome. Their target was not the subjugation of Wallachia, but the removal of its voivod, 'the wicked horseman' as Tursun Bey called him, 'that bloody tyrant and merciless Infidel', Vlad Ţepeş.

The nature of the Impaler's army is far more obscure than that of the Conqueror. Many foreign visitors had the opportunity to observe the Ottomans first hand and were fascinated by them. Wallachia, on the other hand, was a small frontier state lost in its own mountains. It did not possess the grandeur of the Hungarian or Polish armies and warranted little comment from contemporaries. Of those who wrote about Ţepeş' 1462 campaign along the Danube, William of

Wey heard about it secondhand on the island of Rhodes; Chalkondyles, Dukas, Kritoboulos of Imbros and George Phrantzes were Byzantine bystanders. The others were Turks or Turkish supporters who were either there – Tursun Bey and Constantin Mihailović – with their own agenda; or later court historians who simply copied the earlier accounts. All of them concentrated, with reason, on the Impaler's incredible tactics and say almost nothing about the composition of his army.

Ţepeş himself commanded his troops from the front and there is no doubt about either his extraordinary courage or his skill as a soldier. We have no depictions of the Impaler on the march, but it is likely that he wore, in battle at least, the expensive fluted plate armour of 'Gothic' type. Such suits cost a king's ransom and the finest examples come from Augsburg, Nuremberg (where his father had been invested with the Dragon insignia), Landshut and the Austrian city of Innsbruck. These Gothic suits were the best examples of the armourer's craft, light and hinged to allow total freedom of movement. The Impaler would have used a lance for initial contact with enemy cavalry, a wooden, iron-tipped pole fifteen feet long and for closer work a battle-axe, mace or sword. This last was the knightly weapon par excellence; the usual simple 'cruciform' type had a wide, tapering, double-edged blade, a hilt made for use with one or both hands and a slim quillon (cross-piece). There was already the tendency by the 1460s to curve these quillons to form better protection for the hand. On the march, it is likely that Ţepeş wore only part of this armour, perhaps with a leather jerkin or jack. We know that he dressed as a Turk from time to time, both as a subterfuge (as at Giurgiu) and also as a result of living among them in his teenage years.

His personal bodyguard, smaller certainly than Mehmed's *kapikuli*, were mercenaries and few of them were Wallachian. Certainly by 1475, a hardcore of these had been lent to him by his cousin Stefan of Moldavia, although, as we shall see, this had not been the case in the earlier campaign. Some boyars certainly rode with Ţepeş – the messenger Radu Farma was one – and they came with their retinues much after the fashion of the feudal levies of Western Europe. The retinues' loyalty to Wallachia itself was questionable because they were taught to follow their lord and to watch for his banner in battle. In an age before true nationalism few Christians could match the religious zeal of the sultan's janissaries. The boyars may well have worn 'German' armour, but over it they still dressed in their long Byzantine robes.

The nature of the terrain in which he was fighting and of the campaign in which he fought meant that Ţepeş relied far more than the Turks on his cavalry. We cannot be sure about these horsemen. A century after the Impaler, it was impossible to distinguish Wallachian horsemen from the Hungarians to their west and the Russians to the east. After the Wallachian victory over the Turks at Calugareni in 1595, virtually the entire army was mounted. They had learned their skills from the Turks themselves, training their horses to walk like camels, moving both legs on one side at the same time. Three years after Ţepeş' death, Matthias Corvinus wrote to King Frederick of Naples who had been patronizing enough to send him a Spanish riding master:

> With the horses which we trained ourselves we defeated the Turks, subjected Siberia and vanquished all before us, honourably by means of our own horses. We have no desire for horses that hop about with bent hocks in the Spanish fashion; we do not want them even as a pastime, still less for serious business.[23]

Like Corvinus' own armoured *hussars* (light cavalry), Ţepeş' horsemen probably rode the tough little sturdy ponies of the Tarpan breed, now largely localized to Poland, of thirteen or fourteen hands high, normally dun in colour with a pronounced dorsal stripe. In today's Romania, such horses are called Hutuls, ideal for mountain work, sure-footed and needing very little water. They are related to the wild Przewalski breed with its two extra chromosomes.

The rest of the army comprised fighting men raised under a sort of *levée en masse* not known in Western Europe. Like any medieval army, it was supported by its camp followers and numbers of the whole are as uncertain as Mehmed's host. Fedor Kuritsyn talks of 30,900; Domenico Balbi, the former Venetian ambassador to Constantinople, 30,000; the ever-conservative Pietro Tommasi, 24,000. We have no way of measuring the accuracy of this, but a certain proportion of the Impaler's army was made up of men from the towns, from Sibiu and Braşov, however reluctantly bearing in mind the voivod's dealings with them, from Tîrgsov and Tîrgovişte, from the newly-burgeoning Bucharest which lay on the Danubian plain, right in the path of Mehmed's invasion force. It is possible that the richer Saxon towns had the money to pay foreign mercenaries – few armies were without them – like the French and Burgundian *Jacquerie*, the Italian *Condottieri* and, a new force emerging to strike terror into cavalryman and foot soldier alike, the brightly coloured, pike-carrying Swiss *Landsknechte*.[24]

Ţepeş had two advantages over the Turks. First was the element of surprise which had made the Danube raids so successful. Now, of course, that was gone and his was essentially a defender's role against the Ottoman invasion. Second, he knew the territory over which battles and skirmishes would be fought better than Mehmed. True, the Turks had Radu with them, but we have no evidence that the man was a soldier and he had not seen his homeland for nearly twenty years and never as a man, with an adult's perception of things. Ţepeş used scouts, local men who knew every ravine and precipice, the water sources and the fertile villages, to go ahead of his army. Especially, he placed them along the river bank. Throughout that September of 1462, the Danube was scanned day and night.

The drill used by the bulk of the voivod's army, which would have been composed of foot-soldiers, was probably little different from the Ordinances of Charles the Bold of Burgundy, themselves written, usually late at night by the insomniac duke, during the 1460s:

> In order that the troops may be better trained and exercised ... the captains of the squadrons are to ... practise charging with the lance, keeping in close formation ... to withdraw on command, to rally ... and to withstand a charge ... The pikemen must be made to advance in close formation ... [and] kneel so that the archers can shoot over the said pikemen as if over a wall. The archers must also learn to place themselves back to back in double defence or in a square or a circle, always with the pikemen outside them to withstand the charge of the enemy horse.[25]

We have no record of the books that Ţepeş owned, but perhaps one of them was the popular *Regulae Bellorum Generales* of the Roman writer Vegetius who said, 'Only a few men are brave by nature – good training increases their numbers.'[26]

The Wallachian foot soldiers wore long white tunics tied at the waist with belts and thick animal hides to ward off Turkish lance thrusts or sword cuts. This was a variant of the jack or brigandine worn throughout Europe, a sleeved garment made of up to thirty layers of wool and buckled under the armpits or down the front. A sensible foot soldier would have worn some kind of sallet or kettle-hat, an iron headpiece with sloping sides to deflect blows.

A curious reference to Ţepeş' army can be found in the Saxon stories which began to circulate shortly after the 1462 campaign. He forced a contingent of gypsies into his fighting units, although this was probably the normal enlistment process of the *levée en masse* of the time, and:

> clothed them all in cowhide and similarly their horses as well. And as they came upon one another, the Turkish horses shied

away and fled because of the cowhide clothing which their horses did not like.[27]

The story goes on to recount the deaths of both retreating Turks and attacking gypsies by drowning in the nearest water supply, so this incident *may* refer to the parched summer of 1462. It is, however, a classic of the anomalies and non-sequiturs of the 'horror' stories. It is highly unlikely that a gang of pressed men, which the tale says the gypsies were, would have been given expensive horses and the strange reference to cow-hide frightening the *sipahi*'s horses makes no sense at all.

Like the Ottomans, the weapons carried by the Impaler's troops would have varied enormously. It is possible that some of the archers used crossbows, highly favoured by the Germans, the Italians and the Swiss. Relatively cumbersome and slow to fire, these weapons fired quarrels or bolts, short, wooden-flighted arrows that could punch a hole in the most expensive plate armour. Modern experiments with reconstructed bows have produced an average firing rate of four bolts a minute. Other archers would have carried the longbow, made famous by the English, traditionally made of supple yew and six feet long. The arrows, a 'cloth-yard' in length with shafts of ash or witch-hazel and goose-feather flights, could reach a target 350 yards away. An experienced bowman could release fifteen arrows a minute. Ţepeş' pikemen carried the same halberds, glaives and bills as their Turkish opponents, and daggers or short swords for in-fighting. Handling a pole-axe was difficult and took precision timing, especially being able to hook the twelve-foot weapons into the neck or armpit of a well-armoured opponent.

We do not know what artillery the Impaler had with him. The towns of Braşov and Sibiu made guns and it is conceivable that their guildsmen brought with them one or two bombards, or cannon. But these guns were usually used for sieges, their stone or iron shot smashing through masonry as the huge guns of the Turks had done at Constantinople. One such monster, called Griete, was fired in 1411 at Bourges, the Duke of Berry's capital. An eyewitness wrote, 'when it was fired the thunderous noise could be heard four miles away and terrorised local inhabitants as if it were some reverberation from Hell.'[28] The only recorded uses of handguns by the Wallachians refer to their firing as the Turks crossed the Danube and it may be that Țepeș dispensed with them later. His was a hit and run campaign, a masterly piece of guerrilla warfare; and unreliable firearms, whatever their weight, would merely slow him down.

The rations for Țepeș' men would probably have been less frugal than those of Mehmed's. Unlike the Muslim Turks, the Orthodox Wallachians drank alcohol carried in barrels or goat-skin sacks. Bread, biscuits, pork, beans and cheese would have been their staple diet, but raids on villages in Turkish-held Bulgaria produced chickens, eggs and beef. Hunger was a weapon in itself and Țepeș used it very effectively against an army whose very rank titles were linked with food. And throughout the long, hot summer, his men lay in the Danube's reeds and watched and waited.

13

IMPALER PRINCE
THE 1462 CAMPAIGN

In the first week of June 1462, Mehmed's horse-tail advance guard reached Vidin, one of the few crossing points of the Danube the Impaler had failed to destroy. The Grand Vizier Mahmoud had sent these scouts ahead to reconnoitre and they had come back with the depressing news of the extent of Ţepeş' raids along the river. There is some confusion in the accounts as to how the Turks got there. Laonic Chalkondyles refers to their ships, as though they sailed or rowed up the Danube, which is entirely feasible given their command of the Black Sea and its being turned, as the cliché has it, into an 'Ottoman lake' but the Turkish chronicles themselves make no mention of a seaborne attack. Constantin Mihailović of Ostrovitza, a Serbian janissary, however, makes the point clear:

> When night began to fall, we climbed into our boats and floated down the Danube and crossed over to the other side several miles below the place where Dracula's army was stationed.

There we dug ourselves trenches so that cavalry could not harm us. After that we crossed back over to the other side and transported the janissaries over the Danube and when the entire infantry had crossed, then we prepared and set out gradually against Dracula's army, together with the artillery and other equipment that we had brought with us.

This crossing was possibly a second attempt, the Wallachians having driven the Turks back in an earlier clash with volleys of arrows. But this seems unlikely. Ţepeş knew the Turks' propensity for night attacks (he was soon to use the same tactic himself) and surely would have not let the enemy get such a foothold on the Wallachian bank. Mihailović continues:

Having halted we set up the cannon but not in time to stop three hundred janissaries from being killed.

At some point, Ţepeş' scouts down river must have spotted the amphibious landing and the Impaler struck. What is so refreshing about Constantin's account is its honesty, as opposed to the clear propaganda of the Turkish sources. He writes:

The Sultan was very upset by this . . . as he witnessed the great battle from the other side of the Danube and was unable to come over himself. He was afraid that all the janissaries might be killed.

This was Ţepeş' best bet – to attack the Turks while most of their army was still across the river. Amphibious operations and river crossings were notoriously difficult and the army on water, however temporarily, had the disadvantage. Ţepeş had not been caught napping; he was simply outgunned. Constantin went on:

Seeing our side was greatly weakening we defended ourselves with the hundred and twenty guns which we had brought and

fired so often that we repelled the prince's army and greatly
strengthened our position. And Dracula, seeing that he could
not prevent the crossing, withdrew.

It is this that makes it unlikely that the Impaler had much
artillery with him. Constantin does not mention it at all, but
perhaps against Mehmed's impressive cannonade of a probable
120 pieces, the Wallachian guns were too puny to commit to
paper. The sultan crossed the Danube and distributed 30,000
coins to his troops, a bonus over and above the *ulufe* or
thrice-yearly salary paid to the janissaries.

Now, the die was cast. Țepeș was facing an army, organized
and far better equipped than his own and probably three times
its size. He had received no reply to his letter asking help from
Matthias Corvinus in February and trouble was breaking out
to his north-east, and from an unexpected source, from his
cousin Stefan of Moldavia. Chalkondyles takes up the story:

> [Dracula] divided his army in two, keeping one part with him
> and sending the other against the prince of Black Bogdania
> [Moldavia] to keep him back if he tried to invade the country.
> Because this prince [Stefan] had had a misunderstanding with
> Vlad he was at war with him and, sending messages to Sultan
> Mehmed, he said that he was also ready to join him in his war
> against Vlad.[1]

Because Chalkondyles is the only source that contends that
Stefan offered his services to Mehmed, most Romanian
historians have doubted its validity. Kurt Treptow, however,
is quite prepared to believe it, less in the spirit that Stefan
joined forces with the Infidel against his own cousin, but that
he put Moldavia and his own interests first. In no sense were
the two principalities one – the fact that each had its own ruler
is proof of that. This was not yet an age of nationalism,
although some Romanian historians would turn Țepeș into a
nationalist; nor, as we have seen, was the unifying concept

of Christendom particularly strong. Essentially, fifteenth-century politics was a melting pot and it was every ruler for himself. Even so, it casts doubt on most historians' assertions that Stefan was truly a 'great' ruler in the accepted sense of the term. It also makes nonsense of the title *Athleta Christi* (Christ's Champion) given to him by the Pope.

Stefan's bone of contention with Ţepeş was the fortress of Chilia on the Danube delta. It was vitally important to the Moldavians that they, rather than the Impaler's people, control it. On 2 April 1462, the governor of Caffa wrote to Casimir of Poland, highly concerned that these Christian princes were at loggerheads:

> I understand that Stefan, Prince of Moldavia . . . is fighting with Vlad voivod who makes happy war with the Turks. This quarrel not only helps the Sultan but, what is more dangerous, if the Turks enter in these two Wallachias, it will be a great danger for us and for other neighbouring countries.[2]

But it went beyond the acquisition of Chilia. On the broader canvas, Ţepeş and Stefan had drifted apart since their time at Suceava when the Impaler was on the run. He had now thrown in his lot squarely with Matthias Corvinus and Hungary; Stefan sided with Casimir of Poland and paid a yearly tribute to the sultan.

The Moldavian-German Chronicle quoted in Treptow's *Essays* reads:

> In the month of June of the 22nd day the voivod Stefan came in front of Chilia, but he could not take it and was shot in the left ankle . . .[3]

Domenico Balbi confirmed the military pincer movement:

> the naval fleet of the Sultan, together with the Prince of Moldavia, went to attack the fortress of Chilia, they stayed there for eight days, but they were unable to do anything.[4]

In January 1465, Stefan finally took the fortress at the second attempt, but by that time the harm had been done. Ţepeş had been obliged, back in the summer of 1462, to detach 7,000 men to his eastern frontier to defend it against possible attack – that was 7,000 he did not have to stand against Mehmed's janissaries.

Ţepeş' war of attrition now began. Outnumbered, abandoned by one ally, Corvinus, and fighting another, Stefan, he was forced to employ desperate tactics. As his army withdrew northward, skirmishing with Mehmed's cavalry on the flanks and his janissaries in the centre, he carried out a scorched earth campaign, burning villages and crops in their pre-harvest glory. Boyar and peasant alike grabbed what belongings they could and went with him, leaving nothing but destruction for the Turks to find – burned-out villages and demolished walls. Animal corpses were thrust into wells and used to dam rivers. Artificial marshes were created on the Danube's flood plain to slow the Ottoman advance and pits were dug with sharpened stakes in their bases to catch the unwary horseman who rode too fast and too far. Michael Ducas wrote:

> Thus, having crossed the Danube and advanced for seven days, Mehmet II found no man, nor any significant animal and nothing to eat or drink.[5]

Just as the previous winter had been particularly cold, so the summer of 1462 was particularly hot.[6] The humid continental climate of Wallachia in the Impaler's time was probably much the same as it is now, the intervening centuries having been particularly cold. Because of this, the usual four seasons are today often taken merely as two – summer and winter. The highest ever recorded temperature, at Ruse on the Danube, in July was 108°F (42°C). In the mountains, the air was cooler and the rainfall heavier, but after the cold winter of 1461–2, there could still have been snow in the ravines and gulleys until July. Tursun Bey wrote:

> When they got closer to the established place [i.e. a head-on confrontation with Țepeș] the front line of the army announced that there was not a drop of water to quench their thirst. All the carts and animals stopped there. The heat of the sun was so great that one could cook kebabs on the mail shirts of the *gazis* [warriors]. This is why the Sultan accused the commanders of carelessness. At the same time the scouts were scolded and punished.[7]

This was an army that prided itself on its commissariat, where food and water for men and horses were essential requirements. The chronicler Hodja Hussein wrote:

> In this parched plain the lips of the fighters for Islam dried up. Even the Africans and Asians, used to desert conditions, used their shields to roast meat.[8]

Relatively safe in the cool of the oaks in the Vlasia forest and with plenty of water and food, Țepeș' cavalry harassed the struggling Ottomans, galloping out from thickets, loosing arrows and cutting down stragglers, hit-and-run tactics that the Turks had rarely faced. There is a theory that Țepeș in effect used germ warfare against the Turks by paying infected Wallachians, disguised as Ottomans, to mingle with the invaders and spread disease among them; suitably high wages were paid to these men. It all sounds rather unlikely. Lepers were visibly ill and everyone, Turk and Christians alike, shunned them, stoning them in their bleeding rags and kicking them out of civilized society. If, as some contend, the victims had tuberculosis or syphilis these diseases are not that contagious, unless we accept the Western mythology about the sexual preferences of Mehmed's janissaries. In any case, it can take twenty years for syphilis to have a debilitating effect – Mehmed's campaign was all over by August.

According to Tursun Bey, Mehmed detached part of his force to tackle the 7,000 waiting near the Moldavian border in the east. Waiting silently and hidden by reeds on the edge of a forest, the Ottomans under the leadership of Mehmed-Pasha, ambushed the little command. The troop commanders are listed by Tursun, leading the left and right wings. Caught utterly by surprise, the Wallachians tried to fight their way out, but they were clearly heavily outnumbered and 'the victorious *gazis* slaughtered the Infidels with their bloody swords as if they had cut cucumbers.' Tursun Bey estimated that only 700 of the 7,000 escaped and the Turks 'loaded the heads of the Infidels on their camels and mules. Besides this each soldier put on top of his sword [presumably the blade tip] the head of an Infidel; their swords looked like snakes with the heads of men. The sky was an amazing sight.' So far, so dramatic, but Tursun Bey gets carried away with his narrative:

> hundreds and thousands of Infidels were brought in chains to the victorious Court. After the evening service, torches were lighted and the triumphant Sultan sat on his chair. Then the Infidels, resembling dragons and as evil as Ahriman [a Persian god of evil] were brought to him.[9]

Laying aside the Turk's obvious exaggeration in numbers, the defeat of Ţepeş' 'second army' probably did take place. It was as well for the Impaler that Stefan of Moldavia had no plans to invade the neighbouring principality. The survivors of the battle were executed 'with [the janissaries'] bloodthirsty swords'.

Perhaps in retaliation for this defeat, perhaps because Mehmed was marching on Tîrgovişte, Ţepeş decided on the famous night attack of 17 June. According to the papal legate Niccolo Modrussa who interviewed the Impaler at the Hungarian Court at Buda years later, the Wallachian force, numbering by this time about 24,000, found themselves in rough country with the Carpathians at their back. The Turks had looted towns already and carried off Wallachian children as tribute. Using Turkish arrows ripped from the bodies of the dead, Țepeș unleashed a cavalry force, perhaps 7–8,000 strong and rode hell for leather through the Ottoman camp.

Mehmed's camp was far more than a mere huddle of tents; it was a symbol and microcosm of Ottoman society. Chalk-ondyles wrote:

> I think there is no prince who has his armies and camps in better order, both in abundance of victuals and in the beautiful order they use in encamping without any confusion . . .[10]

The camp was built at noon, the professional handlers of canvas, skins, banners and guy ropes breaking their backs in the midday sun. The Grand Vizier's tent was purple, those of the commanders yellow or red. Pietro della Valle saw it in the seventeenth century when the crescent was about to wane, but Mehmed's camp must have been similar. The vizier's tent was half a mile in circumference, entered by a series of rotunda and screened by smaller green tents perhaps for camouflage. Columns supported the high, vaulted roof and carpets were strewn everywhere. The sultan's tent was larger than all the rest, with its distinctive six horse-tail banner flapping over-head. Around it, in three circles, stood a series of war-wagons with guns mounted, a tactical trick the Turks had borrowed from Jan Žižka and the Hussites. A solid rearguard of janissary tents lay beyond that, but the strength of the camp was at the front, covering the ground from which an attack was most likely. Wings of *kapikuli* and provincial cavalry had their multi-coloured canvases on each side of the great circle, ringed as it was with the commissariat and Mehmed's personal bodyguard in two concentric circles. In the centre, guarding the main approach to the sultan, were alternating rows of artillery, infantry and janissary tents. A screen of advance guard tents faced the would-be enemy and two huge rotating circles of cavalrymen, walking their horses slowly, kept watch.

Țepeș' veterans heard the whole camp at prayer an hour before sunset, the imams intoning towards Mecca. A cannon was fired as was the custom and the troop commanders called good fortune and long life to the sultan. With no alcohol and a disciplined regime, the Ottoman camp was utterly unlike anything among the Christians.

The story of the night attack, which would go down in Romanian history, is a classic example of propaganda and historical skulduggery. The Wallachian version, as related by Modrussa, ran as follows:

> Dracula carried out an incredible massacre without losing many men in such a major encounter, though many were wounded. He abandoned the enemy camp before daybreak and returned to the same mountain from which he had caused such terror and turmoil. I learned by questioning those who had participated in this battle that the sultan lost all confidence in the situation. During the night, the sultan abandoned the camp and fled in a shameful manner. And he would have continued this way, had he not been reprimanded by his friends and brought back, almost against his will.

Ţepeş had planned a two-pronged attack, his boyar, Gales, hitting the camp from the rear. The boyar seems not to have done this, however, perhaps panicking at the last moment, leaving the voivod outnumbered. The bias of Modrussa is evident. Mehmed II may have had his faults, but losing his nerve was not one of them.

Tursun Bey has such a different account that we must wonder if he was talking about the same battle.

> [The Wallachians] first encountered the army from Anatolia and they read verses of welcome and death to them, as they deserved ... They were adequately welcomed; their mouths were filled with spears ... Most of them were wounded or killed while they were trying to run away. In the confusion of the darkness they advanced towards the centre of the [camp] thinking that it was the way out ... When numerous candles and torches were lit in each tent ... the mean Infidels lost their

heads and scattered, having lost all presence of mind ... Most of them, leaving their horses and trying to escape, entered the Turkish tents ... Their defeat was so great that even ten-year-old children who were apprentices and servants in the army [the *devşirme*] killed many Infidels twice as powerful as themselves.[11]

Tursun Bey's account is patent nonsense. Ţepeş was brought up amongst the Turks, and he would have briefed his cavalry accordingly. There are even suggestions that he personally wandered the lines himself, in typical Turkish disguise, reconnoitring before the attack took place. They made for the centre of the camp, because that was where the sultan's tent was pitched and he was their target. No cavalryman would *abandon* his horse to escape, but use it for a fast getaway. And the comment on the prowess of ten-year-olds against the Impaler's hard riders is simply laughable.

Luckily, we have the honest and straightforward Constantin, who was sleeping in his janissary's tent that night, to strike a likely balance:

Although the Romanian prince had a small army, we always advanced with great caution and fear and spent nights sleeping in ditches. But even in this manner we were not safe, for during one night, the Romanians struck at us. They massacred horses, camels and several thousand Turks. When the Turks had retreated in the face of the enemy, we [janissaries] repelled the enemy and killed them. But the Sultan had incurred great losses.[12]

There is no doubt that the night attack came dangerously close to succeeding. Had Ţepeş, thundering through the camp, hacking right and left to the Turks' terrified cries of '*Kaziklu-Bey!* Impaler Prince!' managed to reach Mehmed, the result may have been very different. As it was, the gamble failed and the Impaler may have been wounded as his cavalry fought their way out against enormous odds. Tursun Bey ranted:

> It was all the fault of that wicked man with broken wings [a reference to his dragon standard?] and a heart pierced by the spears and swords of brave soldiers.[13]

What a gift for the vampirologists – Dracula's heart pierced!

Whether Ţepeş was pursued into the Carpathians immediately by Mihail-oglu Ali-Bey as the Ottoman sources insist or whether the Turks licked their wounds and were too terrified to follow, as Modrussa's version contends, the fact was that Mehmed's advance continued. Some sixty miles from the voivod's capital of Tîrgovişte, the advance guard came upon a sight possibly unique in the annals of warfare. It is not found recorded in any Ottoman chronicle, but Chalkondyles describes it as follows:

> the [sultan's] army came across a field with stakes, about three miles long and one mile wide. And there were large stakes on which they could see the impaled bodies of men, women and children, about twenty thousand of them ... The [sultan] himself in wonder, kept saying that he could not conquer the country of a man who could do such terrible and unnatural things and put his power and his subjects to such use ... And the other Turks, seeing so many people impaled, were scared out of their wits. There were babies clinging to their mothers on the stakes and birds had made nests in their breasts.[14]

The forest of the impaled is one of the lasting, ghastly images of Vlad Ţepeş. He was not going quietly into that good night. Tursun Bey knew exactly where he was going:

> Trying to escape from the lion's claws, he had chosen the claws of a bird of prey. The Hungarian king [Matthias Corvinus] took him prisoner. And there he sent his soul to Hell.[15]

The end of the campaign of 1462 is a matter of serious dispute among Romanian historians. The chronology of Constantin Rezachevici for instance[16] leads us to believe that the sickening sight of the field of the impaled was the last straw in a psychological battle that Ţepeş had been waging since the previous year. Not only were Hamsa Bey and Catavolinos rotting there, their flesh hanging in tatters as on-going meals for the crows and Carpathian vultures, but so were Ţepeş' own people, his women and children. There is every likeli-hood that Mehmed's army was ill with any one of a dozen infectious diseases that followed medieval armies – the plague, dysentery, malaria – and this is why he did not sack Tîrgovişte, but turned south to Braila, which he destroyed, and then back across the Danube, leaving Radu the Handsome to take the Wallachian throne if he could. The sultan was back in his old palace at Edirne by 11 July. Florescu and McNally have taken up this suggestive narrative wholesale and other Western historians, for example the military expert Tim Newark, have accepted this version of events.

Rezachevici's narrative continues that Ţepeş won victories over his brother's Turkish-backed force in August and on 8 September, the monks on the island of Rhodes having 'tolled the bells and have sung Te Deum to worship the glory of the Romanian prince'.[17] Both Barbu T. Campina and Nicolae Stoicescu have elaborated on this theme, contending that what led to Ţepeş' downfall was the defection of the boyars to the more reasonable and infinitely less terrifying Radu.

Kurt Treptow, however, argues more convincingly that this defection would not have happened had the Impaler genuinely been victorious. The night attack was a gamble that failed. And having failed, Ţepeş knew all too well that his small and increasingly exhausted force had nothing left to throw at the Turks. Endless guerrilla raids in an interminable partisan war was the best he could do. Given this situation, the boyars lost heart. The bulk of the Turkish army had gone home, Radu (after all the son of the great Dracul too) was at Tîrgovişte and his known friendly relations with the Turks would mean, perhaps, stability and a few years of peace, even if that peace came with the inevitable strings of the yearly tribute and the *devşirme*.

There was also a sense perhaps, less well defined and certainly not quantifiable today, that Dracula was betraying his Wallachian and Orthodox trust by allying himself with Corvinus.

The facts bear Treptow out. By the end of August, Radu ruled Wallachia and his brother had retreated north to his mountain stronghold on the Argeş. According to the folk tales – there are no Turkish accounts of these 'mopping up' operations – Radu followed him and positioned his guns on the spot at Poenari still called 'the field of the cannon'. The Romanian stories tell that a spy in Radu's camp got a message to the castle, by means of an arrow through a window, of an imminent attack the following day and Ţepeş and his followers escaped, reversing the shoes of their horses to confuse the trackers they knew would come after them. Such a ruse is almost certainly mythical. If Ţepeş' men rode Arabs, it would be feasible because Arab horses' hoofs are surprisingly circular. If they were Tarpans, the shoes would not fit. The other curious folk take refers to the Impaler's wife or mistress (it is unclear which) who told him on the night before the attack that she would rather be food for the fishes of the Argeş river than be taken as a slave by the Turks. Accordingly, she threw herself from the battlements into what is still known locally as Rîul Doamnei, the Princess's River.

All we can be sure of is that Ţepeş escaped and, clambering down the precipitous gorges and ravines, reached Konigstein, one of János Hunyadi's old fortresses in Făgăraş. He waited here for news of the King of Hungary who was due to meet him at Braşov, to the north.

Matthias Corvinus had probably never intended to go head-to-head with the Turks. As Machiavellian as any Renaissance prince, he watched and waited to see which way

the wind blew. His kingdom would have cause to regret this
in the next generation, when an estimated 90 per cent of the
Hungarian Army, including its King Louis II, were cut down
by the troops of Suleiman the Magnificent at Mohácz in 1526.
Corvinus left Buda with a large army and all the panoply of
war on 15 July. He had only reached Szeged, still on his own
soil, by 10 August. He crossed into Transylvania by mid-
September and waited throughout the whole of October at
Sibiu, deliberating his next move. Mehmed, of course, had
gone home before he even set out.

Finally at Braşov by November, Corvinus met Ţepeş, who
had recently moved into Prince Dan's old Wallachian suburb
of Scheii, outside the walls. Negotiations between them
dragged on for five weeks before Corvinus sent the fierce old
Hussite warrior, Jan Žižka, to arrest him. Exactly where and
how this happened is unknown and the ostensible reason for
it completely out of keeping with what we know of Vlad
Ţepeş. It concerned a series of three documents that had come
into Corvinus' possession and that were dated 7 November
1462. One was addressed to the sultan, another to his grand
vizier Mahmoud and the third to Stefan of Moldavia. All three
purported to have been written by Ţepeş using such crawling
and unlikely terms as 'emperor of emperors' and 'lord and
master' in connection with Mehmed. The letters offered the
Impaler's military service on the sultan's behalf against the
Hungarians and even offered to kidnap Corvinus in person.
The consensus today is that these letters were forgeries. Only
copies survive, but the Latin is bad, the style clumsy and the
idea hardly consonant with a man who had made it his life's
work to cement a principality and take on an enemy (the
Turks) whom he clearly detested.

Florescu and McNally believe that the author was probably
Johann Reudell from the Black Church in Braşov, using a
corruption of his own surname – 'Rothel' – as the place from
which the supposed Ţepeş' letters were sent. The burned and
the impaled of Braşov were having their revenge at last.

The real reason – and the reason that it is even possible that Corvinus dictated the letters himself – is that the Impaler was now an embarrassment to the Hungarian king. He was a political refugee, still no doubt intending to force Corvinus to commit himself to Pius II's crusade against the Turks. Corvinus needed hard evidence to explain to Pius – and anyone else who raised eyebrows at Corvinus' lacklustre performance – that he had been threatened by treachery and had been forced to act against the Prince of Wallachia and, in doing so, spend a great deal of his crusade chest in the process. In fact, of course, Corvinus actually spent this money on buying the crown of St Stephen (see below) which gave him full validity as king.

The Impaler had risen twice as Wallachia's prince, rather as the Count Dracula of vampire fiction kept rising. Now he was a prisoner once more.

The years that followed are a closed book in the life of Vlad Ţepeş. We are not even sure how long he remained a prisoner of Matthias Corvinus, but the best guess is that he was released, on certain conditions, in 1475. It seems likely that his confinement was one of comfortable 'house arrest' and not a musty prison cell, first at Alba Iulia, then at the fortress of Vac before being taken to the summer palace at Visegrád on the Danube's bend. This was the 'paradise on earth' referred to by Castelli, the envoy of Pope Sixtus IV, the thirteenth-century castle undergoing Italian landscaping during Corvinus' reign. Much of the palace that Vlad Ţepeş would have known was destroyed later by a century and a half of Turkish occupation, but recent restoration gives us a clear picture of Corvinus' eye for architecture.

We know that Ţepeş was not kept with other prisoners in the rather forbidding King Solomon's Tower on the crest of the hill, and he probably had his own apartments and the freedom of the place within reason. Corvinus may well have amused himself – and Ţepeş – by wheeling

him out occasionally to overawe guests. Everyone had heard
of the Impaler prince. Niccolo Modrussa spent hours talking
to him about the Turkish campaign; at least one anonymous
artist painted him. At some point, perhaps in 1474, Ţepeş was
given his own house in Pest, across the river from Corvinus'
capital at Buda. It was here that the folk tales tell of the bizarre
incident in which a thief was chased by constables through
Ţepeş' courtyard. Ţepeş killed the leading constable with his
sword. When challenged by Corvinus' magistrates to explain
himself, he alleged that the man had clearly committed suicide
by daring to invade the territory of a prince. Corvinus is said
to have laughed this off.

While Ţepeş accepted this gentle incarceration with whatever
patience he could muster, the world moved on around him. In
June 1463 his ultimate gaoler, Matthias Corvinus, paid an
astonishing 80,000 gold coins, much of it papal crusading
money, to buy the glittering crown of St Stephen from the
Holy Roman Emperor. A reported 3,000 knights carried it
back to Buda where Corvinus was crowned the following year
in the cathedral of Esztergon. Perhaps Ţepeş was there too.
Pius II, disgusted with the lack of crusading zeal of all
European leaders except the Impaler, led his own crusade.
Probably a dying man already, he reached Ancona in the
August of 1464, waiting in vain for an army that never arrived.
His meagre troops were celebrating the Feast of the Assump-
tion when he died.

The fall of Chilia to Stefan of Moldavia in the winter of 1465
saw the beginning of a cold war between the 'Black Bogdan'
(Stefan) and Corvinus. The hot war that erupted was brief
enough, with Stefan's forces victorious at Baia-Mare close to
Christmas 1467. Three years later the usual entanglements
among the Romanians led to open warfare again as Stefan took
on Radu Dracula with the intention of replacing him with his
own puppet, Basarab Laiota, one of Vlad Ţepeş' rivals ten

years earlier. By the end of 1473, Tîrgovişte and Bucharest had
fallen to Stefan and even Radu's wife, Maria Despina, and his
daughter, Maria Voichita, were in Stefan's hands. By January
1475, all that Radu held of Wallachian soil was the fortress his
grandfather had built at Giurgiu on the Danube and it was
there that he died, unloved and unmourned, allegedly of
syphilis, in that month. His monks, no doubt used to burying
Draculeşti, laid his body to rest in the monastery of Tînganu.

The problem that arose now for Corvinus was that Basarab
Laiota had thrown in his lot with the Turks. It was no doubt
at last dawning on the Hungarian king that the buffer state of
Wallachia was a buffer no more. The Moldavians held Chilia,
guarding the entrance to the Danube, but the Prince of
Wallachia was once again paying the annual tribute and the
devşirme to Mehmed. Corvinus' back door was ominously
open. The man to close it was Vlad Ţepeş, close it as he nearly
had in the night attack on the Ottoman camp back in the June
of 1462. But Ţepeş was a maverick and Corvinus knew how
the man could turn on his former captors. Accordingly, he
renewed a proposition that had been floating around for some
time – that Ţepeş marry Corvinus' cousin, Ilona Szilágy, the
daughter of the Impaler's old comrade from the Transylvanian
days. This meant the conversion of the former voivod to
Catholicism.

Corvinus had already proliferated the 'horror' stories about
the Impaler in his own demesnes via the German presses of
Augsburg, Nuremberg and Landshut. That was at a time when
he wanted the world to think the worst of his prisoner. Now,
he was quite prepared to let the Orthodox Church hang
Ţepeş' soul out to dry over the heresy of his conversion. He
needed the man under relative lock and key in 1462. Now he
needed him out and unleashed. We need not see Ţepeş as a
gullible dupe in all this. It is likely that personal faith was not
a major issue for him and he knew the consequences from his
Churchmen in Wallachia. But he was also a member of the
Dragon Order and he had already made Catholic vows there.

Above all, marriage to Ilona Szilágy would give him his freedom. Two sons were born to the couple in the imposing house in Pest where they lived, sons who would carry on the Dragon code and the blood of Dracula for a thousand years.[18]

The Impaler's last campaign began on 18 July 1475. In that year the Ottomans took the Crimea, bringing them ever nearer to a confrontation with Russia that would last for four centuries. In Italy, the artists da Vinci and Botticelli were painting for various patrons. Even here the hard world of politics was rarely absent. Botticelli's *Adoration of the Magi* contained characters that looked suspiciously like members of the Medici family. In London, William Caxton produced the first printed book in English, a romance translated from the French troubadour Raoul le Fevre; and further north in Cambridge, Robert Woodlark founded St Catherine's College, where he insisted that the dubious discipline of law was not to be taught. In Mehmed's Constantinople, now transformed with minarets and echoing to the call of the muezzins, Kiva Han was opened, the world's first coffee house.

And the papacy was on the march again. Although Francesco della Rovere, now Pope as Sixtus IV, was not the crusader that Pius had been and was more interested in the papal indulgence of nepotism and patronizing the arts by building the Sistine Chapel, he nevertheless 'called the kings of Christendom for swords about the cross'. Venice, already under renewed threat from Mehmed, was waiting. So was Stefan of Moldavia. 'We are ready,' wrote Stefan, 'to resume the struggle for the defence of Christendom with all the power and heart which Almighty God had chosen to invest in us.'[19]

Now that Basarab Laiota had effectively joined the Turks, Stefan could afford, in fact needed, a rapprochement with Ţepeş. He sent Ion Amblac, a trusted aide, to Corvinus early in June and the Hungarian king began the usual crusade-launching process. The Wallachian Saxon towns were once again asked for money and equipment, the Hungarian Diet was summoned to pledge its support and Corvinus raised a tax of one gold florin per household throughout his kingdom. Ţepeş was given command of the army that Corvinus sent to Turkish-held Bosnia. Striking out from his headquarters at Arghis he had marched to Merghindel by October and joined forces with Corvinus to inflict a defeat on the Turks in the town of Sabac on 8 February of following year. Corvinus then went home, which seems rather precipitate bearing in mind that the rest of Bosnia was still in Ottoman hands, and he left command of the army to Ţepeş.

Using a ruse that had worked before, the Impaler sent a body of Hungarian troops wearing Turkish turbans and tunics to mingle in the streets and squares of the silver-mining town of Srebreniča. This 'Trojan horse' caused mayhem inside the town walls while Ţepeş' cannon blasted the masonry from outside. As always, the Impaler's vengeance was terrible. At Srebreniča, at Zwornik and at Kuslat, the grim picture was the same – perhaps years of idleness had whetted Ţepeş' appetite. The papal legate Gabriele Rangoni wrote to Rome:

> He tore the limbs off Turkish prisoners and placed their parts on stakes ... and displayed the private parts of his victims so that when the Turks see these, they will run away in fear.[20]

The spring of 1476 saw Ţepeş back in Transylvania. The tide of war and politics had turned again in his favour and at Turda he received not only the good wishes of Stefan of Moldavia in his forthcoming struggle with Basarab Laiota, but, more practically, an army of over 20,000 men under command of Stephen Báthory. In the Magyar town ringed with its gorges honeycombed with deep and gloomy caves, Ţepeş weighed his options. The real commanders, in terms of experience and knowledge of the country, were the Impaler himself and Vuk Branković, the son of George who had long held Belgrade. The plan was to join forces with Stefan of Moldavia before advancing against Mehmed, but the Turks struck first,

defeating the Moldavians at Valea Alba in July. Ţepeş' arrival
reversed the fortunes here and the Turks were driven back to
the Siret River out of Moldavian territory – the second time
that the Impaler had come to the aid of his sometimes less than
grateful cousin.

The campaign now switched to the sustained attack on
Laiota. Ţepeş and Báthory marched from Transylvania with
perhaps 35,000 troops; Stefan brought 15,000 from the east. It
was a classic pincer movement. On 7 October, Ţepeş wrote to
the people of Braşov, whose houses he had once burned,
whose people he had once impaled:

> With faith in the Lord Jesus Christ, I, Vlad voivod, by the grace
> of God, Prince of all Wallachia, My Majesty [had he learned this
> phrase at Buda?] gives this order to the honest, faithful and
> good friends ... to the country, to the twelve councillors and
> to all [in the] great fortress of Braşov ...

Ţepeş proposed a deal in return for their support of him
against Laiota. All previous customs duties on goods, all taxes
were to be wiped; the Braşovian merchants could trade freely
throughout Wallachia. In return he expected their full support
in not sheltering his enemies, as they had, of course, done in
the past.

> If anyone should not respect [this arrangement] they will
> receive the wrath of My Majesty. It cannot be different ...[21]

A month later, Ţepeş had caught up with Basarab Laiota.
Reports to Matthias Corvinus at Buda confirmed that the
pretender's army, 18,000 strong and reinforced with Turks,
had been decisively beaten at Rucăr. Casualties were heavy on
both sides, but by 8 November, Ţepeş was again writing to
Braşov, this time from his old capital of Tîrgovişte. He had not
seen it since July 1462:

Herewith I give you news that I have overthrown our foe Laiota who fled with the Turks. Thus God has given you a free path. Come with bread and goods and you will eat now that God has given us a single country.[22]

Nine days later, Carstian, the governor of Tîrgovişte, wrote to Braşov with news of the Impaler's capture of Bucharest:

Therefore I ask you to give praise to the almighty God with organs, songs and bells, as we have done in our country which is also yours. And you must know that the boyars of all the country have sworn allegiance to Vlad voda . . .[23]

The last weeks of Ţepeş' life are shrouded in mystery. With Stephen Báthory's army now back in Hungary and Stefan of Moldavia's marching home to the east, the man who was now prince and voivod for a third time was exposed to the same dangers he had always faced. There is a kind of monotony in Balkan politics, a sense of ghastly déjà-vu. The boyars who had opposed him in the early part of his second reign had largely been disposed of and replaced. Yet it is clear that even those replacements, presumably trusted men hand-picked by Ţepeş, had gone over first to Radu and some to Laiota in the years since Corvinus took the Impaler prisoner. A bodyguard of 200 Moldavians was left behind by Stefan to defend the voivod; whether Ţepeş had asked for these or Stefan had offered them with a vague sense of unease, we do not know.

At the end of December 1476, Basarab Laiota launched a counter-attack against the Impaler, now based in Bucharest, dangerously near to the Danube. Previous rivals had been killed – Dan and Vladislav – but Laiota had slipped through the net. The clash itself was no more than a skirmish. This was not a great and desperate gamble like the night attack on Mehmed's camp. Even so, Ţepeş would go out in a blaze of glory. According to the Russian account (Kuritsyn of course having met the Impaler's widow and children at Buda, as well as the remnants of his Moldavian bodyguard, see Chapter 14), the voivod had gone to the top of a hill, alone, to watch the fighting below. One of his own men, confusing him for a Turk, hit him with a lance. Under sudden attack from all sides, Ţepeş defended himself with his sword, cutting down five assailants before he died.

This account makes little sense. The only reason that Ţepeş would have moved to higher ground is to reconnoitre and he would not have done that alone. True, he often wore Turkish armour as a ruse, but that would be pointless in a skirmish in open country with Laiota. It is likely that his attacker was an assassin and that the man saw his chance in the clash of arms and went to work, almost certainly killing Ţepeş from behind. According to the legend that has endured, his head was hacked off and taken back to Mehmed at Constantinople who had it displayed, appropriately, on a tall stake visible in the heart of the city.

Vlad Dracula was dead. The world would spend the next five centuries resurrecting him.

14

THE GAPING GRAVES
THE RESTING PLACE OF THE IMPALER

Tradition has it that Vlad Ţepeş is buried in the island monastery of Snagov, one of several he endowed in his role as Prince of Wallachia and one he almost certainly fortified as an excellent strategic refuge at a time when war and invasion were the constants of life.

Snagov strikes its visitor in different ways. When journalist Victoria Clark visited the monastery ten years after Ceauşescu's overthrow, she was rowed across the lake through mist and reeds by a woman to meet Father Emilian Poenaru of the Orthodox Church, the monastery's curator. She was told by her guide, 'Please don't start asking questions about Dracula. Father Emilian is sick of all that tourist stuff.'[1] Father Emilian was hospitality itself, offering coffee, peanuts, pickled peppers and cold meat. He also smoked Marlboro Lights and whiled away his non-guiding hours by knitting! Six years earlier, ghost-hunter and photographer Simon Marsden had a rather different experience:

All was dark save for the flickering of candles that at intervals lit up the rich gold and silver of the many icons. Then, as I neared the altar, the small, dark figure of a nun appeared from behind a pillar and stared at me. 'Was this Dracula's grave?' I stammered. She did not reply, but continued to stare, I felt, straight through me.[2]

There was an oriental rug over the great stone slab and a rather awful vase with Vlad Ţepeş' portrait stenciled onto it, together with a sinister-looking chalice.

Marsden and Clark were looking at the hollow shell of what may have been the Impaler's last resting place. And intriguingly, their different agendas evoked different memories. Clark, researching the Orthodox Church, encounters a jolly priest with modern, Western habits, irked by the visitors' fascination with the Impaler. Marsden, the occultist, sees monsters in the shadows and the weird behaviour of the nun:

I walked to the door, turned once more and saw [her] making strange signs over the grave, gesticulating and waving her arms as if in a trance.[3]

Carol II Hohenzollern was King of Romania when archaeologists first came looking for Dracula's grave. One of many legends of the Impaler is that, trapped in a loveless marriage, he wandered the streets of his capital Tîrgovişte, picking up prostitutes on the way. So too, Carol II had his string of mistresses, like Magda Lupescu who was smuggled into the royal palace in Bucharest against first the knowledge and then the wish of the Romanian people. Or like 'The Crow', a black-clad cocaine addict with short bobbed hair whose nymphomania was legendary in the capital. 'This black whore,' a professor of Cluj University told reporter Robert Kaplan, 'had to be carried out of Carol's bedroom, drooling and half-conscious.'[4]

The insufferable Carol had many of the worst traits of Nicolae Ceauşescu and some of Ţepeş, lending an eerie suggestion that a similar fate overtakes the rulers of Romania no matter when they live. He ran his own extortion racket, receiving monthly fees from casinos and nightclubs. He had shares in all the major companies and grabbed one million pounds in compensation when Stalin annexed Bessarabia from him, not for the country's treasury, but for his own coffers. In 1938, having smuggled a vast fortune out of the country into his personal banks, he proclaimed a royal dictatorship (the 1930s was, after all, the decade of dictators) and declared unofficial war on the country's 800,000 Jews. Forced out, as Ceaușescu would be fifty years later, Carol fled Romania with Lupescu and nine railway carriages of loot. Like Vlad Țepeș, Carol tried to play a double game against opponents who were far stronger and the Fates who were just as unkind. And, like Vlad Țepeș, he lost.

Luckily, not all Romania's sons were as avaricious and twisted as their king. In 1931 the Commission on Historic Monuments appointed an archaeologist, Dinu Rosetti, and a genealogist, George Florescu, to excavate the island of Snagov as part of a national survey of historic buildings, concentrating on the area around the chapel, which was the core of the medieval monastery. Their findings were written up as *Diggings Around Snagov* and they uncovered foundations of buildings, bones and pottery shards which indicated that the island had been a Bronze Age settlement. Its lake, one of the deepest in the country, was not only a source of fresh water, but provided fish for food and a natural defence against attack.

The archaeological team found clear evidence that Snagov was not only a monastery, with its chapel, dormitories, cells and chapter house, but that it was fortified against ravaging armies, with buttresses, trenches and extra-thick walls. It must have resembled, in fact, a small town in the Impaler's time, with its own treasury, mint and printing press. And the bastions reaching to the water's edge gave comfort to boyar and peasant alike who could hide within the sanctuary of the Orthodox Church.

The original monastery at Snagov was endowed in the fourteenth century, but the largest of its three chapels, that of the Annunciation, was built by Vladislav II of the Dăneşti family, the Impaler's enemy, in 1453. It was probably Ţepeş himself who was responsible for the fortifications of the island, although no documentary evidence for this has survived.

Rosetti and Florescu found an unprecedented number of skeletons on the island with their skulls missing. One rational explanation is that these were victims of political assassination and perhaps torture, but the conflict in which they died is less easy to discern. It was Vladislav's island before it was the Impaler's and in 1462 it was captured by Radu cel Frumos, when fighting with the Turks against his brother the Impaler. The missing heads, of course, could have an altogether more sinister explanation in the context of vampire folklore. As we have seen, decapitation is one of the ritualistic means of preventing the return of the undead.

Tradition told the 'time team' that Dracula was buried, in keeping with his rank and the honour done to him as Prince of Wallachia, near the altar. The archaeologists were trying to answer the same question that Simon Marsden had posed – was the altar slab Dracula's grave? The slab itself may once have borne inscriptions and frescoes typical of medieval Romanian tombs, but the constant trampling over centuries by monks, soldiers, prisoners and vandals had removed all trace.[5]

The team knew that Snagov had undergone several transformations since Vlad Ţepeş' time. The Turks burned part of it towards the end of the 1462 campaign and storms and earthquakes had brought about the collapse of the Chapel of the Annunciation. One of the ornate doors, with carvings of saints from the fifteenth century, is now in Bucharest Museum of Art. Despite the monastery's reputation in the seventeenth century as a centre of culture and learning, it had declined by the nineteenth when Paul Kiselev, the Governor-General of

Wallachia converted the place into a prison. By 1867 it had closed and the locals helped themselves to anything they could find, which probably included grave robbery and the exhumation of various bodies in search of valuables.

Under the slab, the team found disappointment. Whether this grave had been robbed – like so many graves from ancient Egypt to that of the actor Peter Cushing, the Abraham van Helsing in a string of Dracula films – or whether it never contained a body in the first place, the huge dank hole merely contained piles of animal bones, and pottery shards that proved to be of Iron Age date.

Near the door of the church, however, was a tomb that looked all the more promising because it had clearly not been touched. Its position was odd and it was the same size as the slab near the altar, implying that this was the grave of someone of importance, but the fact that it was some way from the spiritual centre of the church and in a place where all visitors would walk on it implied that this burial was a deliberate act of contempt. This time, however, the grave yielded information. In it was a wooden coffin, all but rotted, which had been wrapped in a pall whose purple plush and gold embroidery were still discernible. If this was the casket of Ţepeş, then the body inside gave the lie in one sense to the vampiric condition. Far from it being 'incorrupt' and hideous, with blood seeping from nose, ears, eyes and mouth, there was no head at all and the torso and limbs were mere bone.

The dressing of the dead is a fascinating subject. The body near the door at Snagov was wearing the rotted fragments of silk brocade, yellow and brown. And the sleeves were clearly once crimson, fastened with large silver buttons and cords typical of the fifteenth century. From the position of the sleeves it could be determined that the arms had not been crossed over the breast. This is a common European symbol of piety and was the position of the arms of bodies in other graves excavated at the site. However in this case the right hand rested near the hip, as though holding the hilt of a sword.

The problem with this interpretation is that throughout Europe to be left-handed was considered at best unlucky and at worst a manifestation of the devil. Whoever was buried in the doorway at Snagov would surely have been right-handed and would have worn the sword on the left. Historian Mike Parker states:

> The clothing of the dead constitutes a hall of mirrors, representations of representations, in which things may not be entirely what they seem at first.[6]

And the clearly civilian clothes raise all sorts of questions. If this *was* Vlad Ţepeş and if he died according to tradition in battle he would surely be wearing plate armour, either the workaday 'harness' in which he was killed or a more elaborate, ceremonial suit put aside for the purpose.

Near the skeleton Rosetti and Florescu found a battered crown with cloisonné inlay representing claws of terracotta colour, each claw holding a turquoise. All the known portraits of Vlad Ţepeş show him wearing an ornate cloth cap, perhaps with cloisonné beads or pearls, but there are no representations of his crown as Voivod of Wallachia.

Other items, which were again clearly fifteenth century in date, included a small cup, with its fascinating echoes of the golden chalice legend, and a buckle with a gold thread decoration. Most intriguing of all was a ring, once probably attached to the dead man's sleeve. Rosetti speculated, having found similar examples in Nuremberg, that it was a love-token, specifically a fitting for a lady's colours, the heraldic scarf carried by medieval knights in tournaments. It is likely that both Ţepeş and his father, Vlad Dracul, competed in such events but Rosetti went further and saw the ring as part of the Order of the Dragon with which Vlad Dracul was invested at Nuremberg on 8 November 1431. A number of representations of the dragon exist in a variety of forms throughout Europe. One in the Bayerische Nationalmuseum in Munich is of gold fabric, in trapunto work (quilting) and was probably sewn directly to a garment. Another, this time in metal, is preserved in the Kunstgewermuseum in Berlin. What is common to all the examples shown in D'A.J.D. Boulton's authoritative work on orders of chivalry, *The Knights of the Crown*,[6] is that the dragon's tail forms a circle. Is this the significance of the 'ring' found in the Snagov tomb?

Two years after the excavations at the Romanian monastery, two allegedly medieval skeletons were being examined in London. Dr Laurence Tanner, Keeper of the Monuments at Westminster Abbey and Professor W. Wright, President of the Anatomical Society of Great Britain, were tasked with a detailed study of the two sets of human remains found by workmen in the White Tower in 1674 and interred as the likely 'Princes in the Tower' four years later. I use this example of archaeological analysis because of its resonance with the Snagov work. Tanner and Wright, publishing their findings in *Archaeologia* in 1934, found animal bones in the urn along with human ones. This is almost certainly because the collection of the bodies in 1674 was done carelessly and included all sorts of debris. The Tower of London, like the island of Snagov, was a large, bustling community in its own right, with chapels, workshops, kitchens, barracks and even its own zoo. Where the English experts had an edge over their Romanian counterparts is that they were, respectively, a doctor and a dental surgeon. However eminent Florescu undoubtedly was, he was a genealogist and his expertise in the archaeological excavation of a grave must have been minimal. And, in the 1930s, archaeology was still a largely amateur science; it was only twenty years after the Piltdown find had taken in virtually the whole archaeological community – not until 1953 would it be revealed as a hoax.[7]

Tanner and Wright were able to estimate the height of the child skeletons and could tell by the teeth that one was between twelve and thirteen at the time of death and the other between nine and eleven. They could even tell that the elder child suffered from a painful condition of the jaw, probably the bone disease osteomyelitis. What they could not tell was the sex of the children, nor the age of the bones. All the more remarkable then that their conclusion should be that, 'the evidence [that] the bones in the urn are those of the Princes [in the Tower] is as conclusive as could be desired.'[8]

It is the very unsatisfactory nature of the Tanner–Wright research that has led historians to continue to argue the pros and cons of the bodies' identities and the likely guilt or innocence of the princes' uncle, Richard III, for their murder. The Richard III Society has made repeated requests to the Dean and Chapter of Westminster Abbey to re-open the tomb into which the bones were returned in 1933 because modern science could determine age, sex and other imponderables once and for all. Rather like the Catholic and Orthodox Churches with their sacred relics, the Dean and Chapter have said no.

To be fair to Florescu and Rosetti, they probably intended to carry out further investigations into the Snagov bones but this was not possible. The finds were placed in the History Museum in Bucharest, but with the invasion of Romania by Hitler's Panzer Divisions in October 1940, a party of convicts was given the task of removing the Museum's contents to the mountains at Valeni de Murte for safekeeping in the hands of Nicolae Iorga, the country's foremost historian. Somewhere on the journey the finds disappeared and despite rumours of their existence in various parts of the world nothing has been forthcoming.

It may be, as legend suggests, that the empty tomb in front of Snagov's altar originally did house Ţepeş' body and that it was removed to the door tomb or elsewhere for any number of reasons. A similar excavation was carried out years later at the Impaler's stronghold of Curtea de Argeş. Here in the local church, it was the peasant tradition to light candles to the right of the altar only. Excavation there revealed the tomb of an earlier Wallachian prince. Perhaps then, Ţepeş' remains were removed by Orthodox priests appalled by the legend of the Impaler's cruelty or by the fact that he probably embraced the Catholic faith during his captivity in Hungary if not earlier. Equally, it is possible that Țepeș' body was allowed to rot in the forests where it lay. History, after all, is written by the victors.

Perhaps, given the Impaler's murderous reputation, at Snagov and throughout Wallachia, it was inevitable that his original tomb should be desecrated or, at the very least, that the body should be moved. In the 1980s, Dracula experts Raymond T. McNally and Radu R. Florescu approached the Romanian government to fund an American–Romanian archaeological team to continue where Rosetti and Florescu left off in the 1930s. No serious reply was received.

If the body at Snagov is that of Vlad the Impaler, how did it get there?

> Dracula's army began to kill [the Turks] and to pursue them without mercy. Then out of joy Dracula ascended a mountain in order to see how his men were killing the Turks. Detaching himself from the army, one of those around him, taking him for a Turk, hit him with a lance. Dracula, seeing that he was being attacked by his own men, immediately killed five of his assassins on the spot with his own sword. However, many arrows [another translation is lances] pierced him and he died in this manner.[9]

So runs the earliest Russian account of the death of Vlad Țepeș. Its probable author was Fedor Kuritsyn who arrived at the Court of King Matthias Corvinus at Buda in Hungary sometime in the year 1482 as an envoy of Ivan III, Grand Duke of Muscovy. In many ways it is likely that Ivan's purpose in sending Kuritsyn was to open 'the window on the West' rather as Tsar Peter the Great was to do in 1689. The culture of the Renaissance, originating in Italy and spreading north and west to the rest of Europe, had reached Hungary by the middle of the fifteenth century but not further east. Ivan's young state of Muscovy would become one of the greatest powers in the world by the twentieth century but it needed friends in these early stages.

Probably working through an interpreter called Martinco, Kuritsyn mixed with the nobility in the court of Matthias Corvinus, and met the dead Impaler's widow and Mihnea, Vlad's eldest son by his previous marriage. Obsessed with the legends circulating about the Impaler, Kuritsyn visited Transylvania where the man was born and Wallachia which he ruled in a kind of fact-finding pilgrimage. He went to Braşov, whose townspeople Ţepeş had impaled in their thousands and to Bistriţa, another town that had reason to hate him. By the spring of 1484, Kuritsyn was at Suceava, the capital of the Moldavian warlord and Ţepeş' cousin, Stefan cel Mare (Stephen the Great).

Here, the Russian envoy met not only Stefan, who had known Vlad Ţepeş since boyhood, but Maria Voichita, the daughter of the Impaler's brother, Radu the Handsome. Most importantly, Kuritsyn interviewed ten soldiers who had served with Stefan as the Impaler's Moldavian bodyguard near Bucharest eight years earlier at the time of the Impaler's death. It is likely that the account above, with all its infuriating non-sequiturs, came from them and was included in his *Povest o Dracule* (*The Story of Prince Dracula*) in 1486. The actual document which has survived in Leningrad is dated 1490 and was drafted by Efrosin 'the sinner', the monk from the monastery of Kirillov-Belozersky who, judging by his comments, was less of a fan of Dracula than was Kuritsyn.

Another version of the Impaler's death comes from the Austrian chronicler Jacob Unrest:

Dracula was killed with great cunning, because the Turks wished to avenge the enmity which he had borne against them for so long and also the great damages inflicted upon them. They hired a Turk as one of his servants with the mission of killing him while he served him. The Turk was apparently instructed to attack Dracula from the back. He was then to cut off his head and bring it back on horseback to the sultan.[10]

There is no clear evidence as to precisely where Vlad Ţepeş died. That it was near Bucharest and Snagov is certain and the date was probably close to Christmas 1476. Legend has it that he died in a clearing in the dense forest of Vlasia, although mention of his having been killed on a mountain and his body having been found in a swamp does not accord.

The fact that his body may have been found by the monks of Snagov makes sense if Ţepeş died in battle. Routinely, after such clashes, it was the work of priests not only to bury the dead but also to record the names of the famous who had fallen. No such listing exists for Vlad Ţepeş. The version that reached Frederick, the Holy Roman Emperor, in Vienna read, 'The captain named by King Matthias, Dracula, together with 4,000 men was butchered by the Turks.'[11] That number of corpses, even if not literally accurate, would have attracted the vultures that wheeled in the Carpathian skies. The Impaler's body, pierced, bloody and headless was carried through the forest according to legend and buried in the altar space of the church at Snagov. Who stripped the body of his armour, who washed the congealed wounds, who clothed the Impaler in the robes of the Order of the Dragon, if that was what they were, is not recorded.

Another grave, another church, another country, 300 years after Ţepeş. In 2007, a group of historians and archaeologists worked on *Vampire Princess*, a programme made for the History Channel. In an obscure Czechoslovak churchyard near Prague, eleven bodies were exhumed. Carbon dating was able to place their burials between 1700 and 1750 at the height, as we have seen, of the vampire plague in Central Europe. Eight of the bodies were conventionally buried in a Christian east–west position, but three were different. They were buried on a north–south axis and all three had large stones in the coffins with them, as though to weight the bodies down. All three were male and one had the first three bones of the vertebrae missing – a sign of decapitation. The skull was placed between the legs, out of reach of the hands. And there was a circular wound to the sternum which might have been caused by the insertion of a stake.

In other words, for the first time we have archaeological evidence in the heart of vampire country of the sort of precautions that superstitious people were taking in the folkloric tradition we saw in Chapter 6.

To explain these corpses, we have to travel to the nearby town of Cesky Krumlov near the Austrian border. Today, the castle there is one of Czechoslovakia's major tourist attractions, with dozens of ghost stories attached to the place. At the time of the vampire burials recorded above, Czechoslovakia was Bohemia and the area was part of the vast estates of the Schwarzenberg family, close confidantes of the Habsburgs at the court of Vienna. As we have seen, the tales of 'real' vampires of the eighteenth century deal with peasantry or at best artisans. In the case of Eleonore von Schwarzenberg, however, we have an aristocratic vampire. The name undoubtedly appealed to various writers on the vampire theme – Poe's *Lenore* is the best known – and it is likely that Stoker, via Vambery, knew her story too.

The programme makers revealed that in 1996 a contemporary portrait of the princess and her only son was sent for professional cleaning and that X-rays showed that her head had been repainted on a separate piece of canvas. Was this, they wondered, a symbolic beheading of a vampire that no one, because of the woman's status, dare actually carry out on her body? Eleonore was a keen huntress (the portrait shows her in hunting dress) but the one animal on her extensive estates that she would not allow to be killed was the wolf. Instead, she had the beasts caught and kept in cages in the castle, employing her devoted (and brave!) servants to milk the she-wolves. Eleonore then drank the milk.

Already in the folklore of the time we have the *varcolac*, the wolf-coat, the vampire's alter ego. Eleonore drank wolf's milk in the belief that she would conceive as a result. In the classical tradition, of course, Romulus and Remus, the legendary founders of Rome, had been suckled by a she-wolf and for centuries the animal's spirit was said to watch over the Eternal City. The milk-drinking eventually worked because in 1722, at the age of forty-one, Eleonore gave birth to a son. Even today, the pregnancy of a forty-one-year-old woman is considered 'senile'; in 1722 it was either a miracle or witchcraft. Since this was Bohemia, most ordinary people probably chose to believe the latter.

Tragedy struck the family ten years later when Eleonore's husband was killed in a hunting accident and her beloved son was sent to be brought up in the Viennese court.

The rest of Eleonore's life is a long agonising decline. Very superstitious herself, she refused the best medical attention even when the emperor sent his own physician to attend her. It is noticeable that this was Dr Franz von Gerstof, one of those vampire hunters we met in Chapter 6 and who could have been a prototype van Helsing. We know from the copious and meticulous accounts from the castle that Eleonore did permit bloodletting (then accepted modern science) but the obsession with blood of course strikes all sorts of chords. She was certainly a hypochondriac but her weight loss was genuine and almost certainly caused by cancer. She regularly took medicine extracted from crayfish eyes, which she believed improved her failing sight, spermaceti from whales, and elements of 'unicorn's horn' which was one of her prized possessions. She spent the modern equivalent of £3,000 a month on such useless medicines and on 30 April 1739 (*Walpurgisnacht*) she took no less than sixty preparations, smoking a pipe throughout to ease her congested lungs.

When she was clearly dying in the spring of 1741 she consented to being moved to Vienna, where she died on 5 May. Her post mortem was an extraordinary affair. Even in the 1740s, doctors could recognize most of the symptoms of cancer so the need for a post mortem seems odd. The payment to the doctor concerned was an astonishing £65,000 in today's terms, way over the amount usually paid. He found a tumour the size of a child's head in her pelvic area and noted her pallid condition.

Very little of the post mortem makes sense. Today, we would not be at all surprised by the ordinariness of the findings but in fact the doctor did not give a cause of death at all. Aristocrats were never anatomized in this way and why was the payment so enormous? One possible answer is that it was believed that Eleonore, like the anonymous men in the graveyard on her estates who might have infected her, was a vampire, and that the doctor was being paid both hush money and danger money because of a vampire's supposedly infectious nature. In other words, the post mortem was not a scientific fact-finding exercise, but a euphemistic destruction of a vampire. True, her head was not cut off – or at least there is no record of this – but her heart was removed. Was this the polite way to avoid a stake being driven through it?

Traditionally, the Schwarzenberg family had been buried in St Augustine's Church in Vienna; their lavish heraldic tombs are still there. Eleonore, however, does not lie with them. She is buried in St George's Chapel in the castle of Krumlov and her plain tomb with the chiselled inscription 'Eleonore, a poor sinner' is covered with a carpet. It is as difficult to find as the last resting place of the Impaler himself.

In 2007, the church gave permission for the television team to carry out a geo-radar scan on Eleonore's tomb. The camera showed a scattering of human bones which were almost certainly not Eleonore's – raising the question of whether someone else was buried with her – and a huge stone cage surrounding the coffin of Eleonore herself. Was this one last obstacle to the vampire princess returning from her grave?

In an age in which God's justice was still poetic and when 'murder will out', Vlad Ţepeş' end, if not Eleonore's, was almost pre-ordained. According to the Russian Orthodox accounts:

> Dracula loved the sweetness of the earthly world much more than the eternal world, and he abandoned Orthodoxy and thereby forsook the truth and the light and accepted darkness.[12]

This whole book is an attempt to find that light and that truth again. But if we are to find the light, we must first venture into the dark. Eleonore might still lie in her stone tomb, but Dracula has risen from the grave.

15

IN THE COMPANY OF CAIN
THE PSYCHOLOGY OF VLAD

After my death, whoever the Lord God grants the throne of Wallachia, whether it be one of my sons or relatives or, for our sins, one of another family, if he will strengthen, protect and renew this deed of mine, may God grant him His support; but if he will not renew and strengthen it and ruins and destroys it, let God destroy and kill him in the body in this world and in spirit in the hereafter he will be in the company of Judas and Cain and of all others to whom it was said: his blood be on them and on their children, as it is and will be, forever ...

This document, written during Vlad Ţepeş' second reign in Wallachia and now housed in the archive at Bucharest, is a *Hrisov*, a grant of lands to a boyar family. In that sense, it is typical of earlier documents issued by his predecessors. In the case of Ţepeş, however, it takes on a special meaning. Is the line 'for our sins' merely the empty phrase it has become today, or did the Impaler expect little mercy from his God because of the bloody actions of his life?

In February 2002 Slobodan Milosević went to trial at The Hague in Holland. He faced sixty-six charges covering three countries across which Ţepeş once rode. In Bosnia, he conspired, said the prosecution, to wipe out Muslims and Croats over a three-year period in the 1990s. In this case there were two charges of genocide, ten of crimes against humanity, eight grave breaches of the Geneva Convention and nine violations of laws and customs of war. In Croatia, where non-Serbs were 'ethnically cleansed' between August 1991 and June 1992, there were two counts of crimes against humanity, thirteen violations of the laws and customs of war and nine grave breaches of the Geneva Convention. In Kosovo, with its twice fought-over Field of Blackbirds, 800,000 Albanians were expelled in six months of 1999. In this instance there were four counts of crimes against humanity and one violation of the laws and customs of war.

Geoffrey Nice QC, outlining sample crimes for the benefit of the court, chose, apparently at random, 20 November 1991. On that day 255 non-Serbs from the general hospital of Vukovar in Croatia were transported to a farm some three miles away. Here, beaten and tortured for hours, the hapless group was divided into huddles of ten or twenty and shot. Their bodies were dumped, Nazi-style, into a mass grave. In Bosnia on the same day, said Nice, a heavily pregnant woman was forced out of her village home by Serb troops and had to give birth to her baby in the woods nearby, without help, without medical facilities, without a roof over her head. She was one of forty-five local people promised Red Cross help by Serb paramilitaries. Instead they were taken to a house with a strange smell. The smell came from the floor and its carpets which had been soaked in petrol. The doors were locked and someone threw in a match. 'They were all burned alive,' Nice told the court. 'The baby's screams were heard for some two hours before it, too, succumbed.'[1] And on that same day in Kosovo, to the background whine and thump of artillery shells, Serb forces roamed the villages, shooting men and raping women. One woman, separated from her twenty-year-old daughter in the panic, eventually found her body along with seven others she recognized at the bottom of a well, probably thrown in alive to die of thirst and starvation. The *Daily Mail*'s banner headline screamed, with deep relevance to this book, 'Calculated cruelty, medieval savagery.'

In the same issue, criminologist Brian Masters wrote an analysis of Slobodan Milosević, the 'butcher of Belgrade', that beautiful city once owned by another tyrant, George Branković and saved from Turkish destruction by János Hunyadi, the White Knight. Masters told us that the names of hundreds of Milosević's victims were listed by the prosecution and their ages were written alongside. There were many children among them ... twelve, six, three, one ... the results of random slaughter by a megalomaniac. Masters was clearly horrified, as most of us would be, by sitting in the same room as Milosević. He was:

> not a monster who can be readily labelled as such. He shows no signs of psychopathic disorder. Nor does he appear to be a Jekyll and Hyde, or one of Dostoevsky's characters in the grip of a compulsion; he is not a bloody maniac by night and harmless statesman by day. He does not show the signs of the necrophiliac character who cherishes death and loves the proximity of corpses. There is no evidence that he is a sadist, bent upon causing pain and watching its effects in order to find peace within himself. He is not a serial killer or mass murderer ... It is not suggested that he personally strangled, shot or torched his victims ...[2]

Benjamin Disraeli once famously said that there 'are three kinds of lies; lies, damned lies and statistics'. And nothing is more difficult to deal with than crime statistics. Throw into the equation the vagueness of medieval arithmetic and we are quickly at sea. At the end of any battle in the Middle Ages, the clerks and heralds of the winning side would comb the field, looking for corpses. They recognized the nobility by their coats of arms, embroidered on jupons or tabards or painted on the shields still strapped to their bodies. The common soldiery, even those who wore the livery or crest of the house they served, were rarely counted.

If we take English battles that were contemporary with the Impaler's reign of terror (because they are the best documented) we find the chroniclers' figures are fairly consistent. There were an estimated 2,300 dead after the second battle of St Albans on 17 February 1461. By this time, the practice was developing of butchering prisoners after a battle because they were a nuisance and expensive to feed. The figures are much heavier for Towton in the following month (in fact, this is the bloodiest battle on English soil), partly because of the topography of the field – Bloody Meadow was a murderous cul-de-sac created by a loop of the river Cock and by high ground, into which the losing Lancastrians were driven – and partly because it was fought in a snowstorm, making visibility and escape difficult. But Towton illustrates the statistics problem very well. Polydore Vergil, the Tudor historian, estimates 20,000 dead and wounded on both sides, Yorkist and Lancastrian. The contemporary Croyland Continuator claims 38,000; Tudor Edward Hall, an oddly precise 36,776; and the contemporary letters of Margaret Paston, 28,000. Clearly, they cannot all be right. The point at issue is that none of the figure compilers was actually present at Towton. The Continuator was probably a politician away from the action; Polydore Vergil was writing fifty years after the event, as was Hall and for the next generation.[3]

Medieval chroniclers, who were hardly ever eye-witnesses to events, embellished numbers for effect. According to them, a particular hero could kill a thousand men in the course of a battle – physically impossible given the weapons of the time – and perform astonishing feats. In England, the fictional Guy of Warwick killed the enormous – and equally fictional – Dun Cow that ravaged the neighbourhood of the town. John

Lambton slew a dragon causing equal havoc in his neck of the woods, with the particularly unfrightening name of the Lambton worm. All this was recorded as hard fact, without any shred of doubt or qualification.

What, then are we to make of Vlad Ţepeş' own statistics, written in his letter to Matthias Corvinus in February 1462? At Oblucita and Novoselo, 1,350; at Dirstor, Cirtal and Dridopotrom, 6,840 and so on. The tally cited by the Impaler, over a two-week killing spree and involving eighteen specified villages and towns, is an astonishing 20,019. This, however, is a rough estimate, the letter tells us and Ţepeş' grand total is '23,884 Turks and Bulgars'. And we cannot dismiss these figures as lightly as we can those of the Croyland Continuator or Polydore Vergil. Ţepeş was there. And he had a grim tally stick – literally a count of heads. Radu Farma, the boyar who took the letter to Corvinus, also carried with him two bags of heads, noses and ears. What was the point of this? Was Ţepeş trying to impress the uncrowned King of Hungary? He needed his support in what would be a desperate war against the Turks. It is difficult to see how these grisly statistics and the even more grisly bag-contents would help. Presumably, it showed Corvinus that the war had really started and that the Impaler meant business, but it could equally have convinced the wary procrastinator that the voivod did not need his help after all. The account of Antonio Bonfini at Corvinus' court suggests that it was Ţepeş' excessive cruelty that led the king to imprison him for so long. Certainly, these seemingly exact figures are unusual, perhaps even unique in medieval history. We have no way, of course, of verifying them.

If we turn to what could be termed Ţepeş' 'peace time' slaughter and look at the Saxon stories which were already circulating by the time of his imprisonment by Corvinus, a different pattern emerges. Where numbers are mentioned, rather than the ubiquitous 'all' or 'many' who are suffering various forms of butchery, we are given the following statistics: two pretenders (Vladislav II and Dan II); a gypsy;

two priests (one with his donkey); the putatively pregnant mistress; the boyar who complained of the stench of decaying corpses; the wife of the man with the overly short shirt; 200 poor people burned in a Tîrgovişte hall; 600 merchants from the Thunow and Pregel districts in Wuetzerland; 400 young men who had come to Wallachia to learn the language; 500 boyars who could not tell him how many princes had ruled Wallachia in their lifetime; and 30,000 killed at Amlaş on St Bartholomew's Day 1460. Even without the indiscriminate slaughter of Christians, pagans and Jews at Nicopolis (which could be said to be an act of war because this was 1462 and part of Ţepeş' raid along the Danube), the arithmetic comes to 31,707.

If we scale up the 'all's and 'many's that are listed in the Saxon tales, we have an estimate of around 100,000 victims of Ţepeş' 'calculated cruelty; medieval barbarism'. And many people have casually accepted this figure as the truth. Miranda Twiss,[4] for instance, accepts the 500 boyar impalements at Tîrgovişte (this figure does not include their families) and the knifing of Ţepeş' mistress who claimed to be pregnant. The interjection by Twiss of words like 'perhaps' 20,000 forming the forest of the impaled and 'it is rumoured that' over 30,000 died on St Bartholomew's Day get a little lost when we are faced with the enormity of these figures in print.

Two examples of analysis cast doubt on the sheer scale of Ţepeş' depravity. The first is the practical consideration of the prince's palace at Tîrgovişte, the ruins of which still remain and which I visited in 2008. It is most unlikely that 500 boyars, as well as their wives and families (and no doubt retainers), could have fitted inside the Great Hall – it had room for 200 people at most. The courtyard outside, which is the scene of the impaling of the 500, could probably hold thirty or forty upright stakes. The Saxon stories (and the Russian versions agree) say that this impalement was instant, rather than carried out in batches over a period of time. Such slaughter is simply not possible. The second factor is the likely population of

Wallachia in Vlad Ţepeş' time. A reasonable estimate is that the Impaler's principality was about 48,000 square miles of territory with approximately 3,220 towns and villages, but it may have been smaller still, around 29,560 square miles. The towns were tiny by modern comparison and the villages often mere clusters of huts near a water source. Various historians estimate, but do not give their sources, that the total population of medieval Wallachia was about half a million. If this is correct, then Ţepeş' death rate becomes ludicrous. We are asked to believe by the Saxon chroniclers that in the St Bartholomew's Day attack at Amlaş alone, where 30,000 perished, the Impaler was wiping out 6 per cent of the country's entire population. If we extrapolate further, that Ţepeş' total body count is over 100,000, then we are talking about 20 per cent, the equivalent in Britain today of 12 million people. Today of course, it could be done, using modern killing methods, or even those as relatively unrefined as the bullets of the Nazi *einzatsgruppen* or the Zyklon B pellets of the death camps in the 1940s. The sheer *mechanics* of impalement however tell a different story.

If we analyse the Saxon stories – and they are echoed, of course, in the Russian and Romanian versions – we can build up a body of evidence which helps us establish, in part at least, Ţepeş' psyche. Of the thirty-two tales, eleven have a proven basis in fact whereas thirteen can be seen to be examples of gratuitous viciousness. The innocuous young people, up to an alleged 400 men, who had come to learn the language and customs of Wallachia were almost certainly spies; that is certainly how Ţepeş saw them. They were locked in a room and burned alive. Such methods are as old as time and still paraded today among the crimes of Slobodan Milosević. But Ţepeş' execution methods were far more ingenious than that. According to one of the Saxon stories:

> ... he had a big copper cauldron built and put a lid made of wood with holes in it on top. He put the people in the cauldron

and put their heads in the holes and fastened them there; then he filled it with water and set fire under it and let the people cry their eyes out until they were burned to death.[5]

And then he invented frightening, terrible, unheard of tortures. He ordered that women be impaled together with their suckling babies on the same stake. The babies fought for their lives at their mothers' breasts until they died. Then he had the women's breasts cut off and put the babies inside head first; thus he had them impaled together.

And then he put many people on spinning wheels and killed them.

And then this Dracula would roast little children and force their own mothers to eat them. And he ordered that the breasts of many women be cut off and he forced their men to eat them ...

Antonio Bonfini, the Hungarian court chronicler, throws in a nice little addition to Ţepeş' behaviour:

And then he often peeled the skin off the feet of Turkish prisoners and covered their wounds with salt, then brought goats to lick their salted soles.

Torture, 'even unto death', was universal in Europe in Vlad Ţepeş' time. It was not formally abolished in the German states until 1831, in Russia until 1847. In fact the earliest known official abolition in Western Europe was Scotland in 1708. Various statesmen lied about this, like Sir Thomas Smith, Secretary of State to Elizabeth I of England:

Torment or question, which is used by the order of the civil law and custom of other countries, to put a malefactor to excessive pain ... is not used in England ... beatings, servitude and servile torment and punishment [the state] will not abide.[6]

Lopping off ears and noses was standard practice for minor infringements everywhere. In England nearly half a century after Dracula a Dr Leighton had both ears cut off and both nostrils slit open. He was also branded on both cheeks for writing seditious materials during the brief 'reign' of Lady Jane Grey. In another English case in 1552, a fraudster had his ears nailed to a post in Cheapside. The only way to cut him loose again was by slicing off his ears. In France, the 'spider king' Louis XII passed laws known as *essorillement* twenty years after Țepeș' death in which servants lost ears for dishonesty. A third offence meant execution. Such mutilations were also commonplace in the East. In Egypt, adulterous women had their noses cut off[7] and as late as 1779 a horrified visiting Englishman wrote, 'He who commits a rape on a free woman has his privities cut off, that it might be out of his power ever to perpetrate the like crime ...'[8] The Turks themselves hacked off hands and feet. According to Grafton's Chronicle, when the Turks invaded Austria in the early seventeenth century they:

> comitted such cruelties and tyranny as never hath bene heard nor written, for of some they put out the eyes, of others they cut off the noses and eares, of others they cut off the pappes and ravished virgins and of women great with child, they cut their bellies and burnt the children.[9]

Did they learn all this from Vlad Țepeș?[10]

A common punishment in the Turkish army was to whip the soles of a soldier's feet so that marching was excruciating. The 'goat-licking routine' described by Bonfini was used extensively in France. French victims were tied to a bench and had their feet soaked in salt water before the rasping tongue of the goat caused acute agony.

Flaying, which features in the canon of Țepeș' crimes, was also popular in France. The skin was removed from the top of the head first and so on down. Few survived below the chest. In 1366 the Count of Rouci died this way, for treason during the Hundred Years War. Being buried alive, as was the

Impaler's brother, Mircea, was a standard method of dispatch by the Inquisition in Western Europe. The last known instance of it featured Anne van de Hoor, from Malines in the Netherlands, who was buried up to her chin. Refusing to recant, her torturers/executioners merely shovelled on the soil until she died of suffocation. Death by burning was of course a punishment usually reserved for heretics, to prepare them in what remained of this life for the flames of Hell to come in the next. In the appalling *auto da fe* of sixteenth-century Spain, thousands came to their deaths, with dozens being burned together as public entertainment. An estimated 13,000 'heretics' died this way between 1481 and 1517.

Ţepeş' fiendish cauldron had its echoes too. For sixteen years during the reign of Henry VIII of England, murder by poisoning was punished by this means. Because the targets of Richard Roose were the family of the Bishop of Rochester, the king took exception and had the crime made one of high treason by Act of Parliament in 1513. Various methods were used, including immersion in already boiling water, the rather more grim method of heating cold water, or the use of boiling oil or tallow (candle-wax) instead. Similar systems were in use in France until the final abolition by law in 1791. Eleven years after Vlad Ţepeş' death, such an execution went horribly wrong in Tours when Loys Secretan, a coiner, was immersed by the local executioner, Denys. Secretan's ropes worked loose in the bubbling water and he kept bobbing to the surface, screaming for help. The crowd took pity on him, hauled him out and kicked the executioner to death.

The 'spinning wheels' of which the Saxon stories speak were widely used in Western Europe. The victim was spread-eagled, usually naked, onto an iron-flanged cart wheel and the limbs repeatedly struck with hammers or iron bars until the bones broke. A skilful practitioner could achieve this without breaking the skin. In France, the wheel was mounted horizontally on a post while the executioners went to work on arms and legs with an iron bar three feet long and two inches square. By the late eighteenth century this was a more common method of execution than the more conventional hanging practised elsewhere. In Germany the wheel was fixed to a tripod so that a good view could be had by the spectators on every side. Regulations here specified that forty blows were to be given, only the last one aimed at the nape of the neck to snap the spine and deliver the coup de grace.

The Holy Inquisition, already in existence by Ţepeş' time against heretics like the Hussites in Bohemia, the Bogomils in Serbia and Wallachia and the Lollards in England, was developing such torture and execution methods to a fine art. For these fanatics torture served a purpose – to root out heresy which subverted God's laws – and so they also developed an intellectual justification for it to which Vlad Ţepeş may have subscribed. Woodcuts of the torture implements used at Bamberg in Germany in 1508 include everything that Ţepeş employed, except one – the stake for impalement.

It is this means of execution that marks Vlad Ţepeş out from all the other ghastly methods that haunt the late Middle Ages. We have established already that life was cheap, and that in Wallachia, as in most European states, the word of the ruler was law. These were the necessary ingredients, the background against which impaling could take place. *The Devil's Dictionary* originally written in 1911 but not published until 1993 has this definition:

Impale, v.t. In popular usage to pierce with any weapon which remains fixed in the wound. This however is inaccurate; to impale is, properly, to put to death by thrusting an upright sharp stake into the body, the victim being left in a sitting position. This was a common mode of punishment among the nations of antiquity ...

But was it? The dictionary goes on to quote China and other parts of Asia, where it 'is still in high favour' and claims that until the beginning of the fifteenth century it was 'widely employed in "churching" heretics and schismatics'. An authority called Wolecraft refers to impalement as 'the stoole of repentynge' and that, rather as the gallows was 'the drop' and being broken on the rack was 'marrying the Duke of Exeter's daughter' (in England), impalement was known as 'riding the one-legged horse'.

In 1995 the world's first Dracula conference was held in Romania in which experts lectured on a number of related themes.[10] Professor Lloyd Worley of the University of Northern Colorado, who, as well as investigating the 'prenatal and natal foundations of the vampire myth' through literature, pathology and psychology, also looked at the act of impalement in some detail. Worley's description of the act is markedly different from the woodcuts produced to accompany the Saxon horror stories of Ţepeş at the turn of the fifteenth/sixteenth centuries. Impaling, says Worley, was:

> the thrusting of a long stake or shaft through the anus [in the case of women sometimes through the vagina], through the intestines to the diaphragm muscle. The naked victim was then hoisted upward and the pole fixed in the ground. Subsequent writhing eventually forced the stake upward to pierce the heart, causing death (if the victim had not already died of shock or blood loss). Even after death, the impaling process continued, with gravity often causing the stake to exit through the mouth.[11]

The Saxon stories imply that Ţepeş invented those 'terrible, unheard of' tortures. But that is simply not true. Assyrian bas-reliefs as early as 700 BC show Israelites impaled by King Sennacherib after he took their town of Lachish. The term for this is *al ha-es*, meaning 'hanging on a pole' and the phrase is vague enough to mean hanging by the neck by conventional methods. Worley quotes the authority of the Dead Sea Scrolls found at Qumran and probably dating to the second century before Christ. The Bible itself makes a number of references to impalement with examples in Deuteronomy, Joshua, Esther and Ezekiel. It is clear from these examples – 'And if a man have committed a sin worthy of death and he be put to death and thou hang him on a tree' – that the punishment was known before Sennacherib, but this verse from Deuteronomy sounds suspiciously like hanging a body in a gibbet, perhaps as a deterrent, which was widespread throughout Europe until the eighteenth century. Worley makes it clear, however, that in the original Hebrew the word loosely translated as 'tree' is in fact 'staff' or 'timber' and the term 'to hang' actually means to 'fix' or 'make firm'. It is possible that the Egyptians used impalement as a form of punishment for a crime, but likely that Sennacherib was the first to use it as Ţepeş did, as a means of instilling psychological terror into his enemies, be they Ottoman Turks, shifty merchants from Braşov or treacherous boyars. As a warlord and conqueror, the Assyrian king faced many of the same problems as Ţepeş, eventually being murdered by one of his sons, in 681 BC.

The horror of impalement was carried over into the New Testament, at least as a folk-memory, and the victim was deemed to be 'accursed of God'. The Romans, of course, used crucifixion as an alternative method and vague references to Celtic practices by both Julius Caesar and by Strabo, the Greek geographer, if they were talking about impalement, were regarded by the Romans as horrific. There are no known references to it throughout the Dark Ages, despite appalling atrocities by various nomadic bands of warriors including the Dacians in what would become Wallachia. Steven Runciman in his monumental history of the crusades refers to a band of Franks on their way to Jerusalem, marching through Hungary and impaling a boy whose village they were looting. Worley conjectures that this was possibly learned from the Turks, although he concedes that there is no hard evidence for this. The fact that Venetian sailors running from captured Constantinople in 1453 made a great deal about their captain, Rizzo, being impaled, suggests that it was a rare and perhaps even unique spectacle. The very fact that Mehmed II's invading army in 1462 does not seem to have used the technique surely speaks volumes for the fact that it was not a Turkish custom, even in a war of attrition. When Vlad Ţepeş was finally killed, allegedly by a Turkish assassin, it was his head that was taken back to the sultan's court, not his entire body impaled.

The mechanics of impalement are problematic and make it doubly difficult to accept the ludicrous body count of the Saxon stories. When they and others calmly say 'Dracula impaled them', the reality of course is that several men and probably horses would be needed for each impalement. This was presumably the role of the *Armas*, a sort of execution squad-cum-private army 500 years before the Tottenkopf SS. The most probable method was to pin the victim, already naked, to the ground by sheer weight of numbers and hold the legs apart by means of ropes attached to the horses. The stake, presumably a reasonably stout, straight but not too large tree-trunk, was oiled and inserted through either the anus or vagina. The problem with this is resistance. The tip of the stake would probably meet bone at some stage and even if not, it would take considerable force to insert the wood through the tough sphincter muscle, yards of twisted gut and the even more formidable diaphragm. Even the grain of the timber would be a problem here, because wood is by no means as penetrative as metal (hence the need for iron-tipped arrows and spears). If the impalement was carried out with the victim lying horizontally on the ground, that would probably need four men to hold him or her down and a fifth to insert the stake. The woodcuts show an altogether easier and more likely process (which would also explain how babies could be impaled with their mothers) of driving a stake through the body either from the chest or back, like insects on a display board.

I put the impalement problem to physicist Brian Bond who came back after deliberation with a 'nutcracker' force theory. He hypothesized that three growing trees, forming a rough 'L' shape could be used and a long tree trunk cut down and laid between them. Experienced men – the *Armas* – would exert leverage on the free end of the trunk and this would have the effect of driving the impalement stake as though with a mallet into the orifice of the victim, who would previously have been tied on the ground by the ankles to two other trees. Experts, Bond believes, could carry out this operation in about five minutes, although, of course, large numbers would be needed and, at least in 1462, time was of the essence. The method recorded by Dr Meryon in Syria in 1813 of draping a victim over a saddle on the ground, slitting the anus and using a wooden mallet, would not seem to be very efficacious given the numbers involved.

According to some theorists, victims could linger for days like this. Wild Dream Television company, in their *Ancient Discoveries* television series, carried out a fascinating piece of computer-generated forensic work under the auspices of trauma surgeon Mike Edwards in 2008. His task was to discover whether it was possible for a victim to remain alive, impaled, for up to two days, as some of the Vlad horror stories suggest. By using a narrow-ended stake, Edwards posited that it *would* be possible if the stake missed the vital organs of the heart and lungs. Clearly, this could only be achieved in reality by trial and error, so that in practice some people died slowly, others straight away. And of course, it was not Edwards' remit to consider the effects of shock on the body's nervous system.

There are also all kinds of question marks over how the stake, with the weight of their victims, could be anchored firmly in the ground. We know that crosses for crucifixion were hauled upright by means of ropes and pulleys, with the victim in place, but the horizontal beam of the cross made this relatively easy. If we take 'the forest' of the impaled literally, then perhaps living trees were used with the branches cut off. Again, we have the impossibility of being able to hoist the victim onto the top of such a tree. No contemporary records give us any indication of the height of the stake, but even a six-foot trunk would cause enormous problems. And it is worth remembering that this 'forest' was created by an army retreating in front of an oncoming and much larger Turkish force. Tursun Bey, who was with Mehmed's army, specifically refers to a 'field' of the impaled, implying that the stakes were not growing, but driven into the ground.

Such preparation, cutting down trees, lopping off branches, stripping victims, holding or tying them down, inserting the stakes and somehow hoisting into position would be at best a lengthy and extremely difficult process.

In one sense, then, the tortures and executions ordered by the Impaler were probably always actually carried out by other people, so that he becomes physically removed from the crime. Even so, he is removed by yards or feet rather than miles and that makes him a different kind of mass-murderer from, say, Adolf Hitler, Joseph Stalin or Slobodan Milosević. There is little doubt that Hitler condoned wholeheartedly the 'final solution' which exterminated over six million Jews, but there is no evidence that he ever entered the gates of a death camp. There is a world of difference, in terms of psyche, between a Hitler and a Ţepeş. The law and social morality might brand them equally guilty, but the Impaler was a hands-on murderer. There are a handful of telling clues that help us to understand him.

His black humour, referred to in the various stories, just *may* have a basis in fact and it is found in several murderers. 'What a nuisance they are!' he is supposed to have complained to a boyar as they walked below the twitching bodies dying on their stakes and, with an even more sinister connotation, 'How beautiful they look.' This is the stuff of twentieth-century serial killers like Ed Gein, who wrapped himself in his victims' skins, and Jeffrey Dahmer, who kept severed heads in his fridge. Ţepeş seems to have had a strangely puritanical streak at odds with his depravity and this, too, is a not uncommon trait of sex killers. Adulterous women in particular were singled out according to the tales. Their breasts were sliced off, as were their vaginas. One faithless wife was impaled in a square in Tîrgovişte with her skin lying on a table nearby. The mistress who lied to the voivod by telling him she was pregnant suffered disembowelling at the Impaler's own hand. Because we know almost nothing about his sex life, not even the name of his first wife, this line of enquiry leads to a dead end.

Another tale about Ţepeş may hold a clue as to what sort of man he was. This time, the source is not the obvious paranoia of the German merchants but Fedor Kuritsyn, who almost certainly interviewed people who had spent a great deal of time with the Impaler at Buda. The Russian envoy wrote:

> It is said of him that he could not cure himself of the evil habit of catching mice and having birds bought at the market place so that he could punish them by impalement. He cut off the heads of some of the birds; others he had stripped of their feathers and then let loose.

Another version of this and one unlikely to have come from Kuritsyn occurs in a letter from Gabriele Rangoni, the Bishop of Erlau and Papal legate to Pope Sixtus IV, in the year of Ţepeş' death:

> Unable to forget his wickedness, he caught mice and, cutting them up into pieces, stuck them on small pieces of wood, just as he had stuck men on stakes.[12]

The problem with psychoanalysis is that it is all things to all men. Even experts cannot agree among themselves, which is the loophole that lawyers in criminal cases use today – the expert witness for the prosecution is countered by the expert witness for the defence. And that is before we get into the realms of Freud and Jung. The historian, however, has to try. We cannot make sense of Vlad Ţepeş unless we try to see beyond the monster of legend and the dark, saucer-eyes of the Ambras portrait.

Animal torture, especially in young people, is one of the three warning signs of the potential serial killer known by American psychiatrists as the 'triad'. We know so little of Ţepeş' childhood that we cannot apply the other two signs – bed-wetting and obsession with fire – and of course the animal mutilations at Buda, if they really happened, took place when he was in his thirties and early forties. American psychotics like Henry Lee Lucas and Jeffrey Dahmer both tortured animals to death. Edmund Kemper was fascinated by cats, burying one alive before digging it up and decapitating it. Peter Kurtin, the 'monster of Dusseldorf' in Weimar Germany, slaughtered sheep while having sex with them and once decapitated a swan, drinking the blood from its severed neck. If the tale of Ţepeş eating al fresco among the corpses of his staked victims and mopping up their blood with his bread is true, then we have another obsession, what criminologists call 'haematomania', the extremely rare obsession with blood we noted earlier.

Numerous Saxon and other stories deal with enforced cannibalism, the Impaler presiding over one set of victims obliged to eat others. As we have seen, recent studies on this bizarre form of behaviour have established that it was probably common in primitive cultures at the mercy of the weather and bad harvests. Classic tales of survival from the Donner wagon train marooned in the Rocky Mountains in the 1840s to the Andes plane crash in 1972 bear witness to the fact that even this last of all taboos can be broken in moments of necessity. Psychopaths like Fritz Haarmann, who sold human flesh on the black market in inter-war Hanover, and Albert Fish, who stewed twelve-year-old Grace Budd in his life-long search for sexual kicks, are the reality on which Thomas Harris' appalling Hannibal Lecter is based. Even so, we only have the lurid 'horror' tales of the Impaler as evidence of this particular perversion.

Criminologist Colin Wilson rates Timur-i-Leng as 'the most spectacular sadist in world history' with Vlad Ţepeş a close second. Like many modern authorities, Wilson is perfectly happy to accept the exaggerated statistics of slaughter. So Timur, according to legend, bricked up 2,000 prisoners at Sabwazar in 1383 and made a pyramid of 5,000 decapitated heads at Zirih. He slaughtered 100,000 prisoners at Delhi and at Sivas in Anatolia 4,000 Christians were buried alive. Wilson includes Ţepeş' 'estimated' 100,000 victims and assumes that the Impaler received harsh treatment at the hands of the Turks during his teenaged captivity which left him a warped individual. This may indeed be the case. If Radu was the victim of Mehmed II's homosexual urges, was Vlad a similar target? True, the Wallachian was a year older than the sultan's son, but we cannot know what pressures he was under during his years as a prisoner at Egrigöz and Edirne.

An analysis of two other historical multiple murderers may help us understand the Impaler. In the cases of Gilles de Rais and Elizabeth Báthory, we immediately run into the same problem we have with Vlad Ţepeş – the unreliability of contemporary evidence. De Rais was Gilles de Laval, Baron de Rais, who was executed in France when Vlad Ţepeş was nine. He was accused by the Catholic Church of being a:

> heretic, apostate, conjuror of demons ... accused of the crime and vices against nature, sodomy, sacrilege and violation of the immunities of Holy Church.[14]

During his trial in September 1439, de Rais was charged with:

> having taken innocent boys and girls and inhumanly butchered, killed, dismembered, burned and otherwise tortured them ... and has foully committed the sin of sodomy with young boys and in other ways lusted against nature after young girls, spurning the natural way of copulation ...

In echoes of later child killers like Peter Kurten and Albert Fish, de Rais is said to have confessed to his servant Henriet:

that he took more pleasure in the murder of the said children and in seeing their heads and limbs separated from their body, in seeing them die and their blood flow, than in having carnal knowledge of them.

Incredibly, there are echoes of Ţepeş' method of impalement – the stake thrust through the anus which has vague links with the supposed sodomy of Gilles de Rais. It is interesting, however, that whereas de Rais' crimes were overtly sexual in nature, those of Ţepeş were not. What is even more interesting is that the very Church who condemned de Rais recently overturned all charges against him, pouring huge doubt not only on the charges, the evidence of the 110 prosecution witnesses at his trial, but also the alleged confession of de Rais himself.

No such pardon has been given to Elizabeth Báthory. Many books refer to her as 'Countess Dracula' because of her obsession with blood and some claim that she was a descendant of Ţepeş. She *was* a descendant of Stephen Báthory, who had fought alongside the Impaler in his last campaign and she *did* rule in Transylvania, which probably explains the confusion. It was probably Elizabeth Báthory who Sheridan le Fanu had in mind when he wrote his best selling *Carmilla* in the 1870s. Colin Wilson paints a cheerful picture of the dysfunctional family from which she came: 'her brother was sexually insatiable, one uncle was a devil worshipper and an aunt was a witch and a lesbian.'[13] Báthory stood trial – or rather, not, as she refused to attend in person or offer a plea – in the winter of 1611, accused of the murder of over fifty young girls. Her motive was not directly sexual (despite her obvious lesbian relationships with various maids) but she believed that she could remain ever-youthful by drinking the victims' blood and bathing in it, reminiscent perhaps of Eleonore von Schwarzenberg's obsession with wolf's milk. Her accomplices were either beheaded or had their fingers ripped out and she was walled up alive with only a small hole for the delivery of food until her death in August 1614.

Rather as Vlad Ţepeş has been blackened by centuries of propaganda, so was Elizabeth Báthory. The number of her victims ranges from eight to 650, allowing us to challenge *all* the contemporary sources. She and her husband lived at a time when Hungary and Austria were seriously threatened by the last gasp of Ottoman expansion and her husband, Count Francis Nadasdy, seems to have behaved very like Vlad and for the same reasons – the Turks were at his gate. Literature of his own time had him dancing with Turkish corpses dangling from his teeth and playing bizarre games of bowls with their severed heads.

Nadasdy's death in 1604 left Elizabeth exposed to many enemies at the Viennese court. She was too powerful, too rich and above all too female to be allowed to continue in her place and a palace coup led by George Thurzo, the emperor's vice-regent in Hungary, staged a ludicrous show trial in which witnesses were told what their evidence should be.

What is common to all three 'monsters' – Ţepeş, de Rais and Báthory – is that because of their status and the physical enormity of their crimes, they had to have accomplices. Someone had to carry out the impaling, the procurement of children and the draining of blood; all three, according to contemporary evidence, had any number of servants willing to do that.

Modern 'vampire killers' normally have no such aid. And it is ironic that, for the purposes of this book, although we know a great deal about what motivates such people, the structure of today's society means that it is impossible to reproduce a Ţepeş unless they can be found in the 'banality of evil' in instances like Milosević. As Benjamin Disraeli observed as early as 1831,[14] 'The Age of Chivalry is past. Bores have succeeded to dragons.' Many of the killers cited by Monaco and Burt in their book *The Dracula Syndrome* are not truly vampiric – their blood-fetish is only a by-product of the greater elements of sadism involving degradation and power. Psychologist Marc Savlov in an interview in November 1998 said of today's society that it actually *promotes* vampiric values:

> we worship people in power and fall on our knees before people who *take* from us. We give in to co-dependent relationships and want to stay with someone who has power even if they're defeating us. And yet we pretend that what we're really all about is family values and good and charity.[15]

So where can psycho-analysis of a man dead for five and a half centuries take us? If we follow the precepts of the now outdated and frequently attacked Sigmund Freud, we make little headway because we know almost nothing about Vlad Țepeș' childhood and it is from childhood that Freud says all our troubles arise. Other than what may be the puritanical streak we have observed in his punishments for immorality among women, Țepeș' sexuality is a closed book. It may even be that the murder of his mistress was done, if it was done, in the heat of the moment because she had ridiculed him by lying. We cannot get far because we have no idea of the content of the Impaler's dreams. In Freudian terms, a simplistic answer to Țepeș' 'problem' is that he lacked a super-ego which in most people controls their external actions and takes them along conventional paths of what is acceptable. Clearly, even by fifteenth-century standards, mass impalement was not. If we accept Freud's version, Țepeș was driven by the Thanatos instinct, essentially an aggressive death-wish aimed at others. Intriguingly, Freud used the mass trauma of the First World War to analyse the effects of slaughter on human beings. Individuals, he observed, and indeed whole states, discarded morals at the drop of a hat and used war as an excuse for aggressive, brutal behaviour. When he looked more broadly at society's role in controlling human beings, he decided that one major task was to control the baser instincts which includes what he called '*lustmord*', the enjoyment of killing. Clearly in Ţepeş' time, when the leader of the Catholic Church called for crusade to kill the Infidel and the followers of Mohammed were offered paradise by way of jihad, there was little chance of such control in the world of Vlad Ţepeş.

We are even more at sea with Freud's one-time friend and protégé Carl Jung because even though the man's intellectual interests were more wide-ranging than Freud's, embracing archaeology, astrology, alchemy and world religions, he again relied heavily on the portents of dreams, his own driving him in a certain direction. He did, however, specifically address the problem of evil: 'where love stops,' he wrote, 'power begins and violence and terror.' Once again, we cannot know anything about Ţepeş' loves and so trying to put the man on the psychiatrist's couch is in the end self-defeating. He may have been schizophrenic; he may have been self-delusional; he may have been a raving lunatic. We simply do not have the evidence to be sure.

Of two things we can, however, be sure; Vlad Ţepeş was a mass-murderer and he was a psychopath. Opportunities for mass murder were rare in the past. Today, because of the technology of mass destruction, they are far easier. Any terrorist bomb, for instance, with the simplest trigger mechanism, is capable of killing dozens in a single blast. The spectacular attacks on the World Trade Center in New York on 11 September 2001 killed nearly three thousand. It is peculiarly given to men like Vlad Ţepeş that because of the situation in which they found themselves – unrestrained power on the one hand and war on the other – they had outlets for their sadistic impulses and could act accordingly.

Today, psychologist Professor Adrian Furnham of University College, London, explains, 'A psychopath doesn't have to be violent or dangerous,'[16] although, of course, many of them are. American psychologists use a sixteen-point scale of criteria identified by the American Psychiatric Association. There are things we cannot know of Vlad Ţepeş – for instance, whether he had a poorly integrated sex life, one of the sixteen points. Likewise, 'poor consistency in work behaviour' sounds a little modern and banal when applied to a fifteenth-century warlord. Other criteria, however, make good sense from what we know of the Impaler's actions. Clearly, he was 'impulsive' and 'reckless'. His ripping open of his mistress, his nailing the Turkish emissaries' turbans to their heads, his attack in 1462 along the Danube – all this and more betokens a man who does not always weigh things rationally. Lying is another characteristic trait of the psychopath – Ţepeş' evasiveness in failing to pay direct homage to Mehmed at Constantinople, in which he basically pleaded an unstable principality, could well be an example. 'Illegal behaviour' must be viewed by different standards from our own. In Wallachia, he *was* the law, but he certainly broke the basic structure-bonds of Christianity with his wholesale slaughter especially in respect of women and children. He clearly 'took risks', another psychopathic trait – but then, what medieval ruler did not? Even the cautious time-server Matthias Corvinus was *eventually* forced into action against the Turks. Ţepeş' attack on Mehmed was foolhardy in the extreme; he was gambling on Corvinus and Stefan of Moldavia's support and got neither. He evinced an obvious 'lack of shame and remorse' throughout his career. He saw impalement and similar methods of execution as a fact of life as well as of death and rather seemed to relish the notoriety the killings gave him. Those who see in Ţepeş' endowments of monasteries some attempt to atone for his actions and to throw himself on the mercy of God in abject fits of remorse have misread the signs. *All* medieval rulers gave freely to the Church – it was expected. A 'failure to learn from experience' and 'poor judgement' can also be laid at the Impaler's door. Many writers say that Vlad's Turkish prison experiences as a boy taught him to trust no one. But the facts of his life prove that he did. He trusted János Hunyadi, he trusted Matthias Corvinus, he trusted Stefan of Moldavia, and presumably, many of the boyars he had elevated in the 1450s. He was to be betrayed by them all. Oddly, a phrase that sounds very modern – a 'failure to honour financial obligations' – fits Ţepeş perfectly. He refused to pay Mehmed his yearly tribute and consistently reneged on various trade deals with the merchants of Transylvania. He did exhibit acute 'pathological egocentricity'. Who else but Ţepeş could kill the constable rather than the thief as a hue and cry took place through his garden at Pest? The Impaler himself would never have called his 'anti-social behaviour' 'unmotivated'. He killed the poor because they were a blot on the Wallachian landscape. He killed Saxon merchants because they were bleeding his country dry. He killed Catholic monks because, at that time in his life, his alleged Orthodox upbringing made this acceptable. He killed Turks because they were the enemy. We may put a different gloss on all that today.

In the end, the hypothesis that Ţepeş' impaling may have been the twisted result of impotence, that in a Freudian way, the stake represented the phallic imagery of the maypole, a kind of sex substitute, cannot be proven. The jury will probably be out on that forever.

> But his fiercest fury was directed against women. He seems to have been darkly jealous of the perpetuation of the human race. Wives and concubines were strangled, sawn asunder and buried alive if they showed signs of pregnancy . . . Contemporary Arab chroniclers, pondering upon the fierce and gloomy passions of this man, arrived at the conclusion that he was the subject of a strange disease, a portentous secretion of black bile producing the melancholy which impelled him to atrocious crimes.[17]

We are not talking about the fifteenth-century Wallachian voivod here, but about the Arab Ibrahim ibn Ahmed who lived 600 years earlier. It would be of little comfort to the victims of either of them to know that, historically in the annals of murder, Vlad Ţepeş was not alone.

16

RESURRECTING DRACULA
VLAD TODAY

Six of them crept into the little graveyard shortly before midnight. There was Gheorghe Marinescu, Mitrica Mircea, Popa Stelika, Constantin Florea, Ionescu Ion and Pascu Oprea. It was not difficult to find the plot; the earth pile was still surmounted by the temporary wooden cross with the name Petre Toma. They laid the cross aside, knowing it had been moved by hands other than theirs and started to dig.

Two kept watch, although no one in the little village of Marotinul de Sus in southern Romania was likely to ask questions. Any of the villagers would know what those men were doing and why.

The soft patter of flying earth was replaced by the thud of a spade on the coffin lid and slowly, and with difficulty, they raised the casket out of the grave. They had the necessary tools: hammers, chisels, a pitchfork, stakes. But there was more to it than that. Time was of the essence and they could do nothing until they heard the clock chime twelve.

Then there was a flurry of activity, jabbing the chisels into the wood, ripping out the nails and screws, hauling the coffin lid aside. The wavering beams of their torches fell on Petre Toma and even the schnapps they had recently downed to steady their nerves could not have prepared them for what they saw. Petre Toma's arms had been laid across his chest when the undertakers laid him out; now they lay at his side. His face, staring sightlessly skyward before burial, now turned to the side. Most horrifyingly, his lips were brown with dried blood.

Marinescu ripped open the corpse with his pitchfork and the chest cavity with a wooden stake. He cut out the heart of Petre Toma and found it full of blood. The terrified little company saw the body relax and let out a long sigh. Now, they had to move fast. Stakes were driven through the body, pinning the arms and legs to the coffin floor. They sprinkled crushed garlic all over it and replaced the body in the grave, careful to put the crucifix back in position.

It was nearly half past midnight when the six left the cemetery, carrying the bloody heart on the prong of the pitchfork. When they reached the crossroads, Marinescu's wife, son and daughter-in-law were waiting. In a ritual older than time, they burned the heart, dissolved the ashes in water and drank the solution.

The account you have just read could come from any of the thousands of books of vampire fiction, even from Stoker's *Dracula* itself. It could even come from the eighteenth-century 'true vampire' stories we read in Chapter 6. Except that this one is not fiction, but fact. And it happened in Romania in 2004.

Petre Toma was a well-respected local teacher who died at the age of seventy-six and was buried on Christmas Day 2003. Almost immediately, his nephew and his entire family fell ill with an unexplained illness. A witness, as reported by the *Sunday Times*, saw the 'un-dead' Toma leaving his house as crows as black as the heraldic device of Matthias Corvinus flapped overhead. His grand-daughter, Mirela Marinescu, said:

> He sucked the life from us. We were all dying, my husband and my child and we all saw him come to us in the same dream.

The twenty-first century hit home hard in this weird time-warp when the dead man's daughter, Floarea Cotoran, reported the incident to the police. Petre Toma was exhumed anew, this time legally, and the autopsy revealed that his heart had indeed been taken. The police investigation resulted in the jailing of the six men for six months for desecration of the dead, but, more disturbingly, it uncovered evidence of up to twenty similar cases in the area over the past few years. As Marinescu explained:

> We performed a ritual that is hundreds of years old. We had no idea we were committing a crime. On the contrary, we believed that we were doing a good thing because the spirit of Petre was haunting us all and was very close to killing some of us. He came back from the dead and was after us.

In rural Romania, it seems, the vampire myth is not a myth at all. It is fact.

While Petre Toma was haunting his village, the creation of Draculaland was underway. Sighişoara, the birthplace of Vlad Ţepeş and one of the most beautiful surviving medieval towns in Europe, was until recently to be home to a Hollywood-style theme park costing an estimated $40 million to build. The theme park would, its creators believed, be bound to bring much-needed cash to the ailing Romanian economy.

In November 2001 *The Hollywood Reporter* covered an unseemly row between movie moguls Universal Studios and the Romanian tourist board. Universal claimed that Dracula was theirs. The classic elements in the film *Dracula* – the cape, the widow's peak, the blood-filled eyes, the fangs – were, said

Universal, their copyright and Romania would have to pay for their use. Veronica Miclea, head of the Romanian Tourist Office in Prague, Czechoslovakia, countered:

> Dracula is our trademark because Dracula belongs to Romania. [Universal] borrowed from us our Dracula and did these films, but forgot he is our character. When you say Dracula, you think of Transylvania; it is Romania.

Nobody in all this squabbling seems to have remembered the intervention of Bram Stoker. How long will it be before the Irish government wants a slice of the action? And bearing in mind where the Count's ship washed ashore in the novel, what will be the claims of Whitby Borough Council?

Romania hoped to make a killing. A million tourists were expected to visit the park scheduled for opening in 2003 and two new airports, and a road and rail link were underway. As the *Hollywood Reporter* says, an estimated additional $20 million in tourism revenue would be an important kick-start to further investment. The take-home pay of the average Romanian is $125 a month.

In January 2002 *The Spectator* painted a more gloomy economic picture. Agathon Dan, the Romanian tourist minister, found it difficult to interest foreign investors. The monthly take-home pay quoted in this article was an estimated $80 'for those who can find work'.[1] The investors seemed unimpressed with the theme park's attempt to recreate a 'horror castle' in which electronic effects would terrify visitors and an 'Institute of Vampirology' complete with Vlad's torture chamber where the Impaler 'skinned, boiled, burned, fried, buried alive, blinded, impaled, strangled and cut off the noses, ears and genitalia' of his victims.[2] Dan returned to Bucharest claiming victory, however, and batted aside opposition from feeble protest groups. His determination was summed up with the phrase, 'only God can stop this project now'. Perhaps God did, but He did it via the unlikely combination of Greenpeace, UNESCO and Prince Charles. Greenpeace was particularly concerned that an ancient oak forest, already old when Vlad Ţepeş was born, would be destroyed to create vampire rollercoasters. UNESCO, the United Nations cultural organization, complained about the proximity of such *kitsch* to the superb medieval town. Prince Charles is a patron of a society concerned for the preservation of Romanian heritage and blasted the ill-advised scheme on a cultural visit in 2003.

Nothing daunted, Draculaland's organizers said they will simply move the theme park to a site near Bucharest or even to Germany, but it has not happened yet. Instead, tourists are treated to plastic fangs, capes and Vlad T-shirts outside Bran Castle which has no actual links with the Impaler at all. Bran *looks* the part, with its picturesque turrets rising from solid rock, but the interior had a total makeover in the 1920s when it was a royal residence and has, if anything, more of a feel of a Lutyens house.

What would Vlad Dracula, the Voivod and Prince of Wallachia, have made of all this? And more importantly, what are we to make of him? First, we must remember that a great deal of the information we have on the man is biased or second-hand. The Saxon stories, circulating from the court of Matthias Corvinus during the late 1460s, emanate from the merchants of Braşov and Sibiu who not only had been controlled commercially by Ţepeş with trade treaties, but who also had been the target of the voivod's ferocity. The *Vornic* or Chief Magistrate Neagu wrote to the council of Braşov in the late 1470s:

> Remember well who started having people impaled . . . You, because you kept Dan [Dracula's rival] among you and this angered Vlad voivod . . . [who] . . . came upon you with fire.[3]

The historian cannot dismiss such evidence out of hand. It would be like dismissing the holocaust because most of the evidence for it comes from Jewish survivors. We have already established, however, the impossibility of the claimed numbers of Ţepeş' victims and so these Saxon stories become doubly suspect. It was in Corvinus's interests in the 1460s to circulate these distortions with their ludicrous body count, to discredit the man he wanted to keep under lock and key for political reasons. Thanks to the printing press, the Impaler stories took on a life of their own and the presses of Nuremberg and other German cities realized that they were a licence to print money, paving the way for the creations of Byron, Polidori, Rymer and Stoker, long before celluloid took over.

The Turkish accounts clearly have a bias of their own. The Impaler was their enemy, along with half of Europe and they were only too delighted to blacken his reputation. The earliest of these was written by Tursun Bey, who took part in the 1462 campaign, but the account was not written until well over thirty years later. Asik-Pasha-Zade's account also dates from the very end of the century, but it is clearly a truncated copy of Tursun's. Mehmed Nesri's version is some twenty years later still and yet another variant of the first. The last version, that of Sa'adeddin Mehmed Hodja Efendi, did not appear until 1584. Clearly we cannot dismiss the Turkish accounts either, but with the inevitable 'Chinese-whisper-effect' distortions accrue in any narrative the further away from the original we get. The Turkish narratives, like Michel Beheim's epic poem, are 'history' only in so far as they were stories for entertainment and in the Ottoman examples recited to glorify Mehmed and Allah. It is interesting to temper the Ottoman accounts with the altogether more honest versions of the Serbian janissary Constantin Mihailović at once one with the Turks, yet without perhaps their poetry and passion.

The Russian accounts, probably stemming from the work of Fedor Kuritsyn at Buda in the 1480s, are rather more forgiving than either the Saxon or Turkish versions. To the Russians, and to the Dukes of Muscovy in particular, the need for strong autocratic rule was paramount. Statesmen knew that cruelty was sometimes necessary and, had the phrase been current in fifteenth-century Moscow, there would have been much talk of eggs and omelettes.

'Nobody troubles about daily deaths . . . in the middle of a daily massacre,' wrote Graham Greene in *Ministry of Fear* in 1943. He was talking about murder in war-time Britain, but the phrase encapsulates late medieval Europe just as well. Ask any member of the public in the street today whether our society is more violent and anarchic than any in the past and the answer will be, 'Yes, it is.' Historians take a longer view. We are pulverized by the sheer scale of atrocities today: 3,000 dead after two aircraft crashed into the World Trade Center in New York in September 2001; 80,000 died in minutes in the heat of Hiroshima on 9 August 1945; 130,000 in Dresden on St Valentine's Day 1945. The estimated casualty roll for the six years of the Second World War is an impossible 55 million dead. We have become numbed by all this. Casualty rates, lists of bombings, executions by paramilitaries, deaths through rioting, they filter through our television sets or out of our newspapers with only slightly more concern than the latest Dow Jones figures on the stock market. What actually makes it grim is the world's destructive capability – the advent of the gun and the bomb has given killing a new perspective.

The point, however, is that we *are* still shocked by these things. Generations have passed since the Second World War, yet the accounts of Adolph Hitler and his 'willing executioners' continue to appal us. We *do* stand in horror when we see, even for the umpteenth time, those 747s plough like arrows into the rippling skyscrapers of the 'Big Apple', the nickname, ironically, so similar to that given by the Ottomans to their capital – the Red Apple. We shake our heads at the pictures of shattered Omagh and any of us older than ten at the time remember *exactly* where we were when, in six seconds in Dallas, someone blew the back out of John Kennedy's head and a dream died.

Medieval men had no time for such maudlin sentiment. And if we are to understand Ţepeş the man we have to acknowledge and accept this. Medievalists like M.M. Postan and Johan Huizinger are quick to point out that the Middle Ages was rich in culture, with a dynamic economy and laudable aims – there was, after all, a twelfth-century renaissance before the more famous one of the sixteenth eclipsed it. The point at issue, however, is that life to the Impaler's contemporaries all over Europe, whatever their social status, was nasty, brutish and short. In England, Margaret Paston wrote to her husband in the year that Ţepeş first became voivod:

> I recommend me to you and pray you get some crossbows and windses [firing mechanisms] to bed with them and quarrels [bolts] . . . And also I would ye could get 2 or 3 short pole-axes to keep doors with, and also many jackets (padded) if ye may.[4]

This letter was written seven years before the Wars of the Roses erupted, and yet even before actual warfare began a knight's constant care was to defend his home against the threat of attack from any quarter. The same Margaret Paston spoke of her son's education, urging the boy's tutor to 'truly belash him till he will amend'. Their daughter, Elizabeth Paston, at twenty, was getting much the same treatment; in her case she was being difficult about accepting the much older man her parents had chosen as her bridegroom:

> And she hath since Easter the most part been beaten once in the week or twice, and sometimes twice in one day and her head broken in two or three places . . .[5]

War perhaps brought out the worst in people. Of the 1370s, the French chronicler Thomas Basin, Bishop of Lisieux, wrote:

> In the opinion of many, the English are not human beings and men, but senseless and ferocious beasts, which go about devouring people.[6]

Basin was no doubt thinking of the sack of Limoges by Edward, the Black Prince, that has echoes of Ţepeş' work. Jean Froissart wrote:

> There was not so hard a heart within the city an [if] he had any remembrance of God, but that wept piteously for the great mischief that they saw . . . for more than three thousand men, women and children were slain and beheaded that day.[7]

From whatever perspective we view Vlad Ţepeş' age, and whichever European country we choose, the same level of cruelty exists. Historian Jean Benedetti was writing of the fifteenth-century Breton knight and serial-killer Gilles de Rais when he said:

> He absorbed what his society had to offer, reproduced it and refracted it through his own personality and temperament. When his society finally condemned him, it was not from any genuine sense of moral outrage but . . . for the most hypocritical and cynical reasons. His society never ceased to regard him as one of its own.[8]

Much of the Middle Ages was spent in active warfare. The number of battles and skirmishes in which Ţepeş took part is not recorded, but from 1456 until his capture in 1462 and again from 1475 until his death two years later, the voivod was constantly a general, leading troops, sacking towns, orchestrating killing. As Benedetti says, 'War is at worst a kind of organized criminality.'[9] In the decade before the Impaler's birth, the Archbishop of Rheims described the effect of an English attack on the French countryside:

> They took women and children, without difference of age or sex, raping the women and girls; they killed the husbands and fathers in the presence of their wives and daughters; they took nurses and left the children behind so that they died for want

of food; they took pregnant women and chained them so that they gave birth in their chains; the children were allowed to die without baptism and mother and child were thrown into the river; they took priests and monks ... ploughmen, chained them up in various ways and in this tortured state beat them so that certain among them were maimed for life and others driven out of their minds ... Some were roasted alive, others had their teeth ripped out, others were beaten with huge sticks ...[10]

This was the norm. Clearly a French army in English territory would have behaved in the same way.

Miranda Twiss' book, *The Most Evil Men and Women in History*, features a contemporary of Vlad Ţepeş, the 'Black Legend', Tomás de Torquemada. Whereas Margaret Paston's letters reveal the fifteenth century's readiness for blows and warfare and the various accounts of the Hundred Years' War confirm the almost banal routine of violence, Torquemada was a servant of God; in theory he represented the antithesis of evil. As early as 1252 the then Pope sanctioned the use of torture in stamping out any kind of heresy. In hypocrisy that is unbelievable today, the accused had no defence in ecclesiastical law and was not told the names of his accusers. Torquemada was a 'natural' for the muscular Christianity expected of the Dominican heretic-hunters, the 'Hounds of the Lord'. In the space of two months, between September and November 1481, 298 people had been burned alive in the notorious auto-da-fe, having been charged with worshipping the god of the Jews. Torquemada was in fact an anti-Semite and his targets were the *conversos*, the Jews who had nominally converted to Catholicism. His *Limpreza de Sangre*, far more vicious than any law the Impaler passed and foreshadowing the obsessive racism of Nazis Himmler and Rosenberg, banned all Jews from office and effectively condemned them to death as heretics. The number of victims of the early Inquisition, unlike the number of Ţepeş' victims, are believable. In Ciudad Rodrigo fifty-two were burned alive. Up to 5,000 penitents by the end of 1485 had to appear each Friday, wearing coarse clothes and whipping themselves. A ghastly list of torture methods was added to the Inquisition's repertoire: water was forced down the throat of a trial victim; the rack pulled joints apart; the *garrucha* lifted the accused slowly by means of pulleys and dropped them quickly, dislocating limbs in the process. Contemporary woodcuts from Spain show all this and more carried out by professional Inquisitors, while benign-looking clerics look on. Tomás de Torquemada, unlike Vlad Ţepeş, died peacefully in his sleep – as the Catholics have it, 'in the odour of sanctity'.

There is little doubt that by unbiased medieval standards, the Impaler was not regarded as out of the ordinary. Clearly the merchants of Braşov, Sibiu and other Saxon towns hated him and with reason. Obviously, the Turks were at pains to blacken the name of their enemy. But men who were not the targets of the voivod's wrath could afford to be more dispassionate and see things in proportion. Men who fought with him sang his praises. Monasteries blessed him. Anonymous monks carried his body to hallowed ground and buried him. This has led to many Romanian historians not only accepting Ţepeş' metier but also finding merit in it. Anton Balota for instance writes:[11]

> the voivod's cruel methods . . . were actually nothing more than the standard practices of their times . . .
>
> It is evident that the basis of the conflicts between Dracula and the traders of Braşov were of economic origins and not the policy of a sick voivod bent on personal vengeance.

They had, after all, been warned.

Constantin Guirescu[12] writes:

> This merit [Ţepeş' preservation of Wallachia] overrules the extreme harshness of the punishments which terrified his

contemporaries and, in the final instance, causes history to pronounce a positive judgement of Dracula.

Anton Balota goes further than suggesting that the Impaler's means justified his ends:

> It is interesting to note that the contents of the tales about Dracula awakened the interest of authoritarian rulers who considered his personality as an example worthy of being copied.[13]

We have already discussed Tsar Ivan IV of Russia – known as the Terrible – and the similarity of his actions to those of Țepeș. Both men, of course, faced the same problem – unruly, power-hungry boyars, who played the game of politics for real. In 1538 they poisoned Ivan's mother with mercury and skinned alive her favourite, Fydor Mishurin, leaving his bleeding corpse on display in what would become Red Square in Moscow. Ivan's childhood torture of animals – he would drop cats from the Kremlin's battlements – fits absolutely the obsessions of the sociopath and Țepeș' own alleged behaviour at Buda and Visegrád. At the age of only thirteen, so the chroniclers claim, Ivan staged a palace coup with the help of loyal guards and had the boyar leader Andrew Shuisky thrown to a pack of starving dogs that tore him apart.

Perhaps like Țepeș, with his puritanical streak and his firm belief in law and order, Ivan came to believe that God was working through him, not only sanctioning his increasing violence, but also using the deranged Tsar as his instrument. We cannot be sure how far, if at all, the stories of Vlad the Impaler as collected by Fedor Kuritsyn were known to Ivan or whether he used them as a blueprint, but if he did not, the style of his reign followed an extraordinarily coincidental path. The Chosen Council he set up in Moscow was composed of carefully hand-picked men, as was the Impaler's in Tîrgoviște. His *streltsi* were an elite force of officers, elevated from humble origins, very like Dracula's *vitesji*. As Ţepeş was facing a war on two fronts, against the Turks and the Hungarians (and temporarily three, if we include the brief campaign against Stefan of Moldavia) so Ivan was fighting the Tartars, the Poles and the Swedes.

It was the death of the Tsar's wife Anastasia that tipped him over the edge. There is no exact parallel here, because we know so little about Ţepeş' family life, but in the deaths of his father and brother, we see a personal tragedy that probably had a serious psychological effect on the voivod. Ivan's grief turned to paranoia of epic proportions and among his victims were his subsequent wives. Two died of natural causes; Anna Koltovskaya, however, took a lover who was impaled for adultery with the Tsaritsa and she too was effectively locked up in a convent. Maria Dolgurukaya was drowned the day after her wedding to Ivan when he discovered she was not a virgin. In February 1565, the Tsar created the *Oprichniki*, secret police riding black horses who carried brooms and dogs' heads as symbols of their intention to sweep away and destroy any examples of treachery to their master. These hardened criminals were a law unto themselves and they were directly responsible for the deaths of thousands of Russians, boyars and peasants, in orgies of slaughter carried out at Ivan's command; they were the equivalent of Vlad Ţepeş' *Armas*.

One of the Tsar's victims was Boris Telupa, a prince who had annoyed him. He was:

> drawn upon a long sharp-made stake, which entered the lower part of his body and came out of his neck; upon which he survived for fifteen hours, talking to his mother who had been brought to behold the sight. After her son's death, she was given to one hundred gunners who defiled her to death and the Tsar's hungry hounds then devoured her flesh and bones.[14]

As with Ţepeş, we are quickly into impossible figures. Three years after the creation of the *Oprichniki*, Ivan unleashed them onto the city of Novgorod where 60,000 are said to have perished. For five weeks a daily cohort of citizens was brought before Ivan in the main square and men, women and children were tortured by flogging, slitting of noses, castration and having their tongues cut out before they were thrown into the River Volkhov to drown. Novgorod was Ivan's Braşov.

Most historians have categorized Ivan IV as insane, partly because he killed his own son in a fit of rage and partly because his rantings were so public. He would bang his head against the stone floor in front of church altars and scream and cry in full view of his, by turns astonished and terrified, court. There is no record of any of this behaviour in the accounts of Vlad Ţepeş. We have no way of measuring his emotions at all and perhaps that is the clue to his enduring legacy of evil. No one speaks of his temper, his mood swings, his tears or his laughter. We can only try to measure the man through his actions. Was he then a morose introvert? Did he sit on his throne at Tîrgovişte or on his horse in the Vlasia forest or among the impaled on Timpa Hill wearing a mask that men found impenetrable?

Can we hope to understand the Impaler by comparison with more modern examples of tyranny? The Saxon stories compared him unfavourably with monsters of the past, like Nero and Diocletian. And if such comparisons can be made with ancient personifications of evil, why not more recent cases? The whole issue depends on our definition of evil and such a concept is impossibly wide. At its simplest level, the word is defined as an adjective by the *New Penguin English Dictionary*: 'not good morally; sinful or wicked; arising from bad character or conduct; causing discomfort or repulsion; offensive; disagreeable; pernicious or harmful.' As a noun: 'wickedness, sin; the fact of suffering misfortune or wrongdoing; something that brings sorrow, distress or calamity.' This is only of limited use, because concepts of morality differ. Miranda Twiss for example includes the schizophrenic Roman emperor Caligula in the same book as England's King John;

one was a certifiable lunatic, the other merely trying to centralize his power, exactly as Vlad Țepeș did, but without impalement. The bloodthirsty Attila the Hun, responsible for the deaths of several thousand, is included in the same pages as Gregori Rasputin, as far as we know guilty of the murder of no one. And this illustrates the point. As Twiss says:

> We do not really understand evil – often taking it as an absolute rather than as a comparative word. Our concept of evil in the twenty-first century is dramatically different from previous centuries.

So, any attempt to compare Țepeș, very much a man of fifteenth-century Europe, with Josef Stalin, Adolf Hitler, Pol Pot and Idi Amin, very much men of the twentieth century, is, in the end, counterproductive; but the question had to be raised. Concepts of morality and *realpolitik* have changed. In terms of war, for example, the Geneva Convention, breached in the charges made recently against Slobodan Milosević, has established a yardstick the Impaler would not have recognized. The revised version of 1929 provides for wounded or sick prisoners of war to be respected and protected, not mutilated and killed. Pillage is specifically outlawed, but it was regarded as a perk by all medieval armies, Christian and Muslim alike. There is relevance in comparison with all the above dictators, in that they too used terror in their capacity as ruthless heads of state to inspire fear and compel compliance, but there are more differences than similarities. As one of the 'generation dead' interviewed over the Internet in the 1990s by Tony Thorne said:

> The Marquis de Sade, he was considered a very sick, very evil degenerate at one point; they have *clubs* for that kind of stuff now.[15]

And what sort of yardstick brands Adolf Hitler more of a monster than Josef Stalin? How can we measure the enormity

of their crimes against the relatively small-scale ones of Vlad
Ţepeş? People have a habit of forgetting and forgiving in some
instances too quickly and in some instances not at all. So Myra
Hindley, the Moors murderess, died in jail. The paramilitary
bombers, guilty of many more deaths, walk free: 'A single
death is a tragedy; a million deaths is a statistic.'

Or, as Edward Young wrote in the 1740s:

> One to destroy is murder by the law;
> And gibbets keep the lifted hand in awe;
> To murder thousands takes a specious name,
> War's glorious art, and gives immortal fame.[16]

In the Book of Leviticus it is written:

> If any man whomsoever of the house of Israel, and of those
> come from elsewhere who sojourn among them, eat blood, I
> shall set my face against his soul and banish him from among
> his people.[17]

Vlad Dracula has not been banished from his people. The
world's first Dracula Congress was held in May 1995,
organized by the Transylvanian Society of Dracula, based in
Bucharest, together with the Ministry of Tourism and Culture,
the Romanian Institute of Military History, the Institute of
Folklore and Ethnography and (perhaps inevitably considering the West Coast obsession with vampires) the Center for
Humanistic Studies, Santa Barbara, California. The purpose of
the Congress was to evaluate Dracula both as Vlad Ţepeş the
historical figure who died 500 years ago and as the literary and
celluloid myth of more recent origin. Most of the historical
papers were given by Romanian historians, dealing with
written and oral sources. Matei Cazacu, for instance, considered Ţepeş to have been a pawn in the Machiavellian game
played by Matthias Corvinus who made the Impaler arguably
the first victim of written propaganda. When Corvinus judged

the time to be right, of course, he unleashed him as a force of terror. Both of these are examples of manipulation to defend his own kingdom of Hungary. Others stressed Ţepeş' role in the light of infant Romanian nationalism, as a hero defending his country's cause against bullying aggrandisement on all sides.

The Congress took to the road, moving from Bucharest (only just becoming fashionable in the Impaler's day because of its proximity to the Danube and the likelihood of Turkish attacks) to Braşov, scene of some of the most violent of Ţepeş' outrages, then on to Tîrgu Mureş, Bistriţa and the Borgo Pass.

Romania, with its legacy of Ceauşescu and failed Communism is anxious in the twenty-first century to make money out of Ţepeş' memory. After Ceauşescu, who reinvented the Impaler as a pseudo-Communist hero fighting the evils of the 'capitalist' foreign merchants of Braşov, the voivod achieved a new reputation, personified by Mihail Ungheanu with his book *The Falsification of Dracula*. The haunted ruins of the palace at Tîrgovişte, the crumbling relics of Poenari over the Argeş, the gaping grave at the island monastery of Snagov – all these are 'open to the public' in a way unthinkable in Ceauşescu's time and certainly in Vlad Ţepeş'. Yet the Romanians persist in divorcing the real flesh-and-blood man from his literary and mythic counterparts. To them he is Ţepeş, the Impaler, not the over-the-top creation of an Irish civil servant, but a prince of his people, a hero on a white horse whose actions, though grim, are inevitably justifiable against the odds he faced. But, in the end, Vlad Dracula did not preserve Wallachia. His own nature was too unforgiving, his own reputation, whether deserved or not, too terrible. Within less than a generation after his death, his principality was merely the western edge of the Ottoman Empire as the conquests and the absorption continued.

Beyond Romania and the 'land beyond the forests' his legend is different. This was a man who nailed men's hats to their heads, impaled mothers and their babies, swatted friend and foe alike as if they were flies. Before even more callous mass-murderers came along, he was the bogeyman to frighten us all and he became, over time, the dreaded Count of the undead, the bloodthirsty vampire associated with Bram Stoker, with Max Schreck, Bela Lugosi and Christopher Lee. He hovers in the night air of every vampire story written since 1897 and if we cannot see him, it is because he has shifted his shape once again. Gabriel Ronay in *The Shadow of the Vampire* makes some fascinating links between Vlad the Impaler and twentieth-century propaganda. He may be stretching things a little when he equates the Nazi obsession with ritual and purity of blood with the Dracula stories, but is probably quite correct when he refers to the work of the American army's Psychological Warfare Division which produced posters of 'the Hun' as a monster with fangs and gave their G.I.s Stoker's novel as reading matter. As he says:

> The rulers who once used Dracula's deeds to justify their absolution have long since gone, together with their once mighty empires. The Russian despots and Nazi Ubermenschen, who made the myth an important strand in the cultural weave of their societies, have been obliterated. The crusading churches which found the scare engendered by the vampire myth in their dogmatic sparring are now at peace. Only Dracula the Un-dead lives on . . .

Very few people today accept a real link between the Count of fiction and the real Vlad Ţepeş. The only connection, they will tell you, is that Bram Stoker rather liked the name and that there are no contemporary references to the Impaler as a vampire.

This may be true, but it overlooks the fact that although belief in vampires was centuries old, it was not until 300 years after Vlad that the folklore was written down for the first time. The various accounts of Vlad's life were written for different purposes as we have seen. The Saxons, who may not have believed in the undead anyway, branded him a homicidal

tyrant; the Russians were impressed by his power; his native
Romanians believed him a hero. There was no place for a
revenant in any of that. And I believe that the intriguing
parallels between the man of fiction and the man of substance
– the undead and the living – cannot be merely coincidental.
Vlad Țepeș ruled as Prince of Wallachia three times in the
space of a quarter of a century, the third time returning from
an imprisonment and exile which had lasted twelve years.
Many of his contemporaries must have believed him to be
dead, yet he came back, as it were, from the dead, to claim his
inheritance, rather as Count Dracula continued to rise from
his grave. As a military leader, Vlad was known to favour
night attacks, his most spectacular against the invading
Ottoman Turks in the summer of 1462. Stoker's Dracula
operates only at night and shuns the sun; the night-haunting
vampires of Central Europe exhibited the same traits. Traditionally, the only means of destroying a vampire, which
Stoker employs via a vampire-hunting Dr van Helsing in the
novel, is to drive a stake through its heart and hack off its head,
just as Vlad's own head was hacked off as a present for the
sultan. The driving of stakes – impalement – was Vlad's
favoured method of torture and gave rise to his nickname of
Țepeș. There is also something of the undead about Vlad III
Dracula, son of the dragon. I am still writing about him today
and you are still reading about him. To celebrate him, a
commemorative stamp was printed in 1976, the 400th anniver-
sary of his death. Today, he is at the heart of a tourist industry
struggling to establish itself after the grim Communist years
of the *conducator* Nicolae Ceaușescu, himself perhaps a
quirky reflection of Vlad in terms of his dictatorial powers and
the appalling body count for which he is allegedly responsible.
Before his overthrow and execution at Christmastime 1980,
Ceaușescu said smugly to his Health Minister, 'A man like me
comes along only once every 500 years.' Was his predecessor,
500 years earlier, Vlad Dracula, the Impaler?

*   *   *

One of the great problems of history is that, all too often, we can only measure men by their deeds because we cannot know their innermost feelings. We see their faces, painted as copies on canvas or carved into wood and stone, but we cannot see their hearts, and so, in the end, Vlad Ţepeş must remain his country's greatest enigma. Our concept of evil is subjective – each of us has his own interpretation of it. And the Impaler shows us many facets of his psyche, all of them partially hidden in the mists that curl among the reeds at the Snagov Lake where he once lay buried. And hidden, too, by the mists of time. To most of us in the West, brought up on the Stoker and celluloid versions of the Impaler, his name still strikes a chord, still sends a certain shiver down the spine along with the music of the children of the night – the name of Vlad Ţepeş, son of the devil.

BIBLIOGRAPHY

Abraham, Gerald, *The Concise Oxford History of Music*, Oxford, OUP, 1979

Ahmed, Rollo, *The Black Art*, London, Arrow Books, 1996

Alder, L. and Dalby, R., *The Dervish of Windsor Castle*, London, Bachman & Turner, 1979

Ali, Abdullah Yusuf (trans.), *Holy Qur'an*, Birmingham, Wordsworth, 2000

Aston, Margaret, *Panorama of the Renaissance*, London, Thames and Hudson, 2000

Barclay, Glen St John, *Anatomy of Horror*, London, Weidenfeld and Nicholson, 1978

Barraclough, Geoffrey, *The Times Atlas of World History*, London, Harper Collins, 1992

Behr, Edward, *Kiss the Hand You Cannot Bite*, London, Hamish Hamilton, 1991

Benedetti, Jean, *The Real Bluebeard*, New York, Dorset Press, 1971

Bennet, Matthew (ed.), *Hutchinson Dictionary of Ancient and Medieval Warfare*, London, Helicon, 1998

Blackmore, Howard L., *Arms and Armour*, London, Studio Vista, 1965

Bord, Janet and Bord, Colin, *Alien Animals*, London BCA, 1981

Boulton, D'A.J.D, *The Knights of the Crown*, Woodbridge, Suffolk, Boydell Press, 2000

Brady, Thomas, Oberman, Heiko Augustinos and Tracy, James, D. (eds), *Handbook of European History 1400–1600* (2 vols), Michigan, William B. Eerdmans, 1996

Brereton, J.M., *The Horse in War*, Newton Abbott, Davis and Charles, 1976

Briggs, Asa, *Everyday Life Through the Ages*, London, Readers' Digest, 1992

Briggs, Katherine, *A Dictionary of Fairies*, London, Penguin, 1977

Brown, R. Allen, *Castles: a History and Guide*, Poole, Blandford Press, 1985

Burford, Tim, *A Hiking Guide to Romania*, Chalfont St Peter, Bradt Publications, 1993

Carey, John, *Reportage*, London, Faber, 1989

Carter, Francis (ed.), *An Historical Geography of the Balkans*, London, Academic Press,1977

Clark, Victoria, *Why Angels Fall*, London, Picador, 2001

Cohn, Norman, *Europe's Inner Demons*, London, Granada, 1976

Copper, Basil, *The Vampire in Legend, Fact and Art*, London, Corgi, 1973

Corfis, Ivy and Wolfe, Michael (eds), *The Medieval City Under Siege*, Woodbridge, Suffolk, Boydell Press, 1999

Dowley, Tim (ed.), *The History of Christianity*, Tring, Lion Publishing, 1977

Drury, Ian (ed.), *The Times History of War*, London, Harper Collins, 2000

Edge, David and Paddock, John, *Arms and Armour of the Medieval Knight*, London, Guild Publishing, 1988

Embleton, Gerry and Howe, John, *The Medieval Soldier*, London, Windrow and Greene, 1994

Ertug, Ahmet and Koluk, Ibrahim, *Topkapi: The Palace of Felicity*, Istanbul, Ertug and Koluk

Farrington, Karen, *Punishment and Torture*, London, Hamlyn, 1996

Farson, Daniel, *Vampires, Zombies and Monster Men*, London, Aldus/Jupiter, 1975

Fields, Bertram, *Royal Blood*, Stroud, Sutton, 1998

Fine, John, *The Late Medieval Balkans*, Michigan, UMP, 1994

Florescu, Radu and McNally, Raymond T., *Dracula; Prince of Many Faces*, Boston, Little Brown, 1989

Florescu, Radu, *In Search of Frankenstein*, London, Robson Books, 1999

Frayling, Christopher, *Nightmare; The Birth of Horror*, London, BBC Books, 1996

Friar, Stephen, *A New Dictionary of Heraldry*, London, A&C Black, 1987

Goodwin, Jason, *Lords of the Horizons*, London, Random House, 1999

Hay, Denys, *Europe in the 14th and 15th Centuries*, London, Longman, 1966

Hindley, Geoffrey (ed.), *The Larousse Encyclopaedia of Music*, London, Hamlyn, 1993

Hinnells, John H., *A Handbook of Living Religions*, London, Penguin, 1991

Hinnells, John R., (ed.), *The Who's Who of Religions*, London, Penguin, 1991

Inalcik, Halil, *The Ottoman Empire*, London, Phoenix, 1994

Jackson, Nigel, *The Compleat Vampyre*, Chieveley, Capall Bann, 1995

Jacob, E.F., *The Fifteenth Century*, Oxford, OUP, 1961

Jones, Alan, *The Rough Guide to Horror Movies*, London, Penguin, 2005

Kaplan, Robert D., *Balkan Ghosts*, New York, Vintage, 1993

Kightly, Charles, *The Perpetual Almanack of Folklore*, London, Thames and Hudson, 1987

Kramer, H. and Sprenger, J. (trans. Summers, M.), *Malleus Maleficarum*, London, Arrow Books, 1971

Laffont, Robert (ed.), *A History of Rome and the Romans*, London, Macdonald, 1960

Leatherdale, Clive, *Dracula: The Novel and the Legend*, Brighton, Desert Island Books, 1993

Machiavelli, Niccolo, *The Prince*, London, Penguin, 1961

Maclagan, Michael, *Lines of Succession*, London, Little Brown, 1999

Marriner, Brian, *A Century of Sex Killers*, London, True Crime Library, 1992

Marsden, Simon, *Journal of a Ghosthunter*, London, Little Brown & Co, 1994

Marshall, Robert, *Storm from the East*, London, BCA, 1993

Mayo, Stephfordy, *New Moan*, London, Michael O'Mara, 2009

McNally, Raymond T. and Florescu, Radu, *In Search of Dracula*, London, Robson Books, 1994

Mellersh, H.E.L., *Hutchinson Chronology of World History*, Oxford, Helicon, 1999

Monaco, Richard and Burt, William, *The Dracula Syndrome*, London, Headline, 1993

Morley, John, *Death, Heaven and the Victorians*, London, Studio Vista, 1971

Newark, Tim, *Warlords*, London, Brockhampton Press, 1998

Nicolle, David, *The Janissaries*, London, Osprey, 1995

Otetea, Andre, *The History of the Romanian People*, Bucharest, Scientific Publishing House, 1970

Parker, Geoffrey (ed.), *The Age of Calamity*, Amsterdam, Time-Life, 1989

Parker-Pearson, Michael, *The Archaeology of Death and Burial*, Stroud, Sutton, 1999

Peterson, Harold L., *The Book of the Gun*, London, Hamlyn, 1962

Picknett, Lynn, *Encyclopaedia of the Paranormal*, London, Guild Publishing, 1990

Pirie, David, *The Vampire Cinema*, London, Galley Press, 1977

Proctor, Miles (ed.), *The New Vampire's Handbook*, London, Random House, 2009

Ramsland, Katherine, *The Vampire Companion*, London, Little Brown, 1993

Raphael, Frederic, *Byron*, London, Thames & Hudson, 1982

Robbins, Rossell, *Encyclopaedia of Witchcraft and Demonology*, London, Peter Nevill, 1959

Runciman, Steven, *The Fall of Constantinople*, Cambridge, CUP, 1965

Ruthven, Malise, *Islam in the World*, London, Penguin, 1984

Schechter, Harold and Everitt, David, *The A to Z Encyclopaedia of Serial Killers*, New York, Pocket Books, 1996

Seymour, William, *Battles in Britain*, Ware, Wordsworth, 1997

Stoker, Bram, *Dracula*, Ware, Wordsworth, 2000

Sugar, Peter, *A History of East-Central Europe*, Washington, UWP, 1977

Summers, Montague, *The History of Witchcraft and Demonology*, Castle Books, 1992

Summers, Montague, *The Vampire*, New York, Dorset Press, 1991

Summers, Montague, *The Vampire: His Kith and Kin*, Reprint, Kessinger Publishing

Thorne, Tony, *Children of the Night: of Vampires and Vampirism*, London, Indigo, 2000

Thurston, Robert, 'The Spawning of Satan', *BBC History Magazine*, May 2002

Tondriau, J. and Villeneuve, R., *A Dictionary of Devils and Demons*, London, Tom Stacey Ltd, 1972

Treptow, Kurt W. (ed.), *Dracula: Essays on the Life and Times of Vlad Ţepeş*, New York, Columbia University Press, 1991

Treptow, Kurt W., *Vlad III: Dracula*, Iaşi, Centre for Romanian Studies, 2000

Twiss, Miranda, *The Most Evil Men and Women in History*, London, Michael O'Mara Books, 2002

Vuksic, V., *Cavalry*, London, Cassell, 1993

Wilcox, Peter, *Rome's Enemies; Gallic and British Celts*, London, Osprey, 1985

Wilson, Colin, *Mammoth Book of Murder*, London, Robinson, 2000

Woodward, Ian, *The Werewolf Delusion*, London, Paddington Press, 1979

Wyse, Elizabeth (ed.), *Past Worlds; The Times Atlas of Archaeology*, London, Harper Collins, 1992

Young, Lailan, *Secrets of the Face*, London, Hodder & Stoughton, 1983

NOTES

Chapter 1 California Screaming: Vampires in the Twenty-first Century

1. Miles Procter, ed., *The New Vampires' Handbook: A Guide for Creatures of the Night*, London, Square Peg (Random House) 2009.
2. *Bizarre*, May 1997.
3. The spoof *New Moon* book – the first in the *Twishite Saga* by Stephfordy Mayo – is far more specific and of course pokes fun at the heroine's inability to realize what's going on: 'And he doesn't have a reflection and he's got these weird long teeth and he bites people on the neck quite often and he tried to get a blood vending machine installed in the cafeteria last year. You don't think any of this is odd?'
4. Not strictly true. See later chapters.
5. See Chapter 2.
6. Tony Thorne, *Children of the Night*, London, Indigo, 1999.
7. Quoted in Daniel Farson, *Vampires, Zombies and Monster Men*, Aldus/Jupiter, 1975.
8. Paul Barber, *Vampires, Burial and Death: Folklore and Reality*, Yale University Press, 1988, p. 29.
9. As a young historian investigating Victorian death and spiritualism, I visited the cemetery with my wife on a gloriously sunny

day in 1975. Special permission had to be sought because of the vandalism of the previous year. Highgate was appallingly overgrown, with thick impenetrable foliage blacking out the sun of the June day. Mausolea had been broken into, tombs smashed open and funeral-pall-wrapped cadavers were exposed to the dim light. There were some sepulchres my wife would not let me go near and I was secretly pretty glad of that!

10. Quoted in Farson, *Vampires, Zombies and Monster Men*, op. cit., p. 15.

Chapter 2   Reel Vampires: The Undead Cinema

1. Chris Tookey, *Daily Mail*, 20 November 2009.
2. Directed by Neil Jordan with screenplay by Anne Rice from her novel, released in 1994.
3. Thorne, *Children of the Night*, op. cit., p. 247.
4. Alexander Walker, *London Evening Standard*, 1994.
5. Thorne, *Children of the Night*, op. cit., p. 248.
6. *Salem's Lot: the Movie* from the novel by Stephen King, Warner/Serendipity Productions, 1979.
7. *The Lost Boys*, directed by Joel Schumacher, Warner, 1987.
8. Quoted in Thorne, *Children of the Night*, op. cit., p. 249.
9. *Blacula*, written by Joan Torres and Walter Koenig, Movielab, 1972.
10. *The Fearless Vampire Killers* (British title *Dance of the Vampires*), 1967 MGM/Cadre Films/Filmways.
11. *Halliwell's Guide*, op. cit.
12. Quoted in Nigel Blunden, *Encyclopedia of Serial Killers*, PRC, London, 1996, p. 126.
13. *Dracula: Dead and Loving It*, Polygram/Castlerock/Gaumont/Brooksfilm, 1995.
14. *Sunday Times*, 1995.
15. *The Vampire Lovers*, MGM-EMI/Hammer, 1970.
16. *Lust for a Vampire*, Hammer, 1970.
17. Thorne, *Children of the Night*, op. cit., p. 43.
18. Ibid., p. 43.
19. *Dracula*, directed by Terence Fisher, produced by Anthony Hinds, 1958 Rank/Hammer.
20. David Pirie, *Vampire Cinema*, Crescent, 1988, p. 124.
21. Quoted in Farson, *Vampires, Zombies and Monster Men*, op. cit., p. 40.

22. Christopher Frayling, *Radio Scotland* interview, *The Usual Suspects*, 23 December 1997.

23. Basil Copper, *The Vampire in Legend, Fact and Art*, Corgi, 1975, p. 151.

24. *Dracula, Prince of Darkness*, Warner/Hammer/Seven Arts, 1966.

25. Copper, *The Vampire in Legend, Fact and Art*, op. cit., p. 136.

26. The original quotation from Stoker's novel reads, 'I am Dracula. And I bid you welcome, Mr Harker, to my house.' *Wordsworth Classic Edition*, 1993, p. 15.

27. See Chapter 3.

28. The film was cut by seven minutes before it reached the censors, thereby avoiding further problems. By contrast, James Whale's *Frankenstein*, released in the following year, ran into problems from the National Society for the Prevention of Cruelty to Children because of the now infamous scene with Boris Karloff's monster and the little girl at the lake. In the original screenplay, the mad professor's creation throws her into the water; even Karloff's toning down of this caused uproar.

29. Pirie, *The Vampire Cinema*, op. cit., p. 54.

30. Sadly, in his *The Vampire*, occultist Montague Summers (1928), referring to the Hungarian's performance in the stage play, calls him Bela Lugoni! Summers, op. cit., p. 337.

31. Strictly speaking, the *very* first was George Meliès' *Le Manoir du Diable* of 1886 and the second, the now lost Swedish *Vampyr* of 1912. The first full length filming of Bram Stoker's novel was filmed in Berlin in 1920, but was a Hungarian production, *Drakula*.

32. *Nosferatu the Vampyre*, Gaumont/Werner Herzog, 1979.

33. See Chapter 4.

34. *Shadow of the Vampire*, Saturn/BBC Films, 2001.

35. Farson, *Vampires, Zombies and Monster Men*, op. cit., p. 42.

36. Letter from Huntley to the author, quoted in Copper, *The Vampire in Legend, Fact and Art*, op. cit., p. 125.

37. Quoted in Farson, *Vampires, Zombies and Monster Men*, op. cit. p. 27.

38. For a very detailed breakdown of the various runs see Summers, *The Vampire*, op. cit., pp. 335–7. Summers also contends that during the London run, a nurse was on hand for anyone 'overcome owing to the horrors of the drama' [Summers, p. 356]

and that later, the whole cast appeared in front of the curtain to reassure the audience that the play was 'comically intended for their entertainment. So gross a lapse of good manners,' Summers goes on, 'not to speak of the artistic indecorum, is hardly credible.'

39. *Bram Stoker's Dracula*, Columbia Tristar, 1992.

Chapter 3   Bram Stoker's *Dracula*: The Definitive Vampire

1. The vampire as a folkloric myth is discussed in later chapters, but as I focus largely on Eastern Europe, it is best to discuss this Irish version here. The *leannan-sidhe* is a faery mistress who lures unsuspecting mortals into an underworld of the ancestral dead. She can change her shape, usually into that of a white fawn or kid and is particularly drawn to poets or creative people generally. She is invisible to all but her victim. For a brilliant update of this faerie fatale, see Maryanne Coleman, *Goblin Market* and *Pandemonium*. Vampirologist Elizabeth Miller believes that Stoker's *Dracula* has far more in common with Celtic/Gothic traditions than Transylvanian folklore.

2. Christopher Frayling, *Nightmare: The Birth of Horror*, BBC Books, 1996, p. 82.

3. Whitman, son of a New York carpenter, had a number of careers before settling to journalism. His finest collection of poems, *Leaves of Grass*, eventually running to a massive 440 pages, was first published in 1855 and Whitman added to it as his experiences developed. The most telling of these was the four years he spent as a medical orderly with the Union Army in the Civil War and it left him shattered and prematurely aged. He was an invalid and recluse after 1873 and most of his correspondence with Stoker dates from this time.

4. The Pre-Raphaelite Brotherhood dated from the mid-nineteenth century, centring on artists like Burne-Jones, William Holman Hunt, Ford Madox Brown and Dante Gabriel Rossetti. Their themes were usually literary, classical or biblical; romantic medievalism crept into the work of Burne-Jones especially.

5. F.K. Robinson, *Glossary of Words Used in the Neighbourhood of Whitby*.

6. Edgar Allen Poe (1809–49), tragically dead at forty in a Baltimore street and wearing somebody else's clothes, was the

acknowledged master of the macabre. 'Weird, wild, fantastic' are the words used to describe him in *Chamber's Biographical Dictionary*, 'dwelling by choice on the horrible, Poe's genius was yet great and genuine.'

7. Quoted in Frayling, *Nightmare*, op. cit., p. 106.
8. All quoted in Frayling, *Nightmare*, op. cit., p. 106.
9. Summers, *The Vampire*, Dorset Press, New York, 1929, p. 334.
10. Quoted in Daniel Farson, *Vampires, Zombies and Monster Men*, op. cit., p. 40.
11. James Twitchell, *The Living Dead – a Study of the Vampire in Romantic Literature*, Duke University Press, 1981.
12. Quoted in Frayling, *Nightmare*, op. cit., p. 107.
13. Frayling, Radio Scotland interview, *The Usual Suspects*, 23 December 1997.
14. Frayling, Radio Scotland interview, *The Usual Suspects*, 23 December 1997.
15. Bram Stoker, *Dracula*, op. cit.
16. Frayling, *Nightmare*, op. cit., p. 74.
17. Quoted in L. Adler and R. Dalby, *The Dervish of Windsor Castle*, Bachman and Turner, London, 1979, p. 149.
18. Quoted in Adler and Dalby, *The Dervish of Windsor Castle*, op. cit., p. 151.

Chapter 4   Fantasmagoria: Vampires and the Romantics

1. Quoted in Frayling, *Nightmare*, op. cit., p. 82.
2. Summers, *The Vampire*, op. cit., p. x.
3. From Rymer, *Varney the Vampire*, 1846.
4. Quoted in Clive Leatherdale, *Dracula: the Novel and the Legend*, Desert Island Books, Brighton, 1993.
5. Review, *Daily Variety*, 1986.
6. Quoted in Radu Florescu, *In Search of Frankenstein*, Robson Books, 1999, p. 98.
7. Ibid., p. 109.
8. Quoted in Frayling, *Nightmare*, op. cit., p. 75.
9. *The Diary of John Polidori* quoted in Florescu, *In Search of Frankenstein*, op. cit., p. 131.
10. Summers, *The Vampire*, op. cit., p. 294.
11. The hypnotic technique, not always successful, developed by Franz Anton Mesmer 1734–1815.

12. Henry Morley, *Journal of a London Playgoer*, London, 1891. Considering that Morley was Emeritus Professor of English Literature at University College London, he was probably quite difficult to please.

13. Rosemary Herbert (ed.), *The Oxford Companion to Crime and Mystery Writing*, OUP, p. 189.

14. Quoted in Leatherdale, *Dracula; the Novel and the Legend*, op. cit., p. 128.

Chapter 5   Kiss and Kin: Folklore, Sexuality and Bloodlust

1. Summers, op. cit., p. 219.

2. In European witchcraft, the sabbat was a general meeting of witches, usually held at some pagan festival like Walpurgisnacht, in which orgies and sex with the devil took place.

3. Quoted in Summers, op. cit., p. 267.

4. Ibid., pp. 267–8.

5. Ibid., p. 184.

6. Havelock Ellis, *Studies in the Psychology of Sex*, Vol. IV, Philadelphia, 1927, p. 216.

7. Ibid.

8. Summers, op. cit., p. 61.

9. Brian Masters, *Cannibalism, the Last Taboo*, London, Arrow Books, 1992.

10. W.A.F. Browne, *Necrophilism*, May 1874.

11. Summers, op. cit., p. 70.

12. *Daily Express*, 17 April 1925.

13. Quoted in Paul Donnelly, *501 Most Notorious Crimes*, London, Bounty Books, 2009.

14. Summers, op. cit., p. 193.

15. Donnelly, op. cit., p. 367.

Chapter 6   Vampyr: Vampires in European Folk Tradition

1. Nigel Jackson, *Compleat Vampyre*, Capall Bann, 1997, p. 88.

2. François Voltaire (1694–1778) was destined for the Bar and a diplomatic career. His métier however was satire and he was banished from Paris for his outspoken criticism at the age of twenty. In and out of royal favour like a yo-yo, Voltaire spent as much time in exile or the Bastille as he did at court. His

tolerance and cynicism made him the epitome of the Enlightenment in many ways.

3. John Locke's expression of classical liberal ideas struck a chord
with Voltaire when he was exiled to England in the 1730s.
Shaftesbury was the third Earl, a philosopher and politician who
had been taught by Locke. John Trenchard wrote at the turn of
the seventeenth/eighteenth centuries, usually as 'Cato', criticiz-
ing standing armies and the corruption of government under
William III and Anne. He was a keen advocate of freedom of
speech. Anthony Collins was a friend and disciple of Locke and
a champion of the deistic theory that God's existence could be
established by reason, not revelation.

4. Quoted in Jackson, *Compleat Vampyre*, op. cit., p. 3.

5. Quoted in Montague Summers, *Vampire: His Kith and Kin*, op.
cit., p. 128.

6. Ian Woodward, *The Werewolf Delusion*, Paddington Press, 1979,
p. 150.

7. Gervase of Tilbury (*c.*1150–1220) was a lecturer on canon law at
the University of Bologna. *Otia Imperialia* was a collection of
historical and geographical oddities written for the Holy Roman
Emperor, Otto IV.

8. Nicholas of Cusa (1401–64) was a contemporary of Vlad Ţepeş.
Active at the Council of Basle in 1432, he became a diplomat for
the Pope and was made cardinal in 1448. His best known work
is *De docta ignorantia* (1440) but he also wrote on cosmology
and mathematics.

9. Giovanni Cibo (1432–92) was an exact contemporary of the
Impaler, but outlived him by sixteen years. A war-maker and
crusade-urger, Innocent caused a scandal by rampant nepotism
and his involvement in European politics led to the Vatican being
besieged by the Roman nobility.

10. Bill of Innocent VIII 1484. Quoted in James Sprenger and
Heinrich Kramer, *Malleus Maleficarum* with foreword by
Montague Summers, Arrow, 1986.

11. Heinrich Kramer was a Dominican from Alsace who became
Inquisitor for the Catholic Church in the Tyrol, Salzburg, Bohemia
and Moravia in the 1470s, the decade of Vlad Dracula's death.

James Sprenger was born in Basel and became a zealous
Master of Theology at Cologne University. An inveterate

traveller throughout Germany, he died suddenly in December 1495 and was buried at Strasbourg.

12. Quoted in Rossell Robbins, *The Encyclopaedia of Witchcraft and Demonology*, Peter Nevill, 1959, p. 254.

13. Guazzo was a Catholic friar operating as assessor in witch trials throughout Germany and Northern Italy in the early seventeenth century. Hopelessly gullible, he was prepared to believe any nonsense told to him. So a Belgian, according to him, fathered a child by a cow. The offspring grew up instructed as a Christian, but chewing the cud and eating grass! In Guazzo's scheme of things, Martin Luther was the devil's son.

14. Robbins, *The Encyclopaedia of Witchcraft and Demonology*, op. cit., p. 254.

15. Thomas Aquinas (1224–74) was a Benedictine trained at the University of Naples. Canonized in 1323, his writings had huge influence on the medieval Church, especially the Dominicans whose order he joined in 1244. He was undoubtedly a first-rate thinker, although his knowledge of Greek and Homer and indeed of history was very slight.

16. Robbins, *The Encyclopaedia of Witchcraft and Demonology*, op. cit., p. 256

17. *The Undead*, London 1971. Quoted in Jackson, *Compleat Vampyre*.

18. Quoted in Jackson, *Compleat Vampyre*, p. 42.

19. Quoted in Jackson, *Compleat Vampyre*, p. 55.

20. Stoker, *Dracula*.

21. And in Britain too, certainly between the wars. In the Warwickshire village of Bubbenhall, the wife of 'Friday' Watts was a cunning or wise woman who acted as midwife, unofficial nurse and layer out of the dead.

22. Quoted in Jackson, *Compleat Vampyre*, p. 66.

23. The Barguest is a black dog found in Yorkshire folklore. Typically, it had huge glowing eyes and presaged death to all who saw it. Shriker is the name given to the creature across the Pennines in Lancashire and Shuck is the East Anglian variant. For a fascinating recital of appearances by mystic hounds, see Janet Bord and Colin Bord, *Alien Animals*, BCA, London, 1981.

24. Interestingly, Bela Lugosi's eyes were blue. The director of *Dracula* used beams of light shone through a cardboard filter to give them extra reflection.

25. A fascinating and recent example of them are the 'Foo fighters', unexplained lights that appeared to fighter pilots in the closing stages of WWII. For a fuller explanation of these, See Nick Pope and Mei Trow, *Open Skies, Closed Minds*, Simon and Schuster, 1996.

26. Montague Summers, *Vampire: His Kith and Kin*, London, 1927, p. 198.

27. Quoted in Jackson, *The Compleat Vampyre*.

28. Ibid., pp. 81–2.

29. The mandrake or mandragora was a plant believed to have occult and fertility powers. Its roots often resemble a human form and in Germany it was called 'little gallows man'.

30. Montague Summers, *Vampire: His Kith and Kin*, London, 1927, p. 155.

31. Gaius Plinius secundus (23–79) commanded cavalry on the Danubian frontier of the Roman Empire and finished his epic *Historica Naturalis* two years before his death. He made no attempt to distinguish between fact and legend, but his work remains a fascinating collection of Roman lore. He died of suffocation in the choking fumes of Vesuvius in the eruption of AD 79.

32. Henricus Agrippa von Nettesheim (1486–1535) was diplomat, teacher, soldier and an agent of the Emperor Maximilian I. His most famous work was *De Occulta Philosophia*, written in 1510 and enlarged twenty years later. Intriguingly, in connection with the shape-shifting qualities of vampires, Agrippa owned a black dog called Monsieur, which ate off his table and slept in his bed.

33. John Mandeville (probably an alias) wrote *The Voyage and Travels of Sir John Mandeville, Knight* in 1366. The real author was either the French doctor Jehan de Bourgoyne or Jean d'Outrmeuse. The travelogue is mostly a compilation of other works, but involves discussion of Turkey, Persia, North Africa and India.

34. Quoted in Jackson, *Compleat Vampyre*, p. 105.

35. Richard Burton, trans. *The Thousand and One Nights*, London, Vol. VII, p. 361.

36. Stoker, *Dracula*.

37. The exception is the relatively new phenomenon of foaflore (friend of a friend) where such unlikely stories of the choking

Doberman and Freddie Starr eating hamsters are media creations.

38. Farson, *Vampires, Zombies and Monster Men*, p. 18.
39. Quoted in Thorne, *Children of the Night*, p. 63
40. Quoted in Farson, *Vampires Zombies and Monster Men*, p. 18.
41. Quoted in Thorne, *Children of the Night*, p. 63
42. Quoted in Thorne, *Children of the Night*, p. 67.
43. Voltaire, *Dictionnaire Philosophique*.
44. Quoted in Barber, *Vampires, Burial and Death: Folklore and Reality*, Yale University Press, 1988, from a 1728 original, Ranft's *De Masticationi Mortuorum*.
45. Christopher Frayling contends that 'sunlight is Stoker.' In other words, the vampire's inability to cope with daylight is a literary invention for the novel *Dracula* rather as the *tricoteuses* (knitters) clacking away with their needles as the aristocrats' heads bounced from the guillotine in the Place de la Concorde is almost certainly the invention of Charles Dickens for *A Tale of Two Cities*.
46. Quoted in Farson, *Vampires, Zombies and Monster Men*, p. 31.
47. Jessica Snyder Sachs, *Time of Death*, QPD, 2002.
48. Farson, *Vampires, Zombies and Monster Men*, p. 34.
49. Summers, *The Vampire*, p. 34.
50. Montague Summers, *Vampire: His Kith and Kin*, London, 1927 p. 35.
51. Martin Luther launched his attack in 1517 with his famous ninety-five theses nailed to the door of Wittenberg Cathedral. Calvin, Melanchthon, Zwingli and others emerged to become sectarian leaders of the Protestant faith before the Papacy launched its counter-attack in the 1540s, exemplified by the burning of heretical books, the creation of the Jesuit order and the unleashing of the Holy Inquisition.

Chapter 7   Dracula's People: Medieval Romania

1. *Herodutus*, Vol. 2, trans. A.D. Godley, quoted in Kurt W. Treptow, *Vlad III Dracula*, Center for Romanian Studies, Iaşi, Romania, 2000, p. 21.
2. Aeneas Silvinius Piccolomini, *Cosmographia*, quoted in Treptow, *Vlad III Dracula*, op. cit., p. 19.

3. *Slavs and Turks; the Borderlands of Islam in Europe*, published by the Leisure Hour Office, Paternoster Row, London, 1880.

4. Technically, the legions withdrew on the orders of Lucius Domitus Aurelineaus, the Emperor Aurelian, himself probably a native of Dacia, who abandoned the area to the Goths raiding south. Popular and militarily capable, he was given the title Restituter Orbis (restorer of the world), rather ironic in view of his Dacian policy, and was assassinated by his own officers near Byzantium.

5. A violent argument seems to be raging on the Internet currently between J.P. Holding and Richard Carrier on the efficacy of this. The links with Ţepeş seem to me far more relevant.

6. Letter from Batu to Bela IV, 1240, quoted in Robert Marshall, *Storm from the East*, BBC Books, 1993, p. 108.

7. Victoria Clark, *Why Angels Fall*, Picador, 2000, p. 208.

8. *The New Penguin English Dictionary*, London, 2000.

9. For instance, the Percy family held the Marcher lordships on the Scots border in return for halting Scots raids. The Earls of Norfolk became Marshals, officiating at royal ceremonies. The Dymoke family eventually became hereditary Royal Champions and so on.

10. Kurt W. Treptow, ed., *Dracula: Essays on the Life and Times of Vlad Tepes*, East European Monographs, New York, 1991.

11. Guy Bois, *The Crisis of Feudalism*, Cambridge, 1984.

12. Rodney Hilton, *Class Conflict and the Crisis of Feudalism*, London, 1985.

13. The name comes from either the leather jacks or the jerkins worn by the rebels or Jacques Bonhomme, the generic term for a French peasant.

14. Clark, *Why Angels Fall*, op. cit., p. 208.

15. The town was described by traveller Emily Gerrard in 1883: 'The top-heavy overhanging gables, the deserted watch-towers, the ancient ramparts, the crooked streets . . . all combine to give the impression of a past which has scarcely gone and of a present which has not yet penetrated.' Quoted in Burford, *Hiking Guide to Romania*, Chalfont St Peter, Bradt Publications, 1993, p. 277.

16. Letter from Vlad Ţepeş to the Council of Braşov, 1456, quoted from the Latin in Radu Florescu and Raymond T. McNally, *Dracula, Prince of Many Faces*, Boston, Little Brown, 1989, op. cit., p. 112.

17. The Cathars (from the Greek meaning puritan) were a late twelfth-century sect later based at Albi in Southern France. They were considered heretic by the Catholic Church because they believed in two Gods – the God of the New Testament who created a beautiful, invisible and spiritual world; and the God of the Old Testament, representing all that was earthly and evil. The heresy was crushed by Pope Innocent III in 1245.

18. Matthew Spinks, *A History of Christianity in the Balkans*, Chicago, 1933.

19. From Chedomil Mijatovich, *Constantine, the Last Emperor of the Greeks*, London, 1892, quoted in Treptow, *Essays*, op. cit., p. 72.

20. Flavius Constantinus AD *c.*274–337 was the first Roman Emperor to be baptized and Christianity became the state religion of the Empire in AD 324. Having won the throne by intrigue and war – there were for a time five rivals for the purple – he executed his own wife and son for plots against him.

21. Clark, *Why Angels Fall*, op. cit., p. 402.

22. From the poem 'Lepanto', G.K. Chesterton, describing the brilliant naval victory over the Turks by the galleys of Don John of Austria in 1571.

23. In 1943, in removing the Jews of Crakow from their ghetto to the labour camp at Plazsov, the Nazi commandant Amon Goeth told his soldiers that they were ending six hundred years of history.

24. The often misquoted line comes from the poem 'To Helen' by Edgar Allen Poe.

Chapter 8   'A Wild, Bloodthirsty Man': Historical Sources

1. Sheila Bignall, *Who was Nicolas von Popplau?*, Ricardian Register, Vol. XXII, No. 3, 1997, quoted in Bertram Fields, *Royal Blood*, Sutton Publishing, 2000, p. 280.

2. Quoted in McNally and Florescu, *In Search of Dracula*, op. cit., p. 79.

3. Not to be confused with more famous Kronstadt in Russia, the naval base that was the scene of the famous mutiny in 1917.

4. McNally and Florescu, *In Search of Dracula*, op. cit., p. 87.

5. This translation is by Raymond T. McNally.

6. Quoted in Treptow, *Dracula: Essays*, op. cit., pp. 193–4.
7. The translation is from Peter Panaitescu.
8. Herod was Herod the Great, ruler of Palestine in Roman Times. He would have been well known to the monks of St Gall as a tyrant and the evidence against him is quite compelling. Whether or not he ever sentenced the firstborn of every household to death in search of the infant Christ, he certainly slaughtered wholesale on the merest suspicion of opposition to his reign and even ordered the execution of his wife Mariamne and their two sons.

   Nero, Roman Emperor from AD 54–68 was certainly, recent research has revealed, more sinned against than sinning. The story of his violin solo while his city burned around him is nonsense, but he was certainly vain, extravagant and sexually debauched. Unlike Herod, who simply issued orders, there is strong evidence that Nero killed his wife Poppaea by kicking her during pregnancy. He executed Antonia, Claudius' daughter, because she rejected his proposal of marriage and eliminated talented Romans like Seneca and Lucan probably because they were better writers than he was.

   Diocletian was Gaius Diocletianus, proclaimed emperor by the Roman army in AD 284. An inveterate and successful soldier, he spent much of his time defending his empire and holding it together. The probable reason for his inclusion here is his persecution of the Christians in AD 303, in which, in four edicts, he attempted to wipe the sect out. The resulting purge created two victims who would become saints by Vlad Dracula's time – the twelve-year-old Agnes, naked and beheaded under the arches of Domitian's stadium, and the soldier Sebastian, riddled with arrows and bludgeoned to death by the Emperor's guard.
9. The term 'berserker' is usually associated with the Norse warriors, the bear shirts, whose violence on the battlefield was legendary. Interestingly, Bram Stoker uses the term in Dracula where he wrongly attribute the Count's descent from the Szekelys – 'Here, in the whirlwind of European races, the Ugric tribe [Magyars] bore down from Iceland the fighting spirit which Thor and Wodin gave them, which their Berserkers displayed to such fell intent on the seaboards of Europe . . .' A better translation for our purposes in relation to the Impaler is 'madman'.

10. Pagans would be those beyond the extent of the Christian Church, the Ottoman Turks to the south east or the Tartars beyond the Black Sea. Jews, except in Casimir the Great's Poland, were treated with varying degrees of contempt. Heretics, whose definitions would be constantly shifting at the whim of what Orthodox and Catholic doctrine decided *was* heretical, were increasingly the targets of the Holy Inquisition.

11. All translations of the Russian tales are by Raymond T. McNally.

12. Intriguingly, shortly before his hasty and farcical trial in December 1989, Nicolae Ceauşescu offered a bribe to Major Ion Secu, responsible for his captivity, running to one or two million dollars: 'and until I have access to that kind of money, I know a cache here in Voinesti [a village near Tîrgovişte] where I can lay my hands on hundreds of thousands of *lei*.' Quoted in Behr, *Kiss the Hand You Cannot Bite*, op. cit., p. 16. Later searches by the new Romanian government revealed nothing.

13. The classic is *Struwwelpeter*, Heinrich Hoffman's tales for children, 1845.

14. There is a similar gulf, for instance, between the Norman and Angevin kings of England, speaking Latin and medieval French as opposed to the old and middle English of their subjects.

15. Quoted in Florescu and McNally, *Dracula: Prince of Many Faces*, op. cit., p. 219.

Chapter 9   The Sign of the Dragon: Mircea the Great and Vlad Dracul

1. Robert W. Thurston, 'The Spawning of Satan', *BBC History Magazine*, Vol. 3, No. 5, May 2002.

2. Quoted in Stephen Friar, *A New Dictionary of Heraldry*, Alpha Books, 1987, p. 380.

3. Genesis 3, v. 14.

4. *The Anglo Saxon Chronicle.*

5. Peter Dickinson, *The Flight of Dragons*, Pierrot Publishing Ltd, 1979, p. 128.

6. By the sixteenth century, 'dragon' was the name given to the ornately carved dragon's head or serpentine that formed the firing mechanism of wheel-lock pistols.

7. Job 26, v. 13.

8. Isaiah 27, v. 1.
9. Revelations XII, v. 1–9.
10. Quoted in Florescu and McNally, *Dracula: Prince of Many Faces*, op. cit., p. 34.
11. Jason Goodwin, *Lord of the Horizons*, Vintage, 1999, p. 12.
12. The Holy Qur'an, Surah 2, Al-Baqarah, trans. Abdullah Yusuf Ali, Wordsworth Editions, Brighton 2000.
13. Quoted in McNally, *Vlad Tepes in Romanian folklore*, in Treptow, *Dracula: Essays*, op. cit.
14. A promise, astonishingly, still being offered to the hijackers of the aircraft that attacked the World Trade Center in New York on 11 September 2001.
15. Similar weaknesses and divisions in England would lead in the next century to the highly destructive Wars of the Roses.
16. Quoted in D'Arcy Boulton, *The Knights of the Crown*, op. cit., p. 350.
17. Quoted in Florescu and McNally, *Dracula: Prince of Many Faces*, op. cit., p. 38.

Chapter 10 The Crescent Ascending: The Impaler's Apprenticeship

1. Goodwin, *Lords of the Horizon*, op. cit., p. 8.
2. Halil Inalcik, *The Ottoman Empire*, Phoenix Press, London, 2000.
3. Quoted in Inalcik, *The Ottoman Empire*, op. cit., p. 8.
4. Adam of Usk, *Chronicon*, quoted in Steven Runciman, *The Fall of Constantinople*, Cambridge University Press, 1965, p. 1.
5. Goodwin, *Lords of the Horizon*, op. cit., p. 15.
6. Quoted in Burford, *Hiking Guide to Romania*, op. cit., p. 286.
7. For instance Constantin Rezachevici who also claims that the boy was legitimate.
8. Even in the West, kings and scions of great houses acknowledged and looked after their bastards. In late seventeenth-century England, Charles II saw all thirteen of his handsomely taken care of.
9. Florescu and McNally, *Dracula: Prince of Many Faces*, op. cit., p. 46.
10. Quoted in Halil Inalcik, *The Ottoman Empire*, op. cit., p. 90.

11. Documents 80–99 in *Documenta Romanice Historica*, Vol. 1, quoted in Treptow, *Vlad III Dracula*, op. cit., p. 46.

12. The epithet came from the fact that Hunyadi was a Vlach. This, in the welter of languages used in the various courts of Europe, became corrupted to 'blanche' i.e. white.

13. Simon Marsden, *The Journal of a Ghosthunter*, London, Little Brown & Co, 1992, p. 104.

14. Ibid., pp. 105–6.

15. R. Allen Brown, ed., *Castles: a History and Guide*, Blandford Press, Dorset 1985.

16. See Chapter 10 for details of the rigorous training of these boys; see Halil Inalcik, *The Ottoman Empire*, op. cit., pp. 78–88.

17. Unattributed source in Florescu and McNally, *Dracula: Prince of Many Faces*, op. cit., p. 54.

18. Ibid., p. 59.

19. Alexander (356–323 BC) was the King of Macedonia north of Greece. A pupil of the philosopher Aristotle, he may or may not have been involved in the death of his father, Philip, in order to seize the throne. He defeated the Persian Empire, then marched south through Palestine to take Egypt, founding Alexandria. He crossed into India and had plans to conquer Arabia before he died, possibly of food poisoning after a banquet. His military feats are astonishing and it was no doubt seeing Kastrioti in action in the field that led to Murad's nickname for him.

20. All these details can be found in Halil Inalcik, *The Ottoman Empire*, op,cit., pp. 79–83.

21. See *Malleus Maleficarum*, 1486, for one of the most anti-feminist books ever written.

22. Quoted in Malise Ruthven, *Islam in the World*, Penguin, 1984, p. 169.

23. Quoted in Halil Inalcik, *The Ottoman Empire*, op. cit., p. 89.

24. Florescu and McNally, *Dracula: Prince of Many Faces*, op. cit., p. 32.

25. Quoted in Kendall, *Richard III*, op. cit., p. 56.

26. Quoted in John Carey, ed., *The Faber Book of Reportage*, 1987, p. 391.

27. Ibid., p. 284.

28. Lit. a ride out, the term was widely used in Europe at the time for a campaign.

29. Quoted in Florescu and McNally, *Dracula: Prince of Many Faces*, op. cit., p. 62.

Chapter 11   Vlad Voivod: Battle for the Crown

1. *Expuneia istorice*, Chalkondyles. The Greek confuses, as several contemporaries did, Dracula and his father. At this stage, with Dracula still a boy in Hunyadi's eyes and his fate at Turkish hands possibly unknown to him, he did not have any animosity towards him. 'Dracula' here clearly refers to Vlad Dracul.

2. Translated by Nicholae Iorga, quoted as Appendix A, Treptow, *Dracula: Essays*, op. cit.

3. In a curious abnegation of power, Murad abdicated in favour of the twelve-year-old Mehmed in 1444, ostensibly to avoid the usual bout of murder on a sultan's accession. The plan backfired however and a janissary revolt in May 1446 brought Murad back to the throne.

4. Quoted in Treptow, *Vlad III Dracula*, op. cit., p. 58.

5. Ibid., p. 60.

6. Quoted in Florescu and McNally, *Dracula: Prince of Many Faces*, op. cit., p. 75.

7. Ibid., p. 77.

8. Despatch from Niccolo Modrussa to Pope Pius II, *c.*1466, quoted in Florescu and McNally, *Dracula, Prince of Many Faces*, op. cit., p. 85.

9. If we accept 1431 as the accurate date of Ţepeş' birth, he was forty-five when he died.

10. Gonsalvus' condition is the first recorded example of a hirsute child. In terms of Eastern and Western philosophies, journalists in America and Europe use hysterical phrases to describe later examples of the condition – 'freak', 'mutant', 'wolf-boy', 'monkey-boy'. The Chinese just call them *mao hai*, 'hairy children'.

11. All this information is contained in Treptow, *Vlad III Dracula*, op. cit., and originates from Romanian historian Nicolae Stoicescu, *Sfatul domnesc so marii dregatori din Tara Romanesca şi Moldova, sec XIV–XVII* (The Council and officials of Romania and Moldavia from the 14th to the 17th centuries) Bucharest, 1968.

12. These were issued to mark the quincentenary of Dracula's death in 1976.

13. Quoted in Florescu and McNally, *Dracula: Prince of Many Faces*, op. cit., p. 119.

14. Quoted in Nicolae Stoicescu, *Relations with Transylvania, Essays*, ed. Treptow, p. 93.

15. Quoted in Florescu and McNally, *Dracula: Prince of Many Faces*, p. 101.

16. The use of this word is fascinating. It emanates from the Athenian law-giver Draco who in 621 BC revised the city's laws so that death was the penalty for almost any offence. Its similarity to the dragon epithet is merely a coincidence, but an extraordinary one.

17. All quotations here are from Treptow, *Vlad III Dracula*, op. cit., pp. 116–17.

18. Quoted in Florescu and McNally, *Dracula: Prince of Many Faces*, op. cit., p. 188.

19. Kuritsyn, op. cit.

Chapter 12   Enemies of the Cross of Christ: The Fall of Constantinople

1. Quoted in Goodwin, *Lords of the Horizons*, op. cit., p. 41.

2. Ibid., p. 54.

3. Quoted in Florescu and McNally, *Dracula: Prince of Many Faces*, op. cit., p. 127.

4. Ibid., p. 128.

5. Ibid., p. 132.

6. Tursun Bey, *Tarih-i Ebu-i Feth-I Sultan Mehmed-an*, c.1497.

7. Konstantin Mihailović, *Memoirs of a Janissary*.

8. Quoted in Florescu and McNally, *Dracula: Prince of Many Faces*, op. cit., p. 132.

9. Letter from Vlad Țepeș to Mathias Corvinus, 11 February 1462, quoted in Treptow, *Vlad III Dracula*, op. cit., p. 183.

10. Quoted in Treptow, *Essays*, op. cit., p. 316.

11. Quoted in Treptow, op. cit., p. 184.

12. Quoted in Treptow, *Essays*, op. cit., p. 316.

13. Ibid., p. 316.

14. Quoted in Florescu and McNally, *Dracula: Prince of Many Faces*, op. cit., p. 136.

15. From the account of Laonic Chalkondyles.
16. Tursun Bey, *Tarih-i Ebu-i Feth-I Sultan Mehmed-an*, c.1497.
17. Quoted in Goodwin, *Lords of the Horizons*, op. cit., p. 66.
18. Compare Richard III's 'fellowship of steel' at Bosworth and the elite gentlemen corps of the Household Cavalry created on Charles II's restoration in 1660.
19. For the Turkish names of all these ranks, see David Nicolle, *The Janissaries*, Osprey Elite Series No. 58, pp. 18–19.
20. Ibid., p. 20.
21. Bertrand de la Brocquière, quoted in David Nicolle, *The Janissaries*, op. cit., p. 29.
22. Nicolle, *The Janissaries*, op. cit., p. 32.
23. Quoted in J.M. Brereton, *The Horse in War*, David and Charles, 1976, p. 39.
24. The Landsknechtes' distinctive strips of coloured cloth were traditionally first worn in the year of Dracula's death, in battle with Charles the Bold of Burgundy. The cloth came from the tents of his ransacked camp.
25. Quoted in Gerry Embleton and John Howe, *The Medieval Soldier*, Windrow and Greene, London, 1994, p. 24.
26. Ibid., p. 24.
27. Quoted in McNally and Florescu, *In Search of Dracula*, op. cit., p. 198.
28. Quoted in Embleton and Howe, *The Medieval Soldier*, op. cit., p. 75.

Chapter 13 Impaler Prince: The 1462 Campaign

1. From the account of Laonic Chalkondyles.
2. Quoted in Treptow, *Essays*, op. cit., p. 129.
3. Ibid., p. 130.
4. Ibid., p. 130.
5. Quoted in Florescu and McNally, *Dracula: Prince of Many Faces*, op. cit., p. 144.
6. When I filmed with Wild Dream in 2008 there were even extremes of temperature within a single day. On a March morning we passed children on their way to school with scarves, gloves and earmuffs and by lunchtime I was filming in my shirtsleeves under a scorching sun.

7. Tursun Bey, *Tarih-i Ebu-i Feth-i Sultan Mehmed an.*
8. Quoted in Florescu and McNally, *Dracula: Prince of Many Faces*, op. cit., p. 144.
9. Tursun Bey, *Tarih-i Ebu-i Feth-i Sultan Mehmed an.*
10. From the account of Laonic Chalkondyles.
11. Tursun Bey, *Tarih-i Ebu-i Feth-i Sultan Mehmed an.*
12. Constantin Mihailović, *Memoirs of a Janissary.*
13. Tursun Bey, *Tarih-i Ebu-i Feth-i Sultan Mehmed an.*
14. From the account of Laonic Chalkondyles.
15. Tursun Bey, *Tarih-i Ebu-i Feth-i Sultan Mehmed an.*
16. Quoted in Treptow, *Dracula: Essays*, op. cit., pp. 253–63.
17. Quoted in Treptow, *Essays*, op. cit., p. 218.
18. In fact, the *direct* line of Vlad Dracula, via the offspring of his first and second marriages, died out in the early seventeenth century.
19. Quoted in Florescu and McNally, *Dracula: Prince of Many Faces*, op. cit., p. 168.
20. Quoted in Florescu and McNally, *Dracula: Prince of Many Faces*, op. cit., p. 169.
21. Quoted in Treptow, *Essays*, op. cit., p. 319.
22. Ibid., p. 320.
23. Ibid., p. 320.

Chapter 14   The Gaping Graves: The Resting Place of the Impaler

1. Quoted in *Why Angels Fall*, op. cit., p. 229.
2. Marsden, *Journal of a Ghosthunter*, op. cit., pp. 124–5.
3. Ibid., Note 32, p. 23.
4. Quoted in Robert D. Kaplan, *Balkan Ghosts*, Vintage, 1996, p. 86.
5. In theory, Eastern European tombs should have fared better than English ones. An estimated 65 per cent of English medieval sepulchres were deliberately destroyed during the Reformation of the sixteenth century, when grave furniture and Gothic canopies were equated with Popery and the work of the antichrist. They received a second wave of hammer-blow destruction in the rabid Puritanism of the following century. No such systematic destruction took place in Romania.

6. D'A.J.D. Boulton, *The Knights of the Crown*, Boydell, 2000, pp. 354–5.
7. Charles Dawson discovered what he claimed was the 'missing link', the exact half-way evolutionary creature between man and ape, at Piltdown, Sussex in 1912. The cranium has since been proved to be a genuine Pleistocene homo erectus, but the all-important jaw-bone 'found' with it belonged to a modern ape.
8. Articles in *Archaeologica* 1934 by Tanner and Wright, quoted in Alison Weir, *The Princes in the Tower*, Pimlico, 1992, p. 257.
9. Translation by Raymond McNally of Russian manuscripts in the Kirillov-Belozersky Monastery Collection of the Saltykov-Schedin Library, Leningrad.
10. From the account of Fedor Kuritsyn in the Kirillov-Belozersky Collection. Both these versions of events will be assessed in Chapter 11.
11. Quoted in Florescu and McNally, *Dracula, Prince of Many Faces*, Little Brown, 1989, p. 175.
12. Ibid., p. 175.

Chapter 15 In the Company of Cain: The Psychology of Vlad

1. Quoted in an article by Paul Harris, *Daily Mail*, 19 February 2002.
2. Brian Masters, 'The Banality of Evil', *Daily Mail*, 19 February 2002.
3. These figures are quoted in William Seymour, *Battles in Britain*, Wordsworth Military Library, 1997, pp. 134 and 149.
4. In the recent *The Most Evil Men and Women in History*, Michael O'Mara, 2002.
5. All the translations of the Saxon stories in this chapter are by Peter Panaitescu from Kurt Treptow, ed., *Dracula: Essays*, op. cit., pp. 188–196.
6. From a book written in 1583 by Sir Thomas Smith, quoted in Geoffrey Abbott, *Rack, Rope and Red-hot Pincers*, Bouldhampton Press, London, 1993, p. 3.
7. So too, in the Far West. There are photographs from the 1870s showing Apache adulterers with nose-tips missing.

8. Quoted in Abbott, *Rack, Rope and Red-hot Pincers*, op. cit., p. 75.

9. Quoted in Abbott, *Rack, Rope and Red-hot Pincers*, op. cit., p. 76.

10. The Dracula Conference was held in May 1995 at a number of venues throughout Romania.

11. All quotations from Worley are from the Dracula conference website http://members.tripod.com/_Baron91/WorleyImpaling.html

12. Both quotations from Florescu and McNally, *Dracula: Prince of Many Faces*, op. cit., p. 163.

13. Quoted in Robbins, *The Encyclopaedia of Witchcraft and Demonology*.

14. Colin Wilson, *The Mammoth Book of Murder*, Robinson, 1990, p. 59.

15. In his political novel, *The Young Duke*.

16. Quoted in Thorne, *Children of the Night*, op. cit., p. 176.

17. Quoted in *The Mail on Sunday*, byline Emma Hartley, 18 November 2001.

18. John Symonds, *Renaissance in Italy* quoted in Brian Mariner, *A Century of Sex Killers*, Foreword by Colin Wilson, True Crime Library, 1992.

Chapter 16   Resurrecting Dracula: Vlad Today

1. Jessica Douglas-Home, *The Spectator*, 12 January 2002.

2. Quoted in *The Spectator*, 12 January 2002.

3. *Documente istorice slavo-române*, quoted in Treptow, *Vlad III Dracula*, op. cit., p. 111.

4. Quoted in J.J. Bagley, *Historical Interpretation*, Penguin Books, 1965, p. 191.

5. Bagley, *Historical Interpretation*, p. 192.

6. Ibid., p. 197.

7. Ibid., p. 199.

8. Jean Benedetti, *The Real Bluebeard* , Dorset Press, 1971, p. 12.

9. Ibid., p. 15.

10. Ibid., p. 17.

11. In Treptow, *Essays*, op. cit., p. 163.

12. Ibid., p. 24.

13. Ibid., p. 167.

INDEX